MY YOUNG LIFE IN TUNBRIDGE WELLS.

A journey into the past by 'Looking Back' to
the days of my childhood and adolescence.
by

Michael Fane Gardner

My Young Life in Tunbridge Wells

First published in Great Britain by Michael F. Gardner 2006.

ISBN 0 9553640 0 0
ISBN 9 780955 364006

Printed and bound in Great Britain by CPI Antony Rowe

Michael F. Gardner

Dedication

'For Johnny'

Do not despair
For Johnny – head in air;
He sleeps as sound
As Johnny underground.

Fetch out no shroud
For Johnny-in-the-cloud;
And keep your tears
For him in after years.

Better by far
For Johnny-the-bright-star,
To keep your head,
And see his children fed.

John Pudney. 1909-1977.

This book is dedicated to my Mother, Father, Bob, Trevor, Robert and all those who have all played such a role in my life.   I particularly dedicate it to my wife Leila, for putting up with me for all the years we have been married and for giving me the encouragement to compile this work; she has been the inspiration in achieving it.   Finally, but by no means least, it is dedicated to Yvonne, Michael and our dear departed daughter Juliette and to our lovely grandchildren.   I hope they will not get up to some of the things we did when we were young!

My Young Life in Tunbridge Wells

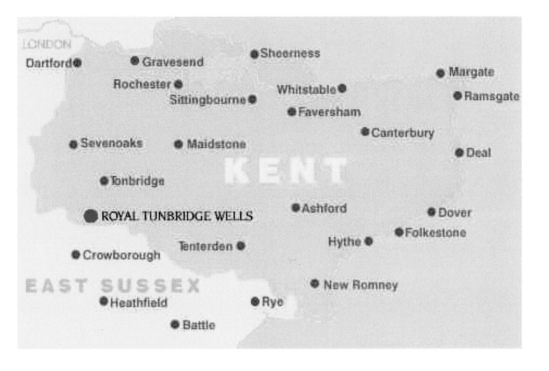

Michael Gardner 2006

Michael Gardner was born in Tunbridge Wells in 1935 and lived in the town with his family, until joining the Royal Air Force in 1953.   After completing four years service in the R.A.F., he joined British Overseas Airways as an Aircraft Engineer in 1956 and then went on to work with Aden Airways, British United Airways, Caledonian Airways (later to become British Caledonian Airways) where he was a Senior Engineering Manager and the Royal Flight of Dubai, where he was Chief of Engineering.

His life in aviation meant that he wouldn't live again in Tunbridge Wells but with family still in the town, is a frequent visitor.   He is now retired and lives with his wife on the South Downs in East Dean.

This work is dedicated to the memory of our dear daughter
Juliette Rose Gardner, 1966 – 1997

Michael F. Gardner

INTRODUCTION

'Looking back'. One should never look back; we are told always to look to the future. I must admit that now I derive considerable pleasure in thinking back to some of the things that have happened in my life, both the good, and the not so good.

My purpose in writing this is to try to pass on to my dear children, and grandchildren, some memories that have stayed with me over the years and I hope it will give some enjoyment to those who read it.

Another reason for 'putting pen to paper' is that I felt that although my mother, father and Uncle Bob, who all had wonderful gifts of narration and could hold us spellbound with their tales of times gone by; the majority of these true stories have been lost. If only we had taken the opportunity to record their memories! During my mothers later years, a single small glass of 'Whiskey–Mac', would bring forth a host of long forgotten stories of events in her life – all told with a little twinkle in her eyes, some humour and possibly, a few regrets!

I am grateful for what life has brought me – the most precious things in my life are my family. I have always felt that a strong family background has been of prime importance to my happiness. I am grateful not only to my own family but also to our joint families and to my wife's foster parents, Mr. & Mrs. Frisby, who took the gamble of allowing me to marry their only daughter Leila before she was old enough to know better!. Also to Leila's Aunt Dolly, who was a good friend to both Leila and I and to the many other people whose names will crop up from time to time in this work.

If you want to savour these things with me, I will enjoy putting 'pen to paper' and begin 'Looking Back'. I hope those who read it will enjoy it as I have enjoyed writing it. When I first thought of doing this work, it really made me realise how fast time has flown by; was it really that long ago when the things I will write about, actually happened?

My Young Life in Tunbridge Wells

Michael F. Gardner

Index

My Young Life in Tunbridge Wells

One of Mike Gardner's earliest memories of being an infant at Christ Church School, in Tunbridge Wells is seeing, day after day, the school motto 'THROUGH' emblazoned in gold along the whole length of his classroom wall.

Mike says that the word, unremarked at the time, entered his character and has helped form his attitude to life. "I have tried to follow its meaning as a principle", Mike says. That principle is triumphantly demonstrated in this marvellous book, in which Mike Gardner conjures up the events, characters and atmosphere of his hometown in a way that makes them seen as real as if the reader had experianced them.

Mike captures the uncertainties of wartime, the excitement of steam travel, and the dilemmas encountered in starting out work - as well as affectionate portraits of family, friends and neighbours, including his father Harry Gardner, who made the unusual journey from Tunbridge Wells to South Wales to stand in Llanelli as the Conservative candidate for Parliament.

Tunbridge Wells is a town that seems almost purpose-made to live vividly in the memory, especially for a young boy. An historic town with an elegance people came from miles to enjoy, yet, for all that, a working town bustling with shops, businesses and trade. An urban place - but one not just surrounded by countryside, but in which the countryside comes right into the heart of town.

Tunbridge Wells, then as now, is a town full of unique places, memorable people - full of life.

This fascinating book will instantly become part of the history of our town. It couldn't have come at a more auspicious moment: it is published during the year in which Tunbridge Wells celebrates its 400th birthday.

I congratulate Mike Gardner on his achievement in writing this book, and commend it warmly to its readers: especially to Tunbridge Wells people - past, present and future.

Greg Clark MP
Member of Parliament for Tunbridge Wells
House of Commons
London SW1

August 2006

Chapter 1:   The Early Years 1935-1939

How far can one actually look back and recall precise details so many years ago? What was important to me as a baby and then a toddler were only part of the whole picture going on around me. All I can do is, hopefully, to put things into chronological order, as they happened and registered with me. It may be difficult to give actual years, particularly when I was very young, but my objective is not to give you a diary of events but, if you like, a verbal photograph of how things were when I was growing up.

My earliest memories go back to the period between 1935 and 1939.

I was born on 11th June 1935.   That made me a Gemini.   (Gemini's are, I believe, noted for their mental agility and love of travel and communication?   Hence, perhaps, my liking for communicative gadgets (fax, telephone, etc) and for a career totally dedicated to the travel concept. I have hardly been desk-bound or remained in one place for long either!).

I was born in Tunbridge Wells, Kent, at a place called 'The Maternity Home'. My mother, Dorothy Ellen Gardner, and father, Henry (known as Harry) Gardner, lived at 14 Sutherland Road, Tunbridge Wells, in a rented flat.   My mother was 33 years old when she produced me, so it was late in life for her, in those days, to begin a family. My birth was to be followed by that of my brothers, Trevor, who was born in February 1937, and by Robert, who was born in March 1949, when Mum was 47 years old.

I don't really have too many memories of the flat in Sutherland Road, where I was initially brought up – I believe we moved on when I was only a few months old to Number 32 Grove Hill Road, where the family would spend over 20 years.   My family took over the ground floor flat there. Looking at my Birth Certificate, I see Dad was recorded as being a 'Furrier' by trade at the time I was born.   My Grandfather, Septimus Gardner, and my Grandmother, had a little shop in Grove Hill Road.   This was directly located where the entrance to 'Week's' car park now stands. ('Week's' was an old family department store that carried out business in Tunbridge Wells for many years. Unfortunately, they have long gone and the site now belongs to 'Hoopers', which is part of a larger conglomerate). My Grandfather's shop was, to the best of my recollections, called, 'R. Septimus Gardner, Furrier & Taxidermist'.

I will talk more about the little shop later but I believe that Dad did some work for his father at the time; hence his occupation being noted as 'Furrier'. I guess that was a unique trade even in those days, when the gentry, and their ladies, hunted animals like Fox and Deer. They would then have them preserved and the carcasses 'stuffed' and mounted in order to hang them upon the wall as trophies. The ladies would wear fox fur coats and foxtail neck furs. These styles were then all the fashion but I'm pleased to say that was a time which has fortunately gone by.

I cannot remember Trevor 'arriving' although, as I began to remember things when I was very young, Trevor seemed to have been there all the time!

Of those pre-war days I can recall a few of the things that happened to us. As I have said, living in Grove Hill Road, we had the ground floor flat at Number 32, and even a little garden at the back. As the living accommodation was lower than the garden, access to it was up a flight of stone steps, which became treacherous in the winter when snow and ice made using the steps dangerously slippery. I remember my Dad was always telling Mum to "mind how you go", when using the steps to get to the dustbin which was located at the top under a lean-to, by the back gate. (This was the pre-equality of the sex's period and before 'Women's 'Lib'!)

By modern standards, our accommodation at number 32 was not large. It comprised of just three rooms and an outside toilet, which was extremely austere particularly in the middle of winter or the night! There was no electric light or heating in the toilet to make it more comfortable so visits to the toilet were always short and sweet!   I do remember that my Dad used to wrap the cistern and associated water pipes in old sacking to prevent it freezing up when the weather was cold; sometimes though, even this precaution didn't stop the inevitable as winters were a lot harder in those days.

A nice sized lounge at the front of the house gave an excellent view of Grove Hill Road at the junction of Mountfield Road (a pleasant cul-de-sac) opposite. The middle room was the bedroom and its 'Venetian' type windows looked straight into a glass conservatory on the outside. (The conservatory was a relic of a lingering Victorian design. The entrance to it was from outside so it was mainly used as a storage place). Many was the time when, as youngsters, we imagined we saw 'Ghosts' in the conservatory on moonlit nights and then spent the night well under the bedclothes, frightened of what may appear! Trev and I used to see who could scare the other the most!

My bed faced the scantily curtained windows. Trev's bed was in the corner, at the side and at right angles to the window, with Mum and Dad's bed between us. Unfortunately, with my bed having the view of the conservatory, there were nights when ones imagination would run riot and prompted by Trev, you could imagine all sorts of figures moving about out there!

The remaining room was the kitchen; which had a cold stone tiled floor. It had a Kitchener Unit (to which the fire brigade had to be called out on more than one occasion to put out the chimney fires!), which during cold weather would make the room the favourite place for all the family. It also had a large 'walk-in' larder.

In the latter years, particularly after Robert was born, this room became the main 'living-room' of our flat, with the front room being used as my mother and Robert's bedroom. Dad still used the double bed in our bedroom for most of the time giving a complement of three beds in that room so it was a little crowded. However, that appeared to be the best solution for the space we had available.

I'm sorry - I am jumping ahead. Let's get back to those very early days. The Calverley Grounds and the Grove Park, were both only a 'stone's throw' from Grove Hill Road and became the places I probably remember most clearly from all those years ago. I can remember my mother buying ice-lollies from an ice-cream salesman in the Calverley Grounds. In those days, ice-cream salesmen had the tricycle mounted ice-cream container and were the original 'stop me and buy one' brigade. In particular, I will always remember the ice-lollies; they were sold in cardboard sheaths and the taste was a mixture of fruit cordial and cardboard. I can still recall the unique flavour to this day!

I have many early memories of summer days in the Calverley Grounds. Mum used to take a flask of tea into the park with her. This was always refreshing - no wonder our family have always been great tea enthusiasts! The Calverley was nice in those days before the Second World War; quite elegant and the place to be. (The grounds were originally part of the 'Calverley Park' estate - the main house, which overlooks the park, has long been a hotel set high above the grounds and is now known as the 'Calverley Park Hotel'). It, of course, had nice gardens with many azalea and rhododendron shrubs, trees and formal rose gardens. There was also a band stand and attractive Pavilion, where flower shows, baby contests and other events were held. I don't think Mum ever entered me in baby shows, not that I can remember anyway.

All children have their 'knocks' as they grow up. My earliest memory of such an incident occurring to me was when I was three year's old. In the kitchen at number 32 we had an armchair, with wooden arms, located just inside the door from the hall, on the right hand side.

As you entered the kitchen, you went down a step. Well, one day I came running through the hall from the living room, misjudged the step and went flying, crashing into the armchair. Unfortunately, I tried to swallow one of the chair arms and in the process split my tongue open. My Mother, who was friendly with a nurse who lived next door, got her in immediately to advise on how to stop the flow of blood, which was by that time, quite a gusher. The nurse recommended my sitting down quietly and eating as much ice-cream as possible in an attempt to stop the bleeding and it worked, but I don't remember how much ice cream I ate!

The incident with the armchair was to remain with me for years - I did and still do believe it had an effect on my speech, which in later years, I managed in general, to overcome. Unfortunately, as a child, you don't have the mental resilience and confidence needed to overcome things like an assumed affliction and it was to give me some embarrassing moments in the years of my youth; but more on that later. (Whether the problems were physical or psychological, or a mix of both, I guess is debatable - probably now, I will never know for sure).

Poor Trev. I remember clearly the time when I tried to bury him!

He was asleep in his pram, outside the back door at home, when, for some unknown reason I decided to bury him in dirt from Dad's back garden. Grabbing the trowel, which was, as always to hand, I proceeded to fill his pram up with garden soil, worms and all! Luckily, for all concerned, Mum, who was in the kitchen at the time, came to the rescue just in the nick of time – my rear end felt her response for some time after!

In another incident, I cut Trev's hair. He had a beautiful head of curls when he was young and I pretended to be Mr Pallant the barber. (Mr Pallant had a barber's shop in Grove Hill Road, just up from my grandfather's shop. My Dad always took Trevor and me to him for our haircuts). Having dressed Trev up with a towel around him I proceeded to 'barber' him. This all took place in the kitchen of the flat above ours, where a lady by the name of Miss Pope lived. She was to become a great friend of the family over the years but on this day, her kitchen, became 'Pallant's – the barber shop'. Fortunately, before I could totally complete the job and 'scalp' Trev, Miss Pope came in and as you can guess, retribution took place when my mother learned about it. When I look back, I sympathise with my mother and father during those early years when I was obviously a 'bit of a trimmer' and had a strong mischievous streak! Having two energetic and highly spirited sons, close in age, must have been a handful for them. My own three children, and now our grandchildren, highlight this fact to me.

Mum and Dad did not have a lot in those days. In fact, for most of their lives, luxuries were never high on their list of priorities. Although my father's family were relatively affluent, with the shop and everything, my father was reputed to being something of a nonconformist and a bit of a rolling stone. I believe this counteracted upon the advantages he had had as a young man. Mum and Dad, when I was a child, really only desired the basics in life. With this point in mind, when I look back at how Trev and I used to play 'rough and tumble' with each other, particularly in the front room where the settee and armchairs really went through it, I realise how demanding we were.

Furniture was not easy to replace in those days and money at that time, wasn't a commodity my family had a lot of.

At this point I believe I have to quantify the preceding paragraph relating to my father. Dad was one of the most intelligent, well read and erudite people I have ever met although his practical aptitude was inconsistent. I remember Dad once made me a railway engine from an old round table leg. The boiler and wheels being made from the redundant table leg and these were mounted on a flat chassis. I treasured this toy and would give anything today to still have it.   Bearing in mind the fact that Dad was not a man to use his hands a lot, his making this engine for me meant so much.   Priceless!

In the pre-war years, I have many warm memories of cosy times in the front room, particularly in the winter, when Dad would have a nice open fire.   I was fascinated by watching the 'fairy lights', made as soot on the fireplace breast brightly sparkled and slowly burnt away. The problem in those days was how cold it was when you moved away from the warm room you were in and made your way to the icehouse known as the bedroom.

A memory I will always have however, was one Christmas just before the war, when Dad had erected a Christmas tree in the front room and illuminated it with little candles. (Electrically powered fairy lights were very rare and expensive at that time). A friend of the family, Margaret Robson, dressed up as Father Christmas. We were all in the front room where Dad had a good fire going, the Christmas tree illuminated with the candles and all was nice and cosy, when Father Christmas came in from the hall to give out some little presents from the tree.

We were fascinated with all this, having never seen a 'real' Father Christmas before – our fascination soon turned to horror as when Margaret was reaching for a present from the tree, and a candle ignited the sleeve of her red gown. Before we knew where we were, she was ablaze. Dad had the sense to grab a small carpet from the hall and wrapped it around Margaret to extinguish the flames.   Fortunately it worked but not before she had received some really nasty burns which required her to go to hospital and which were to leave her scarred, and with a facial impediment for the rest of her life.

Those are the memories we all like to forget but unfortunately all become part of the growing up process and a realisation that not all in life can be perfect all the time.

Chapter 2:   The Clouds of War

As very young children we really didn't know what the war was all about. I guess, in those days, we just seemed to know that we were the good guys and the Germans were the bad guys.   German Shepherd dogs became known as Alsatians, but even renamed they tended to be frowned upon.

I cannot really say when I first realised we were in a state of war. History identifies the start of the war, as far as the people in England were concerned, as 'The Phoney War', and in that period it seemed very little happened.   This is the period of 1939 and early 1940. Life at number 32 with Mum, Dad and Trev, didn't change much initially – I guess when we were presented with our steel air raid shelter, in the form of a table to go in to the kitchen, the realisation that things were going to be different suddenly came home to us, literally.

This contraption, which to us youngsters seemed huge, could only be located in the kitchen as this was the main living area for us all. It had metal grills at each side and at one end with the other end being the entrance.

It was a crawl-in job! Thankfully we were all a lot smaller then than we are now and at a pinch, I suppose all four of us could have got into it. However, time gradually altered that as Trev and I grew bigger. I remember Mum laid some bedding on the base inside of it and in many respects, it was very cosy. As children, making 'camps' was always great fun and in some ways we looked forward to sleeping in this contraption.

When the reality of war really sank in for us it was a different story.   I was five years old when the 'Battle of Britain' began in 1940.   I clearly remember the brilliant blue skies during a really lovely summer and as children, we were always in the fresh air. Mum used to take us out along Mountfield Gardens and then into the Calverley Grounds almost every day. It was a lovely place in those days with abundant greenery and big trees. As there were few cars about or in the vicinity it was a very quiet and peaceful spot although in the centre of what is a fairly large town.

What took our interest as children, was the digging of

the underground air raid shelters in the park. These were built to supplement the table shelters in many people's houses and were located on the right side of the path as you entered the park from the 'dead end' of Mountfield Gardens and about fifty yards along the path on the right. Considering the digging and building of these shelters was all done by hand the shelters were erected remarkably quickly.

There were two public air raid shelters in the Calverley Grounds. Apart from the one at the top of the grounds there was another situated lower down, almost in the area where the footpath from Mountfield Road now enters the grounds. I imagine that the nearby railway ion was seen as a possible target. For some reason or other we were to always use the shelter at the top, mainly because it was the closest to where we lived as there was no entrance to the Calverley Grounds from the nearer Mountfield Road in those days. Anyway, as children we didn't like the lower shelter as we thought it to be particularly "creepy", probably because it was less used that the other one. We always considered it a dark and damp place which it probably was due to the geography of the park.

I will never forget the first time my Mum and Dad took us into the public shelters. It was decided to have a 'dummy run' and see how people reacted and adapted to them. The lighting was by paraffin hurricane lamps and it got a little spooky the further you went into the 'tunnel'. Actually, it did resemble a tunnel although it had a sharp bend in the middle, which prevented you seeing one end from the other. The far end was located almost at a point overlooking the main rose garden with the Chinese Bell in the centre of the 'Calverley Grounds'. A rough estimate would have made it about four hundred yards long, although as a child I did not resort to actually measuring it.

Bench seats ran the full length of the shelter as did 'duck boards' on the floor. (These were designed to allow surplus water to drain away underneath). I will always remember the damp plus strong smell of paraffin that assailed you the moment you walked into the shelter. Funnily enough, I still have memories of the very social, friendly atmosphere in the shelter when we had to use them.

Memories, such as there was always a cup of tea or beaker of squash available and an old man used to ply his trade in the shelter by selling cigarettes and matches, etc, on a tray he used to carry upon his chest. 'Wills Woodbines', 'Park Drive' and 'Craven "A"' still have a memorable ring to me.

The first time we really needed the shelter was one lovely afternoon when we all heard the air raid siren sound for the first time in anger. Before we even got to the shelter, approaching the town from the direction of the upper St John's area, came a big black lumbering German bomber. (later we were to learn that this was a Heinkel HE III) with an RAF fighter plane chasing it. Fortunately it continued over Tunbridge Wells and faded into the distance with the sound of machine gun fire from both aircraft.

When the 'Battle of Britain' took place, it really didn't seem real at first but when aeroplanes appeared to disintegrate in the air and white silk parachute canopies floated in the sky, the reality of what was going on really drove home the meaning to us. Many of the fortunate and the unfortunate men involved in the air battles must have seen our home town as a typical country town as they battled, survived, or regrettably died in its vicinity. (One wonders at the choice of fabric for parachutes being silk – probably few man made fibres were being produced at that time and silk appeared to offer the best in the way of lightness and strength that was available then). I will always remember the dog fights in the clear blue sky at that time, with white contrails and streaks of black smoke as aircraft caught fire after being hit. Watching from the safety of the ground made it seem surreal in many respects and you couldn't believe that men were actually dying up in the skies that we were looking at.

The Pilots of the Royal Air Force were later to become known as 'The Few', mainly through a reference to them in a speech made by Winston Churchill where he summed it up for the nation with the words, "never in the field of human conflict, has so much been owed by so many, to so few". To the common folk of the realm they epitomised the true spirit of the British people and were always spoken about with a certain amount of reverence; a reputation they truly earned the hard way.

From the 'Calverley Grounds', one building that always dominated the skyline was 'Bredbury', located along Mount Ephraim, overlooking the Tunbridge Wells Common which lies right down the side and above the town. Located on the top of one of the building's buttresses was an Observer

Corps Group whose role was to identify aircraft flying over the town and report to anti-aircraft 'ack-ack' gun positions on the outskirts of the town. The observers were members of the Royal Observer Corps, the majority of which were retired military personnel. 'Bredbury', which fortunately still survives today as insurance offices, was a real landmark and enjoyed views right across to the Weald of Kent.

My father, at this time, was a Special Constable in the Police force. We always used to get a low feeling when he went off on night duty, as that was always when the German bombers came and particularly if there was no moon. I well remember walking in the Grove with Mum on our way home from the swings – it was beginning to get dusk and at my very young age, I had the horrible doubts in my mind of would we see tomorrow morning? We had previously suffered several sleepless nights, and I can still clearly remember how ominous the situation appeared to us at that time. I do not think I have ever had such feelings of foreboding since!

I can recall frequently hearing my Mum sing a well known hymn called 'The Day Thou Gavest'. She always seemed to sing this to herself, as she went about her chores during anxious times such as when Dad was working nights. This particular hymn always made me realise just how very vulnerable we were. Tunes really can bring back strong memories. Bombing wasn't a personal war where combatants faced each other, as in the Western films at the Kosmos Cinema, bombing, because of it's nature, is indiscriminate and you were either lucky or unlucky. "If it had your number on it you've had it", was the saying of the day. As a child, I believe that was my first awareness of the vulnerability of the human being.

My mother, by the way, although a 'believer', was not fanatically religious in any way but did enjoy church music, indeed all music, and had in her youth been encouraged to play the church organ but not taken it up. She had considerable musical ability and could play by ear.

Mum would get us to bed at our normal time and we would lie in our beds for what would seem like an eternity because we knew that when the air raid sirens did go off she would come and get us up. She would usually put raincoats over our pyjamas and we would all go into the kitchen table shelter and wait. (My wife, Leila, tells me that as a small child, she and her foster mother slept nightly in their table shelter, which was positioned in their sitting room. With Leila's foster father being away in the army and in Germany for the latter half of the war, the beds went unused in their house. They lived two miles out of Tunbridge Wells, in nearby High Brooms)

To us waiting, the increasing drone of the enemy aircraft seemed endless. All one could do was hope they remained en route to their targets, usually London, without dropping their bombs. Sitting huddled together in the table shelter in the pitch black, with no lights being permitted, is a memory I will never forget. Air Raid Wardens checked on whether lights were showing and occupants could get prosecuted if they habitually broke the "blackout" regulations. One of my father's duties, being in the Police, was that whenever the siren sounded, he had to get dressed and report to the Police Station in Crescent Road as quickly as possible and as I have already said – this was one of the worst parts as we never knew when he'd get back home again.

Our neighbours, in the flats above, used to come down. A favourite neighbour of ours, Miss Pope, was a round stocky person, short in stature that was destined to live her life as a spinster. She was a very nice lady and would remain a good family friend all her life. Above her, in the top flat, lived a Mr and Mrs Longley. I don't remember much about them although they were a pleasant enough but childless couple. I guess it was considered safer on the ground floor so hence the reason why everyone accumulated in our little flat. Mum, sociable as always, would make the inevitable pot of tea and they would all sit around in the kitchen mumbling things between themselves, whilst Trevor and I had the shelter to ourselves. Sleep was something that did not come very easily under the circumstances. In some respects, the sound of their 'mumbling' seemed to take away the frightening noises of the bombers, or worse, when after dropping their bombs on London they would come back over the town on their way home.

Again, the sound of the anti-aircraft guns opening up in the surrounding areas of the town, warned of their coming. We always felt worse when they came back as those aircraft that hadn't dropped their bombs over London, would do so on any selected target they could find, to get rid of the things. So it was on the night that one of the German bombers selected, as his target of opportunity, the Bandstand and Pavilions in the Calverley Grounds. Probably from the air, the outline may have given the impression that it was a factory site; that was what a lot of people thought at the time. We heard the approaching aircraft and shortly afterwards, the whistle of the bombs descending, it seemed an eternity before they hit the ground but when they did, we really thought that was it. The sounds of the explosions, less than a quarter of a mile away from our home, were deafening.

At first we thought it had been the railway station that had been hit but when the flames began to light up the sky, they were coming from the direction of the Calverley Grounds. Our front door had a glass panel and through it, the exploding incendiary bombs lit up the house. As the only buildings in the Calverley Grounds were the lovely old Bandstand and its Pavilions, it was obvious that they had been hit.

My Dad, who was on night duty in his role of Special Constable, came to our house a short time after and confirmed to our anxious family that, as we had assumed, the Bandstand and Pavilions had received direct hits.

Nobody slept for the remainder of that night; the events left a significant mark upon my memory, as night after night, after that event, one had the nagging thought as to how vulnerable we all were to bombing. Fortunately, nobody had been killed during this incident so we were thankful for that.

The morning after the raid, we went to see the damage for ourselves. All that was left of the buildings was a heap of smouldering rubble. The Fire Brigade were still hosing the area whilst being watched by curious and very subdued onlookers. The Calverley Grounds would really never look the same again!

In those early war days, most town houses had solid iron gates and fences as did even the tall, three storied, terraced houses in Grove Hill Road (where we lived), and the two storied houses in Sutherland Road, Mountfield Road, Meadow Hill Road, etc. The entrance to the Calverley Grounds, from Mount Pleasant and Mountfield Gardens had magnificent iron gates and they had always seemed huge to us children. Not long after the war started, men and lorries arrived to cut down all these iron gates and fences, the material was needed for the war effort in the manufacture of military equipment, guns, etc. Seeing the men cutting down the gates with oxy-acetylene cutting equipment fascinated us the sparks would fly in all directions as the flame cut through the iron. You can still see, to this day, the iron stubs of house gates and fences, where they were cut through at ground level. At my parents' last home, 7 Mountfield Road, to which they moved long after the war had ceased, the remaining stubs of the original iron fence work is still very evident.

Unfortunately, the gates to the Calverley Grounds have never been replaced and I believe that in many respects, the character of the place changed forever when first the gates went at the hands of the welders and then the bombers completed the job by destroying the bandstand complex completely.

At this time in our lives as young children, we found it hard to comprehend the aspects of war as it began to affect the direct lives of the people. The changes to the Calverley Grounds alone left a significant feeling of depression as we had grown up with the park and all the fond memories of it in it's hey day as part of our way of life.

The fate of the bombed out Bandstand and Pavilions in the Calverley Grounds was soon resolved. In no time at all it seemed, the bases of the two Pavilions had been dug out and lined as best possible, to become an E.W.S. Pool. (E.W.S. stood for 'Emergency Water Supply'). Many were the times we would see water either taken from or delivered to these pools by fire engines. One of the things that fascinated us were the wicker basket filters fitted over the end of the suction hose of the fire engines – in our opinion, it looked like a waste paper basket but obviously did the job it was designed for!

The Fire Brigade in the war years was known as the National Fire Service. This became habitually abbreviated to N.F.S. A group of us boys would take great delight in going along the road and chanting "E.W.S., N.F.S.– E.W.S., N.F.S." This I guess was an early version of the football supporters chants you hear today! It certainly warned the neighbours we were around but I had no real idea why we chose that as a chant. I guess we just liked the sound of it.

Shortly after this the park was to suffer another destruction of its beauty. This was in the form of the construction of a large drab building which was to become the 'Communual Kitchen'. Because food rationing was in place from very early in the war years, the government established these kitchens in various places, such as town centres, to provide mid-day meals for those who needed them.   Apart from the building in the Calverley Grounds, another was built in the Grosvenor Recreation Grounds at the other end of the town , but quite a distance from those living in High Brooms where my wife grew up. That was about a mile away from us. The construction of the kitchen so near to where we lived, proved to be a source of great fun for us children, much to the frustration of my mother as we used to get black, really filthy, in our ways of 'assisting' the workmen in mixing cement etc. At least, if we vanished, Mum always knew where to find us. I guess we saw every major step in the construction of the kitchen but did not manage to upset the workmen too much! How they put up with us I'll never know!

Some aspects of the building I will never forget like the smell of wet cement and the bonfires the workmen had in attempts to keep warm. You never forget the smell of burning cement bags, which they used to fuel their fires. Once the Communual Kitchen was completed and put into operation, we used to regularly have our mid-day meals there; but more on that later.

Chapter 3:   Early School Days

And so to school. At the end of the summer of 1940, I started school as a pupil of Christ Church School, a Church of England Primary School. The school was located in Vale Road, very close to the Central Railway Station and next to 'Tunbridge's' Garage. The whole area is now part of the 'Safeway Supermarket' site and regrettably absolutely nothing of the school or the garage remains. ('Tunbridge's' Garage was to play an important role as my first place of employment when I eventually left school; but I am moving on too fast.

Next to the garage was a company specialising in the plumbing and heating trade, A.& G. Bridgeland. Something that distinguished this building was that on the side of the building was a large billboard which always had advertisements for 'Guinness'. These were always in cartoon form depicting various animal characters portraying 'Guinness is Good for You' or 'Mind My Guinness' etc, etc. These really fascinated us especially those when its central characters were household names in the Third Reich!

From day one, I hated school. As a parent and grandparent myself now, I must say that when I look back I have to sympathise with my mother as she had a really hard time in getting me to accept that going to school was an important part of growing up. Makes one think of Peter Pan! Eventually, and somewhat reluctantly, I grudgingly accepted matters. The school, the teaching staff, and the pupils and Christ Church School were to play an important role in the process of my education. The staff in particular were all very kind ladies; all of whom were given the title of 'Miss', although I am sure that some must have been married. (Leila remembers from her school days that in fact the majority of the older female teachers were single – having 'lost' fiancées, boyfriends, or husbands during the First World War. The lives of the younger ones were also affected by the Second World War due to the absence of young men in England; having all been called up for military service)

Unfortunately, I cannot now remember all the names of the teachers. Only Miss Turner, the headmistress, and Miss Ritchins readily come to mind as I look back. Miss Ritchins, a matronly lady with a wonderful way of handling young children, will always be associated in my mind with my learning my 'multiplication tables'.   Her method relied heavily on a 'swinging version' of basic facts. i.e. 'two three's are six, two fours are eight, two five's are ten' and so on, all done in a sort of chanting which I guess has stayed with me. The point was, it made us learn what we had to in a fairly pleasant way.

The school building was old, cold and not fully weather resistant.   For heating, we had to rely on a coke fuelled stove located towards the centre, front of each class room.   Many were the times we sat in our outdoor clothes to keep warm and I guess we were lucky not to get frostbite. I can distinctly remember the odours the coke gave off as it burnt. The teachers used to place a dish of water on the top of the stove in an attempt to reduce the fumes.   It wasn't very successful though and during winter days the fumes got quite overpowering. We really needed to go outside at playtimes to get fresh air!

Coal and Coke were rationed along with almost every other commodity during the war so there was never an excess of fuel. Coke was the end product of what was left of coal after the Gas Company had extracted the gas component from the coal. The gas was then stored in the large and unsightly gasometers adjacent to the Gas Works. They were enormous rotunda style constructions and always appeared to give off a distinctive odour to the surrounding area. There was a very large Gas Works at High Brooms in those days, but that has long since disappeared.

Hot water on tap, was definitely not the order of the day back in 1940, especially in the schools during winter. Visits to the toilet block, which was located outside the main school building, had to be a desperate requirement and not for the fainthearted, especially when the weather was cold!

One of the early school memories I have is that during very cold weather, which seemed more often then than in later years, the children would warm their bottles of milk on or around the coke stove! The milk was issued daily, all one third of a pint of it, in Primary Schools during the war years. The milk would normally be consumed at the first break of the day, and by then, if it had been warmed by the stove, would have lost some of its chill factor.   I must admit, however that personally, I always preferred my milk to be as cold as possible and still do.

The school buildings were miserably cold during the winter. The single stoves in each class room weren't capable of efficient heating and as the buildings were very draughty, they fought a losing battle to keep the people therein at least marginally warm. Because of 'blackout' regulations, it always seemed to me that in the most junior classrooms in particular, we worked in artificial light throughout the year. My memories of the first and second year rooms always gave me the impression of gloom, as the curtains were always kept drawn. Actually, in both of the very junior classrooms at Christ Church School, the windows had actually been bricked up as an additional preventative measure against injury from flying glass if there were bomb attacks by the Luftwaffe on the adjacent railway station. All other windows in the school were taped in an X pattern using sticky tape to prevent flying glass. Maybe the gloomy impression I had of those initial class rooms matched my early academic attitude! It was only when we moved up to Class III did we find the classrooms large and airy with plenty of natural light and this was slightly more encouraging to us children.

The precautions at the school against bomb blast were necessary I guess as the school was extremely close to the Central Station, which would have been a prime objective for the German Air Force. When I look back at that situation it was surprising that the school wasn't closed down because of the risk both to staff and pupils. Also, to compound it's strategic importance as a possible target, was the fact that behind the school, a large house had been take over by the military but we never established what it was used for!

Corporal punishment in Christ Church School usually took the form of standing in the corner facing the wall. I guess in the absence of male teachers the ladies did not like resorting to the cane but it did come out in cases of extreme disobedience. To the best of my recollections I only had to endure that once, but I'll say more on that later.

One never to be forgotten memory of my early school days was the school slogan that existed in the room occupied by Class IV. Along one wall at the rear of the teacher's desk, in large gold, rather 'old English' writing, written upon a green baseboard, was the word 'THOROUGH'. I don't know whether it was actually the official school motto and at a young age, the true meaning of the word didn't really register with me. However, as I have grown up, that particular word has played a key part in my attitude and I have tried to follow it's meaning as a principle. In many respects, when I understood what the word actually meant, the significance of the word has retained with me its meaning and it is a word I still do not easily forget.

I guess the location of Christ Church School and its proximity to Tunbridge Wells Central Railway Station probably had much to do with the lifetime interest I have in railways. It was very rare to walk to and from school without the opportunity of seeing a train. Even from the playground, the sound of locomotives and the pungent smell of smoke and steam, kept the awareness of the railway very high for us. In a world at that time when, in our early years, the school period was a matter of survival, because of the war, the railway became a focal point for our leisure interest. Many would be the time when during our school lunch break from twelve to one-thirty, a lot of the time would be spent at the 'Central', much to the frustration of my mother who would be expecting us home for lunch!   It got to the point that most of the station staff got to know us very well, especially during school holidays.

Two long standing friends of my parents were Mr and Mrs Gower. They managed 'Bishops', the chemists, directly opposite the Central Station. The building still stands next door to 'Hoopers', (previously known as 'Weeks') at the bottom end of Mount Pleasant. It is now a Coffee House and it is hard to imagine how it was in the days of my childhood. What I liked about this rather old Victorian building was that Mr. and Mrs. Gower's living accommodation was located at the top of the building, which gave excellent views of the railway station and Christ Church School beyond.

Mrs. Gower, whose first name was Ethel, was a really lovely lady, slightly older than my mother and they were to remain life long friends.   She and her husband really took me, in particular, into their lives. Possibly, it was because they never had any children of their own.   I would spend many hours in their flat, particularly during the school holidays and it became a second home to me. She would keep me occupied whilst her husband looked after the Chemists shop downstairs. The funny thing is that I cannot remember Trevor spending that much time there; in fact at that period of our lives, I guess that Mum was inclined to split us up when she got the opportunity and I can't say I'd blame her for that.   I believe Mrs.Gower kindly used to take me off Mum's hands whenever she could to give my mother a break from coping with two very energetic youngsters. I suspect that being childless herself she quite enjoyed the chance to 'borrow me'. She would never let me forget a saying I used to come out with when I was still quite young, 'No bus aye, no bus?' For some reason or other I must have had a thing about not wanting to get on a bus although I can't really remember why! Was it the fact that buses in those days always seemed to be noisy and there was always a residual smell of diesel oil? She would never let me forget that saying and right up to the time she died, she would always remind me of it as we said 'cheerio' to her after one of her many visits to see my mother. It is a catch phrase that I will always associate with her.

It was during my visits to Mrs. Gower that I was introduced to the electric vacuum cleaner. We never had one at our house so it was quite an experience to get my hands on it and at every opportunity, I would offer to vacuum the carpets for her. I must admit that in those days, they were very noisy things and the first meeting with it frightened the life out of me. Eventually, I grew to love using her vacuum cleaner and went around her flat with it at every opportunity. I don't know what sort of a job I made of the carpets, and my actions probably helped to wear them out, but it sure had a fascination for me and kept me occupied! Compared to modern cleaners this was definitely an antique, but it gave me a lot fun and I really enjoyed doing it.

The chemist's shop was a very 'up-market' shop, in a very nice part of the town and very accessible for high class trading as well, with 'Weeks' department store being next door. As a child I remember the very large painted china containers along the shop wall behind the serving counters, the glass counters and the smell of medication which greeted you, whenever you went into the shop. As I got older, I began to appreciate what a nice and efficient shop it was. Mr. Gower really managed it well in my opinion. Whenever I was 'let loose' in the shop, outside of normal opening hours, I always wanted to have a go at measuring things out using the small brass weighing scales that were used in the shop. I was not often given the opportunity may I say and I don't blame them, bearing in mind the minuscule quantities of medication one would normally work with plus compliance with medical regulations etc. In later years, Leila purchased and gave me a small set of antique, brass 'sweet' scales which do remind me of the ones that fascinated me as a lad.

Obviously, as I grew up during the war years, I became increasingly aware of my brother, Trevor. We were then and still are very close and the best of good friends. As I've already said, there were incidents between us when he was a baby, i.e. trying to 'bury' him in his pram, but in the early 1940's, when I guess we were both 'little terrors', we were to become inseparable mates. I distinctly remember photographs of the pair of us with others, appearing in the Kent and Sussex Courier, our local newspaper, at a couple of 'war effort' functions. (My mother kept these photographs and I have included them in this book).

One of the photographs, taken during an exhibition of war aspects held at the Tunbridge Wells Town Hall shows the pair of us looking at silhouettes and models of aircraft, both Allied and German. I guess this was probably my first encounter with an aspect of aviation, a subject that was to become so important to me in later life. Another photograph was taken, again by the 'Courier' as it was known, and showed us looking at the 'mile of books' appeal which was in aid of under privileged children and homeless refugees

The photograph was actually taken outside of the then, 'Goulden & Curry's' stationers and bookshop, situated in the nearby High Street at the bottom of Grove Hill Road, probably in about 1942/3. The appeal was in fact an eye-opener to us both and the fascination of seeing a continuous line of books, virtually spanning the main roads of the town, left a lasting impression upon me. This line of books stretched from the Pantiles (at the lower end of the town), up the High Street, past the station and onwards up Mount Pleasant. It certainly required a large number of books to cover that length of distance and I wondered how many 'helpers' were required to move them all at the end of the event! I am sure it was all to the common good at that time and I have to admit, I have never seen such an impressive appeal since.

Chapter 4:   First Acquaintances

At about this time, one became aware of people outside of the immediate family; our Grandparents, Gardner and Stringer. The Gardner's, living close by in Grove Hill Road and Mum's family, the Stringers, living in Hawkenbury. There was also Miss Pope, who lived in the middle floor flat at No. 32, and Mr and Mrs Longley, who occupied the top floor flat.   Then there was a gentleman by the nickname, my mother privately gave him, of "Crackers", and a Miss Snashel. 'Crackers' and Miss Snashel both worked at 'Raisewells' Grocery Shop in Grove Hill Road.

'Raisewells', was a high class grocery store located just above the nearby 'Courier' offices. (They also had a larger branch half way up Mount Pleasant hill, where, in days gone by, the 'gentry' used to come in their horse and traps. Parking these outside, they would patronise the store with its large and comprehensive range of dry stores, many exotic at that time, and high class groceries, etc. All as told to me by my mother. After all, it was a little before my time!). When I was a bit older, I would be lucky enough to take a 'Saturday' job in the Grove Hill shop and would thoroughly enjoy it, but more of that later.

Then there was Mr Scott of 'Garlinge & Scott', the greengrocers, located next door to the little 'Mission' type church opposite Raisewells in Grove Hill Road, and Mr Pallant, the hair dresser (or barber as we knew it).   His shop was almost next to my Grandfather's Taxidermy in Grove Hill Road.   There were of course, many others whose names will crop up as we continue. Supermarkets as we have today were still very much a thing of the future at that time and we relied on the small shops in those days.   Then, and very important to us at that time, were our childhood 'mates'; John Warrener, who I have always called 'Wack', Bill Constance, Fred Till, Alan Clarke, Sid Jefferies, Cedric Gibbons, David Harris, Brian Cornford and the Pugh brothers, but I'll say more about them all later. (Jack Warrener and I are still very good friends I'm glad to say and his name will crop up from time to time in this writing. Brian Cornford's family lived at 7 Mountfield Road for sometime. Little would we have guessed as children that one day it would become our family home when my father bought it in 1957)

Girls didn't figure much at this period of my life but I do remember a girl at Christchurch School by the name of Cynthia Appleton. We were in Class III, and must have been around eight years of age. I do recall she was the first girl I ever took home and that was when I asked her to my birthday party which I remember was held in the front room of number 32. As you can imagine, this was a purely innocent boy/girl relationship. After I left Christchurch School I don't think we ever saw each other again. I wonder what happened to her?

However, at primarily at school; we were friends. One bears in mind the fact that I did not have the experience of sisters, and nothing really came of it – I suppose the fact that I still remember her relates particularly to her being my first 'girl friend'. At the tender age of eight, and especially in those days, what else would you expect?

I remember my paternal Grandparents very well. My father's parents ran a little Taxidermist and Furrier business in Grove Hill Road, just below where we lived but on the opposite side of the road in a block of old wooden shops located between 'Weeks' and the 'Kent & Sussex Courier' building. As a child I had no idea of what specialist businesses the Taxidermists or the Furriers were. Septimus looked after the taxidermist side of the business and his wife was the furrier – I wish I knew more about them and what they did before the time I knew them. They enjoyed a business monopoly in the Tunbridge Wells area, an area of the country with a lot of 'gentry' in and around it. I do recall the names of Lord Abergavenny and Lord De Lisle, both being very much local 'landed gentry', from way back, who would bring all their small hunting "Trophies" to Septimus for stuffing and mounting. He made a very professional job of his work and had a very good reputation.

He was a real craftsman, having studied animal anatomy from many books, some of which are still retained within the family. Sadly not the case with actual taxidermy specimens although I believe there are some examples in the Tunbridge Wells Museum but what lack of forethought that we, the remaining family, do not own at least one example of his work. Not surprisingly, he was very well respected for the skills of his work. The shop wasn't very large but it had a large glass window front and in it, my grand parents would display many of their items of work, ranging from really striking fur coats to fox heads etc., mounted on polished wooden boards, alongside other examples of taxidermy.

Even fish were subjected to the 'trophy' scenario, although usually mounted in a glass case with imitation river plants. I guess those who could afford it could at least prove it wasn't just the case of 'the one that got away'

As children, Trev and I had been instructed not to go into the shop if my grandmother had a customer so we would just walk on past. If we were in the shop at any time a customer came in, she would shoo us up the short flight of stairs which led to a middle room that they used as their living room. This was located between the shop at the front and my Grandfather's workshop at the rear. A set of heavy drape curtains divided the living room and the shop. To the best of my recollections, the only natural light in the middle room came from a skylight window in the flat roof so they had to use the electric light a great deal.

My grandmother was a furrier and designed and made fur coats to order but I do not know more about her activities as such details did not lay within my juvenile interests. However, fur was a popular material at that time and usually a sign of a person's affluence. Most ladies, at this time, would own a neck warmer made of a preserved fox head and pelt. These were very popular. I knew that her services were always in great demand and the little shop was a fairly busy place.

One of the half dozen shops was the little 'Tuck Shop' at the end on the corner of the passage way that led to Grove Hill Cottages. The tiny shops were of wooden construction and could well have been built long before other adjacent buildings. In the case of my Grandparents shop, apart from the sales area at the front, there was a living room, workshop and kitchen at the rear of the building on the ground floor and one upstairs bedroom, although we never actually saw that.

Because of the sort of work my Grandparents were engaged in, there was always a very strong smell of mothballs and it hit you the moment you walked into the shop and I will always associate mothballs with their shop and with them. They were lovely people and my Grandfather, who was in his prime, very handsome judging by a photograph taken when he was the cycling champion of Sussex, was a little, stocky person and in many ways my father was the image of him, although taller and a lot slimmer. My father had a head of hair exactly like that of my Grandfathers, grey and bushy.

One treat they used to give us in the winter was a very small glass of 'Stones' Ginger wine, totally harmless. My Grandmother had a big heavy wooden sideboard on the left of the living room as you went into the room from the shop. The living room was reached by climbing the wooden stairs from the shop and was separated from the shop by the long heavy curtains described earlier.   There were times we would hint for a taste of the Ginger wine which Grandma' always kept in the sideboard. When questioned by Septimus about us having a taste of the amber nectar, she would always create a 'valid' reason to him as to why a little wouldn't do us any harm!

There was a popular song about that time called "A little bit of what you fancy, does you good" and was associated with George Formby. My Grandmother probably believed this to be the right attitude when the subject of the Ginger Wine came up! That was my first introduction to 'Stones Ginger Wine', it being the brand still in production now, that she always seemed to have had to hand. I guess that's one of the reasons why we nearly always buy 'Stones' when we need to; it has sentimental memories for me. Anyway, that's my story and I'm sticking to it!

Sometimes, she would give us each a silver Three-penny piece to buy some sweets; although the choice of the 'off ration' sweets was extremely limited and one would finish up usually buying cough sweets as a last resort if nothing else was available. As a child the little Three-penny pieces were often put in Christmas puddings I suppose enticed the eater to devour the pudding to find the 'treasure'.

I must admit I've never had a problem eating Christmas puddings and they are still a favourite of mine to this day and I need no inducements to encourage me!   However not too many coins came our way, pocket money was a commodity we didn't have a lot of in those days – anyway there wasn't a lot you could spend it on during the war years with rationing strictly in force.   One got fed up with continually crunching cough sweets like 'Hacks, for hacking cough's'!

As kids, when we did have some money, our first stop would be at the nearby little 'Tuck Shop'. Naturally enough the proprietor got to know us, and many of the youngsters in the area, and would if possible let us have sweets etc. from 'under the counter', and off the ration!   A footpath ran between this little shop and Weeks department store, which led to Grove Hill Cottages, where many of our friends lived i.e. Wack, Bill, and Fred. These tiny, wooden, cottages were owned by Mr Weeks the family department store owner. 'Weeks' dated from the 1860's; unfortunately, the little cottages along with the row of shops and the newspaper printing works, have all long been demolished to make place for a customer car park that now exists there and modern flats overlooking the area. These cottages had been erected in a similar style to my Grandfather's shop. They certainly weren't very big and it amazed me how some of the families managed for space as most seemed to have several children. But I guess we were not over endowed with space where we lived either.

On my mother's side, Granddad and Grandma Stringer lived in nearby Hawkenbury. I lost count of the number of times Mum would take us to see them. In later years, we would go on our own but at our young age Mum would always go with us. Usually we would go there by Maidstone & District bus number 82 and walk home although when we were bigger it would entail walking both ways. Not that we really minded that as I quite liked walking and in my younger years, Mum was also a very good walker. The bus for this route, for which the headboard read 'Hawkenbury Cemetery', was usually one of the AEC single deckers.

The bus used to stop at 'Sibbies Corner' in Hawkenbury, where we would get off. The name related to a little shop on the corner, named Sibby's. This was a little grocers and vegetable shop and at the time of my childhood, I believe, it was the only shop in the area. For those who lived in Hawkenbury, being on the outskirts of Tunbridge Wells, it did not make shopping easy for the then non-car owning Hawkenbury folks. This was the case for the majority of the British population at that time though.

The origin of bus services in and around the area of Tunbridge Wells is a story in its own right so we were told. In the early days, there were stories of serious fighting between the different bus companies in the 1930's with the Maidstone & District, Southdown and the long distance London Green Line buses, appearing to have come out of it as the winners. Leila's father used to talk about this a lot when he was alive. Today, as in many other provincial areas and towns, the bus services throughout Kent and Sussex are provided by a host of different transport companies. Both the Southdown and London Transport

Green (Country) buses are now just memories of the past; both companies no longer in business as individual companies.

My grandparents lived at 74 Napier Road in a nice end of terrace house which, to the best of my recollections, had two bedrooms upstairs, a front room, middle room and a kitchen which acted as a bathroom when the tin bath, that was usually hung up in the garden shed, came into its own on Friday nights.

I guess the tin bath used to work overtime when my mother was a young girl as she was one of nine children in the family. Heating sufficient water for such a large family bath time must have been a real problem even though my Grandparents had a big copper gas fired water heater. This large contraption took up quite a bit of floor space in the kitchen and transferring its contents into the tin bath, was a hazardous task. This water heater always made me think of a witch's cauldron to which, in my opinion, it had a striking resemblance.

Their house was very nice and everywhere you went you would see pictures and memorabilia relating to the family. The house appeared big compared to our flat in Grove Hill Road. When we used to visit, at the age we were, we would normally stay in the 'middle room' which acted as the dining and everyday room. The lounge, or front room, was definitely only used on special occasions. I remember my Grandfather kept a very large family bible in this room. It had its own reserved place on a little table next to the organ and by virtue of its position, you noticed it immediately you came through the door.(I often wonder what happened to it after my Grandparents passed away) I can distinctly recall my Grandfather reading from it. Although not an overly religious family the Bible did play a specific role in the way they conducted their lives.

My Grandfather had a striking personality, which probably came from his years as a policeman in Tunbridge Wells. He was a strongly built man and although not particularly tall, always had an authoritative manner about him. What I liked about him was that he always showed an interest in what we had been doing. When you consider just how large a family the Stringers were, that was quite something. My Grandmother was a relatively quiet person and always made us feel very welcome when we went to see her. She would always find something from her storeroom to give us to eat if we arrived unexpectedly.

I do not know the origin of the problem that existed between my father and the Stringers. I think it was the fact that my Grandfather didn't want my mother to marry my Dad! It was not a hostile relationship between them but more a case of just not meeting each other. This meant that whenever we went Hawkenbury, it was always without my father. It is a shame that families fragment and I know that after my Grandparents passed away, a long period of strained relationships between my mother and some members of her family took place due to arguments about who should have had what from my Grandparents estate.

The organ to which I have referred to, was a really beautiful piece of furniture. It took pride of place in my Grandparents front room and many would be the time when my mother, who had a natural aptitude for playing the instrument, would play it and we'd all join in the songs and hymns which came forth. Winter afternoons, when it would get dark early, were a favourite time for the Stringer/Gardner ensemble to perform. Mum would 'pump up' the bellows using the foot pedals, select the various stops etc. she needed and away we would go.

If my memory serves me well, the Stringer's were pretty good singers but I can't recall how we performed. The lovely old organ, was a real family heirloom. After the demise of my Grandparents the organ did finish up at my parents house in Mountfield Road, but after I was married and moved away from home, it was disposed of as they considered it took up too much room. This was a most regrettable decision as beyond doubt it was an antique piece of furniture with great family memories and connections.

My mother told me that it had been made in America so was quite unusual and I must admit I have not seen one like it since. It was a shame but these things happen in life and probably at the time my folks weren't conscious of the true value of the item and space was a higher priority.

One thing in my Grandparents house that always caught my eye was a little picture, which hung in the dining room on the wall next to the dining table. You couldn't miss seeing it when you went into the room and it was only in later years, when I could read and understand it that I fully appreciated what it meant. The picture was a two part black and white drawing depicting, in the top picture, an old man walking along the pavement carrying a bundle on his back. People were taking no notice of him.   The lower picture showed a memorial to, what obviously was the old man after his death, and people were flocking to this memorial with wreaths and flowers. The captions to these pictures were 'In Life Neglect -- In Death Respect'.   Of all the expressions I have heard in life I believe there are none truer than this one. I think we can all see examples of this statement around us.

My Grandfather was a very keen gardener and he had an allotment not far from 'Sibby's Corner', in Halls Hole Road adjacent to a footpath which led to the High Woods, about a quarter of a mile away. Since the days when he was a young man, according to my mother, he had always had an allotment and a vegetable garden at home.   I guess with their large family they needed the extra source of fresh food although Mum used to suspect that, as a child herself, she sometimes thought that my Grandfather would use the allotment as a reason to get out of the house at times!

Mum would tell of the quantities of rhubarb he grew and quite a large proportion of it went towards his homemade rhubarb wine, which I believe, had quite a name in the neighbourhood.   In fact my Grandfather was a real expert in the art of winemaking and several of his 'brews' were extremely potent.   Unfortunately, I was too young to partake in many of them but did get the odd sip now and again. It tasted good to me! He had spent his working life in the Tunbridge Wells Police Force although he was retired when we were children and therefore we would often go to find him working on the land when we visited them.   As I have said, he was a big built man, not overly tall, but I guess he would have looked very impressive in uniform and he certainly wasn't one to argue with.   There was something about him that gave the impression he was a strict disciplinarian but to us he was always a kind and considerate person.

The toilet at my Grandparents home, was located in a lean-too at the back of the house overlooking the Hawkenbury recreation ground. This building comprised of the toilet and a gardening store and I can still remember the distinct smell of onions hanging up to dry.   There always seemed to be a lot of them, and of other produce, so I guess Granddad was pretty successful with his garden.

My mother often used to tell us the story of when she was a young girl she had a fear of frogs and this was something she would have all her life.   One of her brothers once played a trick on her by catching a frog and placing it on the toilet seat one dark evening. He must have guessed it about right as to when she would go to the toilet and there sitting on the seat was this frog!   I can only imagine the reaction that followed – the folks in the house thought someone had been murdered! Bearing in mind that the toilet didn't have electric light and Mum would have seen the frog by the light of a candle she was carrying, it must have been a shock to her.   Anyway it appears Granddad was less than amused and the unfortunate brother was to feel his wrath. I don't think he played that sort of trick again.

From the time we first heard this story we hated going out to the toilet in the dark and would always insist on Mum going out there with us. The fact that there was no electric light was something we were used to as it was the same for the toilet at number 32, but we always thought it was a little spooky!

The house in Napier Road had a very nice garden which my Grandfather carefully nursed and on the little lawn they had a garden seat which had a vantage view of the recreation grounds. Having such a small garden at our flat really made us appreciate how nice it was to sit out in the garden at their house and the fact that they had such a nice open view, really made us very envious. One of the assets of their being able to see the goings on in the 'grounds' from their garden was that we could play out there on our own, providing we remained within view. We always considered this a real treat and would make the most of it whenever we could. There were swings, a roundabout and slide there so we could really enjoy ourselves; there was also the proverbial air raid shelter but that one was built above ground. We often wondered what would happen if a bomb had landed anywhere near it as the above ground shelters didn't give people a lot of confidence that they were well protected!

One of my mother's brothers, Frank Stringer, who lived in Hawkenbury, had three sons, Frank, Roy and Ken. Because they lived in the same little village as my Grandparents, they were regular visitors to Napier Road and we saw quite a lot of them.   Their house was in a road on the opposite side of the Recreation Grounds facing a school which I believe was run by Dr. Barnardos for children from London who had lost their homes in the war. To the best of my memory, this road was, and still is, a back road from Forest Road to Frant, and was originally the main road from Hawkenbury and

Tunbridge Wells to Frant Station, a narrow but very scenic route.

To be quite frank, we didn't always get on that well with Frank, Roy and Ken. They were older than us so I guess that was one of the reasons why our relationship wasn't to be a very close one. Another factor was that their father, Frank, was not one of the friendliest people I have ever met and this feeling was shared with other family members. For some reason or other, he and virtually the rest of the Stringer family did not really have a very harmonious rapport with each other and this would become more of a problem after my Grandparents passed away. My mother being the eldest daughter and he being the eldest son may also have had some effect on the family relationship. I can distinctly remember that whenever we were at Napier Road visiting, if Frank and family rolled up, the atmosphere would noticeably change. This may have been another reason why my father didn't try to build bridges with my mother's side of the family.

Roy and Ken were strong members of the Tunbridge Wells Sea Cadet Force and played key roles in the Band. Roy was particularly impressive as he was the mace bearer and would lead the band through the town on numerous occasions. I guess he was somebody my young friends looked up to as one of my friends used to insist that Roy was his cousin. (Roy certainly made an impression at the head of the band so I can understand my friend's enthusiasm, but he certainly wasn't his relation!) The 'Courier' newspaper would often print photographs of the band on the march and display them in their shop window. Of course with Roy leading, he always seemed to be in the picture but he did make a very good job of it however. If I remember correctly, Ken was the leader of the bugle section.

Apart from my mother's brother Frank and his family, all her remaining brothers (five) and sisters (two) lived away from Tunbridge Wells. We would see them whenever they visited the town but this wasn't very often. Travel, in the war years, wasn't very easy so the result was that we were not as close to them as we would probably have liked. Most of her brothers were in Police Forces in various parts of the country. Uncle Arthur was in the Eastbourne 'force, Herbert in Coventry. There were also Uncle's, Charlie and Bob (I can't remember what occupations they had) and finally Uncle Jack who had emigrated to the U.S.A. when he was a young man. My mother used to talk about him quite often and we were to meet him after the war but more about that later.

Mum's younger sisters were Violet and Ivy and in many respects we got to know their families much better than those of her brothers. Violet lived down in Dorset, at Ferndown, and had an only son, Barry. Her husband's name was Stanley and he was an Insurance Collector. In our young opinions he was the perfect example of an 'old woman' and no more so than when it came to his motorcar; even breathing in the vicinity of this beloved car was sometimes too much for him! He was a very religious person and this way of life was impressed upon the rest of his family and even to this day, Barry follows this tradition with his own family although we always thought that Aunt Violet was a more down to earth character.

She is a very nice lady who really enjoys a laugh. I must say that all in all we always got on well with them and looked forward to their visits to the 'Wells.

Aunt Ivy, who lived on the outskirts of London, was married to Uncle Arnold and they had a daughter named Jennifer. During the war years, Arnold was an Officer in the British Army and therefore we didn't see that much of him. He was to become a reporter for the London Evening News after the war, specialising in the political scene.

Unfortunately, Aunt Ivy caught Tuberculosis (TB) in 1942 and was to spend several years in a Sanatorium at Lenham in Kent. T.B. was a very serious complaint in those days and Ivy was pretty lucky to survive considering the fact that she had to have one lung removed. Jennifer, who is about Trevor's age, spent quite a lot of time at Hawkenbury during the war years as with her mother in hospital and her father in the army, we were able to see quite a lot of her. I would say that of all the Stringer Grandchildren, we saw more of her than any one else and we still have a good relationship with her.

As we boys grew older and our walking ability increased, the bus journeys to Hawkenbury would be relegated to walking both ways, weather permitting. To be fair though, I must admit that the walk from the town was a very pleasant one and the route we used was very rural. From our home in Grove Hill Road we would walk up the hill, past 'Weeks' furniture storage buildings and the old horse pound on the left. (My father, in his role of a Special Constable, would often tell us that he'd found stray horses in the town, especially at night and had 'shepherded' them to this pound for safe keeping. Their owners, usually Gypsies, would collect them the next day; after a suitable reprimand from the Police, I guess.)

Where Grove Hill Road finishes, Camden Park begins. At this point there was a Lodge House on the right known by and named as the 'Crocodile Lodge'. In its front garden was located a pair of wooden 'crocodiles' and this place was quite well known because of them.   To the best of my knowledge, this house still exists today. Actually, in latter years I was to learn that Robert's wife Anne's parents were to live in this place at some point in their lives.   I was to get to know this part of the 'Wells extremely well during my duties as a paper-boy.

Once   past   the   'Crocodile   Lodge'   the   footpath proceeded down the hill for about a quarter of a mile and at the bottom, open fields on both sides gave lovely views towards the St. Peters area of the town on the left and Farncombe Banner Farm on the right. This farm no longer exists; the land being converted to housing many years ago. Once past this, the 'road' became nothing more than a track and at this point ran alongside a thick wood. A small lake in the woods was fairly well hidden from the footpath but at certain times of the year, when the leaves were off the trees, you could see it.   Being kids, the lake had a certain fascination for us, but it would be some time before my mother would let us do this walk on our own which would then give us the opportunity to investigate the woods and the lake and woods in more depth.

These woods were known as the 'Charn Woods' but I do not know how this name originated. Once past the woods, the path ran parallel to the fields on the left as it approached Hawkenbury. (The area on the right was later used for the building of some very large Government Offices, where for some years now, Simon, one of Trevor's sons has been employed in the Land Registry offices).

This walk came out almost opposite 'Sibby's Corner' when it reached Hawkenbury and it was surprising how quickly you could do the journey by foot. I have some nice memories of walking this route at all times of the year and I can remember it as though it happened only yesterday! (I must revisit it the next time I'm in the area, I know it will bring back some memories even though I'm sure it has changed a lot.)

The war years continued but after the London Blitz in 1940/41, German bombing raids over our hometown appeared to subside; or did we get a little blasé?   And we still had the VI's and V11's to come!

Chapter 5:   The Love of Railways Begins

At this point in my life, my interest in railways began. In fact, it has never ended!

I guess the fact that all trains in and out of Tunbridge Wells in those days were hauled by steam engines really started my 'love affair' with the steam railway engine. Because at this time in our lives, with the war in progress, there weren't too many things you could take a lot of interest in, the railways were something readily accessible to us. With Grove Hill Road conveniently situated next to Tunbridge Wells Central Station, we were to pass the railway almost every day on our way to and from school and we never missed the opportunity to stop and observe the activities; even if it sometimes made us late either for school or our meals.

In later years we would begin many a prolonged railway 'expedition' from this station as part of our 'loco spotters' and 'Engine number' collecting activities. We were fortunate also to get friendly with a number of engine drivers on this line. Many of them would, as time passed and we became older, break all the rules by giving us footplate rides!

We would spend hours at the 'Central, watching what was by present day standards, intense activities. The railway activity on that line these days is a shadow of what it used to be. Tunbridge Wells Central was the last station on the line from London before the track divided at the southern end of the Grove Tunnel at Grove Junction.   At that point, the main line continued on to Hastings and the other forked right just before the signal box, to run via a single track to Brighton, Eastbourne and London (Victoria) via Tunbridge Wells West station. The 'West was a favourite venue for us as it was a very active place, ideal for us railway enthusiasts with its large marshalling yards and engine shed.

There was always something going on there. We got to know most of the railway staff and they would let us roam relatively freely excepting on the days when they had a visit from one of their Inspectors. I guess the location of the station, being on the outskirts of the town, allowed a much more relaxed way of life there, compared to its close neighbour, the 'Central'.

The 'West', as we always called it, had so much character about it.   Being built about 1890, it was a lot older than the 'Central and was well established and with many original buildings. Unfortunately today, not much that was the original remains.   When the railway shut down several years ago, it was allowed to become heavily overgrown and derelict before Sainsbury's purchased the site and turned it into a supermarket. Although the trains have long gone, there is hope that some railway activity will remain in the form of a preserved railway which will run from the old 'West Station site to Eridge.

A lot of the credit for this must be given to Sainsbury's who, at considerable expense to themselves, have paid for most of the alterations to allow this to happen.   They converted the area for shopping and altered the site whilst retaining an outer facade of the old railway station building, which has become a Steakhouse.

The section of line that remains towards Eridge, now forms the basis of the new "Spa" railway preservation group. The preservation group had the unfortunate abbreviated name of 'TWERPS'– being short for 'Tunbridge Wells, Eridge, Railway Preservation Society'. This title was not thought dignified enough for Royal Tunbridge Wells; hence the decision to rename the preservation group to the 'Spa Valley Railway'!   The connection being the town's historic connection with health giving mineral waters, a favourite with visitors in the past, had been the custom of coming to "drink the iron water".

As I have already said, the railway lines from the 'Central' as they went south, divided at the Grove Junction. From our 'spotters vantage point at the end of the down platform at the 'Central, you could look right through the Grove Tunnel to the junction at the other end, a distance of about one third of a mile.   The Grove Junction signal box, located in the middle of the junction, looked directly into the tunnel and was easily visible from our usual position on the station platform.

Actually, it was easy to see from which direction the trains were coming from when they approached the southern portal of the tunnel, heading towards the station. As with the case of the 'West', in general, we made many friends of the railway staff; however we did fall foul of some who didn't like young children being around what was, in hindsight, a rather dangerous place!   I must admit that as an adult, I would share their concerns and would have probably aged considerably if I had youngsters 'loose' in my place of work!

Access to our vantage point on the platform was through a green gate off the approach road to the yard at the bottom of Grove Hill Road. This was on the left as you approached the main road bridge, from Grove Hill, directly opposite Weeks department store. Today, this yard accommodates 'Graham Ford' the builder's merchants. The present day showroom on the corner as you approach the yard used to be a printing works for a company by the name of 'Clements'.

One of the things that fascinated us was that they had some of their printing machines in the front window of the shop. Whenever they were carrying out a long printing run, we'd often stand outside the building just watching the gyrations of the machinery at work. It was only a little family firm and was engaged in the production of high class printing. I remember once they produced a booklet on the London, Brighton & South Coast Railway. In those days it would have been made as a glossy black and white item. One morning, knowing that we were avid railway enthusiasts, the owner, Mr Clements, came down to our usual spotters point and gave us a copy of the latest booklet. It was actually a first trial copy which was basically a 'second', but we thought a lot of his kind gesture.

Unfortunately, not long after that, a fire virtually destroyed the little printing works and it went out of business. One of the two local newspapers, 'The Tunbridge Wells Advertiser', then took over the site before they in turn were swallowed up by its bigger brother, the 'Courier', which as I have said, was located in Grove Hill Road just up from my Grandfathers shop. This all took place in the late 1940's and since then, the building was associated with the 'Graham Ford' organisation and is now a large music shop where Leila bought her electric piano. One of the advantages of our access point to the platform was that we didn't have to purchase Platform Tickets! At a cost of a Penny (in pre decimal currency; there were 240 to the   Pound Sterling) it would have become expensive for us on our very limited means as we certainly didn't get a lot of pocket money in those days.

On the opposite side of our platform 'spotting' point at the Grove Tunnel, facing the printing works, was the Neville Bakery. They had a bread shop come teahouse located in the

High Street, just down from the bridge, with the bakery at the rear overlooking the railway.   I have already said that there certainly wasn't an abundance of food during these war years and I can still remember the fantastic smells of fresh baked bread and currant dough buns that used to drift across to where we watched the trains.   During school holidays, when the platform became our second home and we would spend most of the daylight hours there, the bakers would often give us a whistle and summon us up to the bakery where they would give us a bag full of piping hot dough buns which we devoured in no time at all!   I really can't think of a more appetising smell than those freshly baked buns; its one thing I'll never forget.   When we got the signal to get the buns, we'd hot foot it across the railway bridge and up a passage way to the bakery before the bakers changed their minds!

I guess the Neville Bakery was the real place to be seen in during the 1930's, before the war, and the venue for the 'gentry' to take their morning coffee and afternoon tea. Located in the attractive old Tunbridge Wells High Street, the 'Neville' was a very elegant place, having a serving counter at the front of the shop with a tearoom at the rear and another tearoom upstairs.   The upstairs area had a magnificent full length glass window which gave a panoramic view of the High Street and the approach to Mount Pleasant. This probably dated from Victorian times.   Let me say that as children we certainly never went into the shop for anything other than bread but in later years, when we were old enough to appreciate these things, it made you realise what a nice place it was and I do recall actually having tea there on a couple of occasions when I was a few years older.

I can't honestly say when it was that I joined the choir! All I can remember is that one day, whilst Trevor and I were playing quite happily at home, the vicar of Christ Church arrived and my mother, who I suspect had planned the whole thing, summoned us to meet him.   If I remember correctly, the question of joining the choir came up very early in the conversation and I think we gave a very unenthusiastic reply. It wasn't exactly what we wanted to do believe me and as I was the oldest, the question was apparently aimed directly at me!   I was to be the Guinea Pig.   In fact my mother didn't really give me a lot of choice in the matter and I really couldn't say much in front of the vicar.

Anyway, before I knew much about it, I was a member of the Christ Church Choir. To this day, I'll never know why my mother was adamant I would make a Chorister as I did not consider my singing voice to be much good.

Trev was to join the choir at a later date and when that happened, I felt a lot better about it. Mum had her wish; we were members of the Christ Church choir! The only plus was that my mother agreed that we could drop out of Sunday school once we were taking a full part in the choir activities. In a way this arrangement suited me as I really didn't like Sunday school very much. The sessions were held in an annex of the main church and they were really a total bore to me; I simply hated Sunday afternoons and having to go there and would have been a lot happier spending my time at the railway station! When I think of it, I guess Sunday Schools were set up to give the parents some peace after Sunday lunch, it certainly worked in our case, although during the war years with my Dad being in the Police Force, he wasn't always there for Sunday lunch. Anyway it gave Mum a break so that was the main thing. I really did not consciously absorb much of the religious instruction from Sunday school! I can't actually remember exactly when our enrolment in the choir took place. I guess I was about nine years of age at the time, so that would put the year about 1944.

The war was still in full swing and we were getting used to the military presence in and around the town. For some time we had been aware of a lot of foreign troops being about especially American and Canadian personnel. What was distinctly obvious, even to our young minds, was the way so many of the local girls seemed set on being on extremely friendly terms with these guys. Especially the Americans! I think we used to make ourselves a little unpopular at times when in the Calverley Grounds, we would, in the course of our children's games come across various couples wanting peace and quiet! It was surprising what the soldiers would offer us to vacate the scene. The Americans would give us Chewing Gum and Candy and the Canadians would give us army badges, buttons etc. We finished up with quite a collection. We used to give the badges, etc, to my mother who would put them in her button tin and even up to the time of her passing, when she had cause to look for a button, she would still came across little odds and end's from that time. The candy never made it home though!

In some respects, we felt a little sorry for the British troops who didn't seem to have the same amount of luck with the girls as the other nationalities seemed to do. At this time, leading up to the invasion of Europe, there were Army camps all around Tunbridge Wells.   The Grove, which wasn't far from where we lived, was converted into an army camp and of course was of great interest to us lads.

There used to be a Bandstand in the Grove at the top end adjacent to Buckingham Road, which had a large paved area originally used for deck chairs when there was a band concert in the pre war years. This area was ideal for the army to utilise as a Transport Workshop facility when they moved in and the Bandstand became a control office and stores. Vehicles and equipment of all shapes and sizes were deployed there although it wasn't used for anti-aircraft action because of the proximity of houses and civilians nearby.   The army used it simply as a marshalling area for large equipment storage pending the D-Day invasions.

The Grove these days bears little resemblance to the place it was when we were young.   The bandstand was demolished soon after the war as the army left it in very poor condition and as far as I can remember, the whole area was in a very run down state. It looked as though the war had taken place there! The army pulled out just before 'D Day', in June 1944. I can remember going exploring around the remains of the camp including the bandstand after the army had left. Everywhere you went there was the strong smell of engine oil; in fact there were numerous used engine oil dumps around the Grove and you couldn't get away from the stuff. Apart from the lingering smell there was also a good chance you'd walk in it, as they certainly hadn't taken a lot of care to clean the place up. The poor old bandstand was in very poor shape; during their tenure of the site the army had made the bandstand into various offices as I have described. When it had served its purpose, not a lot of effort was made to make good the building.

Everywhere you would find rubbish such as a few pin-up pictures and slogans like 'Kilroy was here' and 'Hitler – here we come' etc, I suppose there was little incentive to make good the place, probably, the decision had already been made to get rid of the old bandstand after the war so it wasn't important at the time; also there was still a war to be won.

There was certainly an uncanny atmosphere around the place after the inhabitants left; something like the feeling of a ghost town took over! For a time this situation suited us as it was the ideal place to play and nobody seemed to take much notice of us. (Eventually, after the war the Council did indeed demolish the bandstand, clean up the area and build a children's play ground on the old site). It really hasn't changed much since then. I can still remember some rather excellent swings and a seesaw that used to be located near to the Mount Zion part of the Grove which we played on when we were children; the present ones are a poor substitute as I recall!

In 1944, we were very conscious that the war was still having a big impact on people's lives. The father of one of my friends, Colin Miles, whose mother was a good friend of Mum's, was taken prisoner by the Japanese after the fall of Singapore; they would never see him again.

Another memory I have is that of a young man in Royal Air Force uniform walking down Grove Hill towards the station on a Sunday evening to catch his train back to camp whenever he'd managed to get a weekend break at home. His family lived in one of the roads further up Grove Hill and we would look out for him as he came down the hill heading towards the station with his gas mask over his shoulder. He always carried a little package under his arm and I guess it contained sandwiches his mother had made for the journey back to camp. He wore the brevet of an Air Gunner and probably flew in one of the R.A.F. heavy bomber squadrons. When we didn't see him for some time I asked my Dad if he knew why he didn't appear to come home anymore. Dad told us that the young man was an Air Gunner on a Lancaster Squadron in Lincolnshire and that his aircraft had been shot down over Germany; he and the rest of the crew were missing in action. (It was only after the war had ended that we were to learn that no trace of him or his colleagues was ever found; a situation that would unfortunately be repeated many times)

Much nearer to home however were the sights and sounds of the war as it affected everyone. I clearly recall the day an American four engined B24 Liberator was returning from a mission. It flew over the town with smoke and flames streaming from it. The crew were parachuting out of the stricken machine as it flew on towards Pembury. We watched this from within the Calverley Grounds and I recall a passer by making the comment that he thought all the crew would have been able to get out of the aircraft before it flew into the ground somewhere towards North Kent, several miles away.

At this time in the war the Germans had unleashed their

Mk 1 'terror weapon', the V1 Flying Bomb, onto targets in England. These flying bombs, as they were called, carried no pilot but had a built in guidance system to fly to selected target areas in the proximity of London and its suburbs and were nicknamed, 'Doodlebugs'. They were in fact a small aircraft with a rocket motor mounted on the top of the rear fuselage. The fuselage was filled to capacity with high explosive so it was a pretty potent weapon. The engine was planned to cut off when they got to their target at which point, they would dive towards the ground.

'Doodlebugs' had a distinctive sound which was produced by the staccato effect of the engine exhaust and sounded something like a lorry with no silencer with an engine running at constant speed. You could hear one coming from some way off and as the target was primarily London, they hadn't far to run by the time they passed over Tunbridge Wells! All we hoped was that the darn thing would keep going and we kept our fingers crossed and prayed that it's engine wouldn't expire as it went over us, and the thing would make it to open countryside.

Unfortunately, this wasn't always to be the case and they were to inflict considerable devastation wherever they fell. (I believe that nearly as many people were to be killed by the 'Doodlebugs' as those killed during the whole of the German bombing offensive earlier in the war!) Many would be the time we would feel mesmerised as we watched a 'Doodlebug' fly across the town with an Air Force fighter hot on its heels firing in an attempt to bring the flying bomb down in open country before it reached London.

I'll never forget one day we were at an open air Church service being held on the Lower Cricket Ground in Tunbridge Wells; suddenly, we heard the sound of an approaching 'Doodlebug' which seemed to be coming straight for us. When we caught sight of it, it was indeed heading right across the area of the Common where we were standing. To our horror there, on its tail, was an R.A.F. Tempest fighter firing its bursts of its machine guns as it tried to hit it. They passed directly over the cricket ground, right over our heads and not very high and as they went, empty shell cases cascaded down from the 'fighter, all over the place. We would have been sitting ducks had the thing decided to expire in our area as there was no form of cover anywhere. It was a pretty frightening experience.

I can still remember people running in all directions

fearing the worst, but luck was on our side as both aircraft disappeared over Mount Ephraim and a few minutes later we heard the sound of the flying bomb exploding. As the pilot of the fighter must have hoped; it happened over open countryside near Penshurst. That was one that fortunately didn't make it to the capital!

One of the methods used by the Royal Air Force to bring these things down was to fly alongside the 'Doodlebug' until the wing of the fighter aircraft was underneath the flying bombs wing and then quickly lifting the wing to tip the enemy machine over. Once this happened, the inertial navigation system of the flying bomb went haywire and the machine went out of control. Hopefully into open countryside! I must admit it must have taken considerable nerve to do this but the 'fighter pilots got the manoeuvre off to a fine art and it did work when they got the opportunity.   The secret was locating the flying bomb early enough whilst there were still open areas ahead to allow the pilot to bring it down. With the birth of the Jet Engine, the first jet fighters made their appearance about this time and were primarily engaged in the anti 'Doodlebug' role. Because of their greater speed, they could out perform the flying bombs, something their fast piston engine brothers couldn't always achieve!   I remember the first time we saw one of the new jet fighters flying across the town. It was like something out of one of our comics; no propeller and with a sound like a wailing dog it simply streaked across the sky (The R.A.F. had introduced their new 'Meteor' jet fighters in 1944 and this was to be the first type of jet aircraft we would see.)

It was a case of 'being in the wrong place at the wrong time' for the old tramp when a flying bomb came down and exploded on Tunbridge Wells Common.   When we were young, there was a small summer house on the 'common, located about half way between London Road and the Higher Cricket Ground. Apart from the cricket pavilion, this was about the only building on what was otherwise an area, totally covered in gorse, trees and grass with only the occasional rabbit to be seen. Free grazing of locally owned cattle, on common land, was very much a thing from out of the history books.

The old tramp, who we had seen on many occasions when we had spent time on the common, had on that fateful day gone into the summer house for a sleep. It was his very bad luck that when the 'Doodlebugs' engine cut-out, the bomb made a direct hit right on this summer house!

We were in the Calverley Grounds at the time on what was a very nice summer's day when we heard the noise of the approaching 'Doodlebug'.   Being in the vicinity, we made for the air raid shelter, which was conveniently to hand.   The one thing we got to know about 'Doodlebugs' was that from the time the engine stopped, and an eerie silence began, there was about ten seconds before the thing hit the ground and the shattering explosion took place. This silence was deafening and it seemed an eternity between the engine stopping and the inevitable blast taking place. Once this had happened, we were out of the air raid shelter and scanning the horizon for the tell tale signs as to where the bomb had come down.

From our position in the Calverley Grounds, which was fairly high up, we could see that the smoke came from the part of the common we knew well. We made some excuse to leave my mother on some pretext or other and made our way rapidly to the common. (I recall that we were pretty quick on our feet in those days and were at the scene in no time at all) Because of its remote location, only a few people had got to the area before us so the scene was one of complete devastation when we arrived.

Trev and I were speechless about the scene that greeted us; there was no sign that the summer house had ever existed.   All that was left was just a big hole in the ground with smoke coming from it!   It had been a direct hit. It was only later that a Policeman, who knew us as one of his colleagues children, told us that the old tramp had been in the summer house when it was hit.   He told us that after he'd asked us "what the hell are you kids doing here"!

With that knowledge we went back to find our mother; our mood was in total opposition to that when we'd gone to the common to see what had happened.   We were very subdued at what we had seen. Even though we'd won a couple of fragments of the awful 'Doodlebug', it certainly gave us no peace of mind to know that the poor old tramp had been killed.

To cap it all, my mother took a pretty dim view of the fact that we had gone to the scene in the first place especially when we'd deliberately told her a white lie as to where we were going! This was emphasised when my father came home from his duty.   The Policeman who had seen us on the common had also told my Dad and that compounded the issue; we were to feel his hand and an empty stomach that evening!   To be honest, Trev and I did give my parents a few headaches at times!!   The 'Doodlebug' incident was only one of several such examples of us 'doing our own thing' and not always telling Mum and Dad the whole truth (If my children had gone about doing the things we did, having got their parents permission to do something entirely different, I'd have gone completely hairless – at least at an earlier age!)

Another good example of this was the day we went all the way to Guildford, train spotting, having persuaded my parents to reluctantly agree for us to only go to Tonbridge! At this time, in 1944, Trev had been a member of the Christ Church choir for quite a while and we had received our pay, which was paid every three months and certainly didn't amount to very much!   To the best of my recollections, I seem to recall that our 'quarterly' salaries came to about six Shillings each! (in today's money, that equates to 30 Pence!!) By modern day standards though, it actually bought quite a lot and on the day in question, the rail fare to Guildford represented only a small proportion of our total funds.

Anyway, on the premise that we were going to Tonbridge 'loco spotting, Mum had packed us up some sandwiches and a drink each to accompany her instructions "make sure you only go to Tonbridge, don't go talking to strangers and don't get too close to the edge of the platform."

Her final instructions were "you're only to go there and back."   Well, following Mum's advice, we embarked on our expedition to the very active railway centre of Guildford, a place we'd been planning on visiting for some time. (The prime reason for going to Guildford was because it was a large junction located at a point where the South East & Chatham Railway, S.E. & C.R., met the London & South Western Railway, L. & S.W.R. elements of the Southern Railway, in the pre nationalisation days of the British railway system.)

We had a very successful day. Locomotives that never visited our part of the railway network were in abundance there and our 'Ian Allen Locomotive Numbers Books', in which we faithfully recorded all the engine numbers we'd seen, reflected the results of a very useful and much enjoyed day. That was until we got home.

All had proceeded according to plan until the evening when we were sitting down in the kitchen at number '32, having our tea with my mother and father. To the best of my memory, I guess we were pretty tired and for a moment, I let my guard drop! This came about when the subject of 'Barrage Balloons' came up.

'Barrage Balloons' were used in the anti-aircraft role to prevent attacks by low flying aircraft. The balloon was attached to a strong steel cable and launched to an altitude of about 1000 feet; the theory was that aircraft flying below this height would fly into the steel cables and crash. The idea worked very well and a large number of planes, both German and, unfortunately our own, were to fall foul of these things with catastrophic results.

Anyway, these devices were predominately used to defend London and other major cities. The balloons over London could be seen from certain parts of the Home Counties from some distance away. However, when I told my Dad that we had seen these balloons from Tonbridge, I really shot myself in the foot. My Dad immediately said that you couldn't see them from Tonbridge and then realised that we'd been somewhere we shouldn't have been. (From Guildford, you could however see the balloons very clearly!)

My Dad really hit the roof when he extracted the truth from us; it was a case of straight to bed, after not being allowed to finish our tea and a couple of whacks from his trouser belt. It goes without saying that any further railway expeditions were severely limited for some time after that.

Chapter 6:   My Life Gets More Interesting

Another example of the headaches we used to give our parents occurred when the John Browns Dairies milk float ran away!

Our 'gang' had been playing in the 'Grove and in and around Meadow Hill Road, which was a cul-de-sac just up from number 32, and led directly into the `Grove. Apart from Trevor and I, there was Jackie Warrener, Bill Constance and a complete nut case by the name of Alan Clarke, who lived in Buckingham Road, which was located alongside the Grove.

The milkman on the day in question was partaking of a cup of tea in one of the houses in Meadow Hill Road leaving his milk float parked about half way along the street, in the middle of the road. (There were no cars about in those days so the street was completely empty.) I can't remember what we were doing at the time but I seem to recall a ball game of some description was in progress. Now I know it's easy to forget some things, but I will never forget suddenly realising that the milk float, loaded with its cargo of milk bottles, had started moving. It was running down Meadow Hill Road, which was on a decline, heading towards Grove Hill Road!

To be absolutely honest, Trev and I actually tried to stop the thing by attempting to pull on the hand brake as it trundled past us, but to no avail. (In the subsequent enquiry a lady witness interpreted our actions as letting the brake off in the first place!)

The speed of the 'float got faster and faster as it approached Grove Hill which it met at a ninety degree junction. It careered across the road and hit the high wall of the house opposite Meadow Hill Road with a tremendous crash. Milk bottles went in all directions followed by the milk crates and parts of the 'float as it virtually disintegrated.

To be fair in my description of this incident, I saw what I saw from the entrance of the Grove which I passed rapidly, running as far from the catastrophe as legs would carry me, turning my head to see the scene of devastation behind me as I went! Who, if anyone, let the hand brake off in the first place is a question that was never to be answered. That question was very academic as we hastened from the scene of the crime as fast as we could; all I wanted was to be as far away, as I could get, as there was no doubt about it that some embarrassing questions were going to be asked!

Trev and I met up with each other somewhere down in Madeira Park, not far from the Tunbridge Wells 'Neville' Cricket Ground. We had travelled quite a distance from where the incident had taken place. I remember us comparing notes on what the next line of action would be and the prevailing sense of panic that we would really be for the 'high jump' when my father found out what had happened, let alone the John Browns Dairies! I can recall visions of us all being seen as hooligans and being hauled up in a Juvenile Court as being "totally out of control"; which of course we were not! But to a casual observer the whole thing must have looked bad!

Anyway, after some time considering our position and doing a double check on our stories to make sure we both said the same thing, we sheepishly made our way back to the Grove and towards our home. As we approached Grove Hill Road, we could see the place where the milk float had hit the wall and the milk stained road and footpath. Most of the mess had been cleared up and the battered 'float was back on its wheels but looking decidedly the worse for wear.

Some of the neighbours had helped to clear up the mess and a Policeman was amongst them with his note book and pencil recording any relevant points and eyewitness statements in an attempt to 'assist with his enquiries'.

Surprisingly, as we found out later, nobody actually saw the whole of the incident. However, several ladies had seen us lads playing in the street immediately before the 'float ran away and I guess they got the impression we were involved. The lady who reported that she'd seen Trev and I at the side of the runaway 'float when it was in motion, (that was when we were trying to apply the brake!) assumed we were responsible for the whole incident and told the Policeman so! (we weren't to know that then but her theory came out when the Police came to our house in the evening.) This was much to the embarrassment of my father and mother!

One of our last impressions of the incident as we left the scene was of the poor milkman trying to explain to his boss, a big man wearing a bowler hat, that he had parked his vehicle safely with the handbrake definitely 'on'.

When we got home my mother wanted to know where we'd been and did we know anything about the incident of the runaway milk-float? We told her a story like "we were playing in the road when the milk-float just ran away!" When she asked who we were playing with, once the name of Alan Clarke came up I can remember her saying "I bet that little devil knows something about it, that's just the sort of thing he would do, the little blighter!"

My mother was convinced we didn't do it and this sure did help our case when the Police finally came to the house in the evening. My Dad took a neutral approach to the whole thing and by the time the Police and a representative of John Browns Dairies left our house, Trev and I had been complemented for trying to stop the thing! All of us, including our parents, thought Alan Clarke was the culprit and I suppose over a period of time, the story did filter back to his mother.

I can distinctly remember his mother, a little wizened old lady with a tendency to stoop forward, pointing her finger at Mum one day and saying "my Alan didn't have anything to do with the milk float accident, he was at home with me at the time"! We really didn't know where to put ourselves to stop laughing when she said that. We always knew her as "my Alan" after that and I can remember us still having a good laugh about it in later years. Fortunately, no other vehicle was involved and most of all, no personal injuries either; that was the main thing.

Believe you me, we were not angels but consciously, would never have done anything deliberately as silly as that; would we?

I do recall that Trevor had a mania for lighting fires about this time in our lives! We lived a great outdoor life in those days, especially during school holidays. Our "gang", which lived in the Calverley Grounds as much as possible, had a 'camp' located in an area of scrubland between the Great Hall cinema and the Communal Kitchen. At that time there was a small car park, for use of visitors to the 'Calverley, located between Grove Hill Cottages, where most of our mates lived, and the scrub area where we had our camp. Quick access to the 'camp' site was obtained by climbing over the wall between the two areas. Some time later, access was a lot easier when a large section of the wall fell down one night opening up a great access point!

The area in question bears no resemblance today to how it was when we were children. Hoopers, previously Weeks department store car park now occupies the land where the cottages and the little row of shops used to be which included my Grandfathers. The Communal Kitchen has long since vanished; the Great Hall Cinema is now a high class shopping arcade and home of BBC South East Radio and TV and the scrubland has finished up as another, much needed, multi-storey car park! The 'Courier' printing works and associated buildings have also long disappeared.   A large complex of Insurance Offices and luxury apartments, all in that area, have now replaced them. We were to spend many a happy hour playing in the scrub area and the camp became a second home for us. As I've already said, Trev was usually in charge of lighting and stoking the campfire and he made a pretty good job of it. The trouble with Trev was that he got a real liking for making fires and would take the opportunity of lighting one whenever the chance came up. If we went to play elsewhere, Trev would always explore the chance to light up. Unfortunately, this didn't always please the constabulary and many times there would be awkward questions to answer!

I remember once we were playing in the ruins of a building in Clanricarde Gardens just off of Mount Pleasant. Trev had done his usual thing and 'lit up'.   A neighbour nearby saw smoke and thought that the building was on fire and so called the Emergency Services!   The first we knew of it was when we heard the fire engines arriving accompanied by the Police! Again, what was becoming fairly regular to us, was the sense of panic that came over us as we were confronted by a burly Policeman, and several Firemen, all wanting to know what we were doing and did we know anything about a fire.

They certainly weren't impressed when they realised that the fire was nothing more than us kids mucking about! Fortunately, the Policeman recognised us as one of his colleague's children (again!) and apart from giving us a good telling off on the spot, sent us on our way. However, later that evening, when my Dad came off his beat, he really took us to task about this incident and swore that if he ever caught Trev playing with matches again he would make sure Trev wouldn't forget it! (the ruins in question are now part of the 'Elizabethan Barn' restaurant and night spot, at least it was when I last saw it)

We had a lot of fun in and around the Calverley Grounds and our camp was the focal point of our activities. At least my mother usually roughly knew where we were when we out to play. Our mates were a good bunch of lads in the true sense of the word, if one took out the milk float incident and Trev's inclination to set the town on fire!

We would spend many an hour in the primitive comfort of our second home constructed of old boxes, odd bits of corrugated iron sheeting and the fallen branches of trees etc. (some tree branches were assisted in 'falling from the limb'!)

Many would be the time we would all gather inside its primitive construction and feel quite snug, particularly when it was one of those wet days when normal out of doors play activities would be severely curtailed. In those days, with very little traffic about and when the 'Doodlebugs' didn't disturb it, life was a lot quieter than now; on wet days, sitting in the 'comfort' of our second home, the sound of the rain coming down was deafening! I won't forget the drip, drip of the raindrops as they found their way inside; the frantic efforts to 'bung up' the sources of the leaks and the strong damp smell of well wetted leaves and branches.

Trev, who had rigged up an area for a little fire as one of the priorities in the construction of the camp, usually managed to get something to burn and that certainly cheered things up on dismal days. Although his fire had a chimney, constructed from a section of household water drainpipe, its ventilation qualities were not of the highest order and it didn't perform that well. It wasn't very successful in removing the smoke and fumes from inside the abode and we usually went home, smelling just like kippered fish!

Again I must say that my mother's task in bringing up two 'right Herbert's' in the war years was a full time job and in looking back, I wouldn't have envied her. In these days with modern conveniences such as washing machines, detergents, hot water on tap etc. and most homes having a shower or bath readily accessible, I guess it wouldn't have been too bad. In those days my mother had none of these 'luxuries' available to keep us clean and presentable. I can now imagine that the regular filthy state of us both would have tried the patience of a saint!

She had to resort to hand washing everything in the kitchen sink using blocks of yellow 'Carbolic' soap. This had a strong pungent smell about it. It surely must have been hard work ensuring that her two sons didn't walk about smelling like a couple of bonfires on legs!

Surprisingly, nobody appeared to mind us having our camp in the Calverley Grounds. The area we were using was waste ground anyway and not used for anything else. The occasional policeman would sometimes be attracted to its location by the signs of rising smoke coming from Trev's chimney but after finding the source would invariably go on his way without giving us any problems. This was because both the local police and the grounds men, of the Calverley Grounds, who looked after the park, had got used to us always being there. They even got to know us all by our Christian names as we became increasingly familiar to them.

There were times however when they would get rather upset with some of our activities and would make concentrated efforts to chase us out of the park. They got very upset when we started playing our version of 'war games' in the Rhododendron bushes located in various parts of the grounds!.

The usual format for these games was that having dressed up to resemble something looking like soldiers, or Cowboys and Indians. We would split up in two teams and, with the whole of the Calverley Grounds at our disposal, one team would set out to find the other and 'ambush' the other team. In our opinions, the 'Calverley was the ideal place for these activities having plenty of cover, usually in the various shrubbery and flower beds, and lots of places where particularly good ambushes could take place.

The 'ammunition' for these exploits came from the flower beds themselves in the form of the freshly dug clods of earth which were in abundance. The resulting 'battles' left trails of these clods on the grass and footpaths and a thick dirt dust in the air whilst the battles were in progress. We all found this to be great fun; unfortunately, our enthusiasm for these exploits, wasn't shared by the grounds-men, who saw all their hard work being totally wrecked by the dreaded Gardner brigade!

In various attempts to put an end to these activities, the grounds men themselves tried to lure us into traps by letting us think our 'war games' hadn't been seen by them. Their plan was that as we were absorbed in taking out each other with these clods of earth, the grounds men would creep up on us from various directions and attempt to catch us or chase us all out of the grounds.

As you can imagine, once the grounds men were seen by either of the opposing forces, we ran like merry hell. With us all going in different directions, it was almost impossible for the grounds-men to catch us, and to the best of my recollections, we were always one step ahead of them.

We could certainly shift in those days! As far as I can recall, they never did catch us but it wasn't long before the head grounds-man got to know where we lived and went to see my father about his unruly sons and their associates. Mr. Dann, who was the head grounds-man, lived in the house just inside the Calverley Grounds as you entered from Mount Pleasant. I guess the location at least allowed him to monitor the goings on in the park, especially in the out of hour's periods. I sometimes got the impression that in a way, the grounds men used to get a bit of fun out of their exploits in trying to get us out of the park. It probably broke up the sometimes monotony of their job.

Whenever this happened and we got a strong telling off by my father, we usually packed up this particular line of activity for a few days to let the situation cool, before we went back to doing the same thing all over again. (I believe I said earlier we certainly weren't angels at this period in our life!)

This particular activity came to an abrupt end one day, when playing our War Games. By pure accident, one of the clods of earth hit one of my friends, Raymond Fabb, (Fabby) in the middle of his back. Normally this wouldn't have done any harm but on this occasion, the clod contained a piece of iron! When the accident happened we all thought the lad was seriously injured as he dropped like a stone; fortunately, he was only winded and bruised but it gave us all the fright of our lives and nobody suggested we play that game again! The incident did more to curtail the 'war games' exploits than any amount of being chased out of the grounds had done.

'Fabby' lived with his mother in Claremont Road, located at the top of Grove Hill Road. He was of the same age as myself and we were good friends and eventually went on to secondary school together before the family moved away from the town. On the night of the above incident, I remember his mother coming to our house demanding to see my father whilst she 'dragged' Fabby behind her. She was understandably furious and anxious at what had happened but within a very short time, moderated her attitude as my Dad managed to persuade her that it had been an unfortunate accident, it hadn't been carried out with any evil intent and could have happened to anyone of us. My Dad had a way with him when it came to situations like this; he had the charm of 'old Nick', in many respects, which was a very good thing when you consider the sorts of problems we caused which he and my mother had to deal with from time to time.

Surprisingly, we didn't hear anymore about the clod throwing incident from my Dad.

At about this time, another of my friends, David Harris, who lived at the Calverley Grounds end of Mountfield Gardens, found an injured rook which had fallen from its nest in one of the nearby trees. After a lot of effort we managed to 'capture' this bird and David took it home. Now a rook is a pretty big bird and this one was no exception. It was also one of the ugliest birds I've ever seen!

Anyway, David and his mother persisted in their efforts to tame the bird and made such a success of it that it was destined to live the rest of its life, with them, in the house! This bird was to become a character in more ways than one. It was to feature in several reports in the 'Courier' during it's lifetime and in the opinion of David's mother, it was better than any guard dog! The bird lived in their kitchen and I can remember, whenever I went in their house, it would jump down from its usual location, on top of a large cupboard in the corner of the living room, and swoop towards you; squawking its head off as it flew. For any unsuspecting soul entering the room, it would have been quite a shock as it was a rather frightening experience if one wasn't prepared for it.

I can't remember what they named it but it certainly became a key member of their family and lived for a very long time. Whenever you thought of David and his mother, the bird always came to mind; it was as though it had always been with them. David's mother, who was a long time friend of my mother, used to run a little 'Bed & Breakfast' business at their home when we were children.   I wonder what her paying guests thought of the rook?

It couldn't have been easy in the war years running that

kind of business; what with the rationing, etc. As I've already said, they had a very large house of three stories, on the right hand side and just before you entered the Calverley Grounds. Whenever you went into the house there always seemed to be the smell of cooking lingering in the air. To the best of my recollections, she did pretty well for trade in those difficult times so the bird didn't appear to frighten off the customers! I never gave it much thought at the time but I don't ever remember seeing David's father.

That sort of question never really came to mind when we were children; I suppose that with so many men away fighting a war, if you didn't see a man about the house, there was a general assumption they were away in the Forces. As my father was in his early forties and was in the Police, his position was fairly secure and I guess he would only have been called up in dire emergency if things weren't going well for Britain.

It was about this time that we began to see Prisoners of War working on the land and places like building sites, etc. In the majority, the prisoners we saw around Tunbridge Wells were Italian and they were easily recognisable by the uniform P.O.W. clothing they wore. We never did find out where they were camped, but it couldn't have been far from the town, as they became regulars around the place. In our curiosity, we got to know a few of them and once we got to know how to communicate with them they always seemed very pleasant to us. Their knowledge of the English language was pretty poor. We never saw any German prisoners although I can remember my father saying, on several occasions, that the Police Station had hosted several at times, pending their collection by the Army. These were usually crews of aircraft which had been shot down in the area of the town and I guess they had been rounded up by members of the 'Dad's Armies' (Home Guard's) in the outlying districts.

There were, however, several German aircrew buried in the Tunbridge Wells Cemetery at Hawkenbury. We first saw the graves there during one of Mum's, 'ride there, walk back' evenings out. I know cemeteries aren't everybody's idea of the place to go for an outing, but in those days, on a lovely summer's evening there was something so very peaceful about the place.

The grounds were always immaculate; there were magnificent Golden Firs and Green Conifers and excellent views of the surrounding countryside. We were fascinated with some of the statues of Angels and other figures on the gravestones; they were so elegant. Some of the mausoleum type places were a little awe inspiring, but on the whole, the peace of the place had a certain attraction and was such a change from the everyday way of life. We didn't mind going there and in a sombre sort of way, we quite enjoyed it! When we were children the Cemetery always appeared to be such a tidy and well cared for place.   I guess in respects, it really hasn't changed much from those days although it must cover a much larger area of land, nowadays in order   to accommodate   the   increasingly   huge   numbers   of   the Tunbridge Wells deceased.

What has obviously changed the place is the addition of the Crematorium, which did not exist in the days of our youth and was built post war.

In a remote part of the Cemetery, there was an area allocated to German airmen's graves. It always appeared to us that they had been hidden away from the rest of the graves in a little area of their own where not many people would bother to go. I never did understand why this had to be the case, particularly when I thought back to my Grandparent's picture, which always depicted the 'In Death Respect' motto! Somebody must have had some regard for those fallen airmen as I recall there were usually flowers on the graves? We liked to think that similar treatment of our forces took place in village and town churchyards in the parts of Europe where they fell. The German airmen's graves are not in the Cemetery now as they were moved some time after the war, to the German Military Cemetery at Cannock Chase, in the North of England.   At least they now lie with their comrades.

Another one of my mother's evening outings was to the village of Speldhurst, about three miles from Tunbridge Wells. Again the formula would be to bus there and walk back. Speldhurst, in those days, was a quiet little village which was located in the area between Fordcombe and Penshurst. As I recall it, the road there went only to the village itself; a sort of 'end of the road' type of place being as far as the bus went. I do remember that it had a little pub near the bus stop and if we'd been good, which of course we always were, Mum sometimes bought us a shandy before we started our walk back to the 'Wells. She would also get us a packet of crisps, when they were available, but that would be the exception as, bearing in mind the impact of food rationing, those kinds of things were rarely in stock.

The walk itself was always very pleasant especially on a summer's evening. The route from Speldhurst led towards Rusthall along our way and across some lovely open countryside. In 1944 however, a large proportion of this area was occupied as a tented camp for Canadian and American soldiers, G.I's, as they were known. One of the attractions to us was that the walk progressed around the perimeter of the camp and many of the soldiers would come over to the fence to talk to us and usually gave us some candy or chewing gum. I think also they liked the opportunity to talk to the 'natives'.

On many of these walks, we would usually be accompanied by Miss Pope, who lived in the flat above us at number 32. There certainly wasn't any physical attraction for the soldiers regarding Alice Pope, she was a short round type of person and wore heavy horn-rimmed spectacles; she had a heart of gold however and was always good cheerful company and I guess in those days, leading up to the 'D Day' offensive, she brought a little light relief to the soldiers in their conversations with us.

After passing the army camp, the route brought us into Rusthall at the far end of the village. From there it was a straightforward walk across Rusthall and the Tunbridge Wells Common, home. I lost count of how many times we did that particular walk but we never declined the opportunity of going whenever my mother suggested it. However, it never seemed quite the same after the Invasion of Normandy; the G.I's were there one day; and gone the next!

The first time we did the walk soon after June 6, 1944, the field where the Americans had been was now completely deserted with the outlines of where their tents and equipment had been, being still clearly visible. All that was left were the memories and the ghosts of pleasant young men from a long way away who had always welcomed us as we passed their temporary home. We would miss their conversation and good humour and, in particular, the chewing gum and candy! It was never the same after that and our interest in that particular walk declined rapidly after they had gone.

Chapter 7:   The End Of The War and Life Moves On

I clearly remember the Invasion of Normandy. That day, June 6 1944, dawned with the sound of aircraft roaring overhead. When we first heard the aircraft we really didn't know what to make of it; the sound was reminiscent of much that had gone on throughout the war years. However, this day was to be completely different.   The aircraft were not outbound on another bombing run, but were towing gliders and their route was in a Southerly direction towards France.

When we ran out of our home to find out what all the noise was about, we found the sky full of aircraft and it was an unbelievable sight.   Having never seen anything like it before, we didn't realise that the close formations were in fact aircraft with gliders in tow; this was something we knew nothing about and it was my Dad who explained the significance of what we were witnessing. The sky appeared to be black with aircraft of all shapes and sizes. There were Halifax and Stirling, heavy four engine bombers, smaller twin engine fighter bombers and Dakota transports, all towing their respective gliders which we were to learn, were loaded with troops and equipment. It was a sight we would never forget; I have never seen so many aircraft airborne together at the same time.   It took some considerable time for the invasion force to pass overhead en route to their final destinations.   We were concerned that there could be collisions as the formations were extremely tightly packed together, not leaving much room for error.

Their passing over the town seemed to take a very long time.   It was a true case of aluminium Overcast'! (In later years the Americans were to knick name the British Royal Air force Vulcan, delta wing, bomber aircraft an 'Aluminium Overcast').

Life really did not change much as we approached the last year of the war.   There was an obvious relief in many people's attitudes that at long last, we were going to get our own back and with luck, would finally rid the world of Hitler and his cronies.   I felt it was an optimistic period for everyone; we all knew there would be setbacks but, all things being equal, we would soon see the end of the war.   What would life in 'peacetime' really be like? The thought was too good to believe, as the war seemed as though it had been with us forever.

Food supplies were still strictly rationed and although my mother got on well with key people like 'Crackers' in 'Raisewells', in Grove Hill Road, and this produced some little extras from under the counter, it was not an easy task for her to keep the "wolf from the door". All in all though our Mum did a very good job but I am sure she herself often went without and gave the priority to her always hungry sons!

She had an arrangement with the fruit and vegetable department of 'Raisewells', on Mount Pleasant, that they would let her have any speckled or unsellable fruit. Often she would come home with quite a selection of apples and even the occasional orange! That was a real treat! Usually there wasn't a lot wrong with the things she got and they went a long way towards filling us up.

In hindsight though, and with the benefit of being adult, I wonder whether Mum had these things given to her, as to the best of my recollections, money wasn't a commodity we had an abundance of. Maybe folks were happy to give little bits, like the speckled fruit, to her, knowing she had two sons who probably ate her out of house and home. Its things like this that make me so grateful for everything my parents represented. and did. Both my mother and my father were not the sort of people who made a priority of having a lot of possessions and in general, they lived a very simple life. I think however in that respect, I am completely the opposite!

I guess it was about this time that Trev and I became aware of my cousin, Peter. As I've already said, the connections between my father's family members, wasn't that harmonious and the relationships were, in my opinion, cool. The reason for this is something I never really got to the bottom of and it resulted in the fact that we, on my father's side, were virtual strangers to the family of his sister, Vera.

They lived in a different part of the town to us and not far from the Grosvenor Railway Bridge. I can't remember the actual name of the road but it was about three hundred yards from the bridge as you went up the hill which was opposite the bridge. The name of their house was 'Sunny Ridge'. I can remember my parents often talking about the house although I got the impression that my father found the whole subject a sore point.

—

As I've already said, in my opinion, there was an extremely strained relationship in the Gardner family and with the benefit of hindsight, I believe the main factor was 'Sunny Ridge'. When I discussed this once with my Mother many years later, she confirmed that my Father had in many respects, felt aggrieved about the fact that the house was funded to a large degree by his parents.   Unfortunately, such an arrangement wasn't reciprocal to him, at least not when he was fathering a family.   This, coupled with the preferential treatment that Vera's family appeared to receive from my Grandparents, didn't really help the situation. We have always tried to treat our own children as fairly as possible.

Peter was caught up in this scenario and could certainly do little or nothing wrong, particularly in the eyes of my Grandmother.   I must say that I believe that towards the end of his life, some many years later, Septimus did try to put things right with my Father and helped my parents considerably with their purchase of 7 Mountfield Road.   I don't want to make it sound as though we were hard done by as I really liked my Grandparents and in general, we always got on well together.   They were nice folks and I guess they, at different times, did what they could for both of their children.   It just seemed to me, as a young child at that time, that it wasn't quite a fair equation but of course hindsight is 20/20 vision. By the time matters had been somewhat righted the lack of communication between aunt Vera's and later Peter's households, and ours, had sadly become a habit.

To the best of my recollections, I believe that as a family, we never actually went to 'Sunny Ridge' and I was in my 'teens before I saw the house for the first time. I must admit that every time I pass the house these days, usually in my roundabout routes around Tunbridge Wells in attempts to beat the traffic, it always brings back the thoughts of the significance of the role the house played in the lives of the Gardner family.

The one exception to this situation was that Trev and I got on reasonably well with Vera's son Peter. Our usual place to meet was, if you couldn't guess, at the Central Station. Peter was a few years older than us and was in many respects, very much a loner. Maybe this came about by the fact that he was an only son and very much guarded and 'protected' by his parents and grandparents. I always got the feeling that my Grandmother especially was overly protective towards him to the extent that he was mollycoddled and nothing was too good for him.

Peter was readily identifiable even from a distance, by the long dark raincoat he appeared to live in and by his distinctive style of walking. For a young man, his posture, whereby he appeared to lean forward as he walked, was very much that of a much older person and probably contributed to the impression that he was a lot older than he was.   I don't know exactly what the age difference was, probably no more than four or five years, but it seemed a lot to us at the time.

We would often meet up with Peter at the 'Central during our train spotting sessions and because he appeared to be something of an expert on the subject of railways, would usually believe all he told us.   However, it wasn't long before Trev and I learned that not all that he told us was always to be believed!   This was highlighted once when he 'swapped' some postcard photographs with us of supposedly, some of our favourite locomotives in their very early days of service with the Southern Railway. He had told us about these pictures several times and generated our interest to the point whereby he promised to let us have them in exchange for some we had which were of interest to him. Anyway, when the time came for the swap he turned up with a load of postcards of engines that would never see our part of the country as in the majority, they were all engines of the London Midland Railway!

I guess we were a little naive in many respects and I think this could have been an early example of learning the rule that you should never believe all that people tell you; even if they're members of the same family!

Anyway, we enjoyed Peter's company on our railway spotting exploits and many were the hours spent at the 'Central pursuing our shared enthusiasm.   Regrettably, I was to lose contact with Peter from the time I joined the R.A.F. and feel remiss in stating that I honestly do not know what became of him.   Having not lived in Tunbridge Wells from the age of seventeen, has contributed towards losing touch with many associates of my childhood.   Unfortunately, these situations are all too frequent in families I'm afraid and ours appears to be no exception.   I believe that Trev sees him from time to time around the town so that's reassuring in some respects.   He was a sad character in many ways but at the time we were young, you didn't appreciate loneliness and really didn't have any understanding of it.

As 1945 approached, my years as a pupil at Christ Church School were beginning to come to an end and the daunting thought of moving on to Secondary School, from the relative tranquillity of Christ Church primary school, was something I really didn't relish.

At this time I was in the 'top class' run by Miss Turner and in general, I probably enjoyed school as much during this period as at any time in the whole of my academic life. I got on well with Miss Turner and did fairly well in my studies, particularly in subjects of 'Geography', 'Art' and 'Science'. In those days, one's achievements were rewarded by annual assessments. Those who did well were given prizes, usually in the form of a book choice.

The prize giving usually occurred towards the end of the term preceding the summer holidays and formed part of the 'winding down' period. I was fortunate that certain of the subjects I enjoyed the most resulted in my doing fairly well in them and therefore put me in line for a prize or two. In my last year at Christ Church I was lucky enough to win two books; one for 'Geography' and the other for 'General Progress', whatever that meant! I still have one of these books in my collection (sic, Library!) and whenever I see it, it brings back the pleasure of the occasion and the pride I felt when I brought it home to show my parents.

At this time, assessments of pupils were being carried out to establish their potential for Grammar School secondary education. In particular, suitability for 'Skinners School' was my prime objective and I was successful in passing the written element. However, having passed the first hurdle, I was faced with the daunting task of facing an oral examination for final selection and this possibility terrified me. Self confidence was a little lacking in me at that age and the thought of sitting in front of a panel of learned people gave me nightmares. My mother went out of her way to make me look the part. She bought me a new jacket, trousers and flannel shirt from her much treasured wartime clothing coupons and I guess I looked as smart as I could when the time came to attend the assessment.

To be honest; I hated flannel shirts. In general, my mother used to replace these shirts about twice a year, in the Spring and again in the Autumn was about the schedule and

I can remember that as we approached the replacement time, we made every excuse to prolong the life of the old, and more comfortable ones.   Of course, the new shirts always seemed to make their debut on a Sunday morning so that when we attended the Church choir, we were feeling less than comfortable and I'm sure, gave the impression to the congregation that something wasn't quite right with us as we really itched beneath our cassocks!   The subject of flannel shirts still brings home to me just how miserable to wear they were when worn for the first time.   I realise that my mother bought them because they gave long hardwearing service, essential with growing boys, but, in my opinion, they were the most uncomfortable garment one could wear and I know that Trevor also felt the same way about them as I did.

From the moment you put it on the 'itchiness' began and it was a full time job not to give people the impression that you weren't suffering from a form of 'Saint Vitus's Dance'!   The only time these shirts were comfortable were just before the time came to throw them away when the fibres of the material rendered them only suitable for domestic jobs, i.e. cleaning cloths etc.

The oral interview went very well after the initial few tense minutes. Being the first most important interview of my life, one did the best you could but I got the distinct impression fairly early on that I wouldn't be successful on that occasion and it did indeed prove to be the case.   The biggest disappointment I felt was to the people who had given me all their support, from my parents and the teachers at Christ Church School.   Even at that age, you really didn't want to let people down and in many ways that was more important than the disappointment to yourself.

Anyway, one learns that life is rarely as smooth as we'd all like and in fact, we never stop the learning process so I guess my first interview had to go down to the learning curve of life.   I reckon we learn as much from our failures as we do our successes but of course at the time, it was a great disappointment to me.

As 1945 dawned it became very noticeable to us that the numbers of military personal around the town were becoming much fewer in number.   In the pre 'D-Day' period there were always a lot of soldiers about and, as already mentioned, numerous camps were located around the outskirts of the town.   After June 1944 it would never quite be the same again and as children, we really missed them after the invasion of Normandy began.

There was a general realisation that the war would not go on for much longer and I guess people began to think about life getting back to normal. It didn't really have a great significance to us at the time; at our young ages, we had really grown up in a wartime environment and it was hard to visualise life without the drab and rather dull existence the war had brought with it.

At this time life was much the same for us. We still had lots of fun particularly in the Calverley Grounds with our 'camp' located on the scrubland at the rear of the 'Great Hall Cinema' Trevor in all his wisdom, probably learning from the examples of the German 'Doodlebugs', had perfected a unique method of turning cast iron water drain piping, usually removed after dark from some building site or other, into a sort of primitive flame thrower!

His secret was to stuff the inside bore of the pipe with dry grass, place the pipe upwind and light the opposite end. The wind accelerated the burning process and within a few seconds, the grass would ignite along the entire length of the pipe with a considerable roar which turned the outside of the pipe white hot in no time at all. We nicknamed it 'Trev's Rocket'.

Actually, the original example of this came about purely by accident. One morning when we were trying to get the fire going in our camp, Trev, more out of frustration than anything because he couldn't get the fire to light, came up with the brilliant idea of influencing the burning process by inducing the fire in the 'chimney'. I don't think he bargained on the fact that it would indeed be so successful; before we knew where we were, there was a huge roar and the chimney turned red hot!

Unfortunately, the camp wasn't designed for such a heat source and before we knew where we were, we had to run for water to put the fire out as there was a distinct danger that the camp would go up in flames. Unfortunately there wasn't a ready water supply to hand and we had to resort to drastic methods i.e. like virtually destroying the camp to put the fire out. Trevor's name was mud believe you me; anyway, not to be outdone, he perfected his 'drain pipe rocket' instead so I guess something came out of it.

It was about this time that one day when my Dad came home from his Police 'beat', he told us that a British aircraft had made a forced landing in open countryside; just the other side of the Cemetery. As you can imagine, this was something we just had to go and see so at the first opportunity, later that afternoon, we trekked up to the Cemetery to see what it was all about.

We found out that the aircraft had actually come down on open countryside as Dad had said, on the other side of the Bayham Road almost opposite the Cemetery. It was a good walk for our young legs but we were glad we made the effort. The aircraft was Supermarine 'Walrus' of R.A.F. Coastal Command, a single engine amphibious biplane, mainly used for observation of shipping lanes and rescuing downed aviators etc. It had a crew of three and fortunately, wasn't badly damaged. It had come down on its hull and skidded across the field; fortunately, there were no obstructions in its path so it didn't come to much harm.

At the end of it's slippery 'landing run', having no wheels down and relying on the hull for support, it tipped over on to its wingtip. We gathered from somebody who seemed in know, that the aircraft had an engine problem and the crew decided to make a forced landing. They chose a good place for it as it so happened, as it was a very large field.

I guess that was to be my first encounter with a real aeroplane; I know at the time, both Trev and I were amazed as to how big this thing seemed to be although, in fact, it was a relatively small machine, especially by modern day standards!

The Air Force were very quick to remove the aircraft. Within a few hours of its arrival, a large truck, affectionately known as a 'Queen Mary', was on site; the wings were taken off and together with the fuselage all was then loaded onto the truck and driven away. Coincidentally, the site of this incident was no more than two to three hundred yards from the house that Trevor now lives in. Before the death of Mr Baker, Trevor's future father in law, we discussed the incident of this force landing. I know that Trevor's in-laws and their daughter Pauline, who became Trevor's wife, did not move to the family home in Tangier Lane until after the war, but Mr Baker surprised us by saying that he never knew anything about the forced landing incident! Probably, if it hadn't been for my Dad mentioning it, we wouldn't have known about it either and the incident would have gone unrecorded as far as we were concerned!   It wasn't the sort of item that local newspapers covered at the time as I guess it would probably have been considered as giving information to the 'enemy'.

Chapter 8:   Peacetime Begins

It's hard now to say exactly how we reacted to the news that the war in Europe was over. As children, our thoughts probably centered on the possibilities that there would suddenly be an abundance of everything and food and sweets would be in plentiful supply before we knew where we were. Unfortunately, the reality of the matter was that everything took far longer to get back to 'normal' than anyone could have envisaged.   Food and clothes rationing were destined to remain with us for many years to come.

History records, the war in Europe finished on May 8 1945. What I can remember was the relief everybody felt with the realisation that hostilities, so close to home were finally over. The fact that war with Japan was still being waged didn't reduce the relief we all shared as peace became a reality in Europe.   How close our country came to losing the war earlier on was not to become clear until many years later. As a ten-year-old boy, it was difficult to imagine what life would actually be like in peacetime. The years between five and ten are very impressionable. The war had been something we had in a way, grown up with and without the background of the uncertainty that had become a part of everyone's way of life the future took on a markedly different complexion.

It was about this time that I was told that I would have to go into hospital for a minor operation. Mum had been concerned for a time about two little lumps that had appeared on my stomach, just above the 'tummy button'; no, I wasn't changing sex! After discussions with our doctor, he arranged for an exploratory operation in the Kent & Sussex Hospital to get to the bottom of the problem. The thought of going into hospital filled me with trepidation and I knew I wasn't going to look forward to that event whatsoever. I can remember my last day at school before I went into the hospital. I almost got the impression that it was unlikely that I would be returning! Miss Turner, the Headmistress, made reference to my forthcoming absence at school assembly and I can recall the looks of childish sympathy on the faces of my classmates as if to say, "it has been nice knowing you"! I kept telling my friends that it was only a minor operation, mainly in the hope to give myself confidence as much as anything!

When the fateful day arrived to be admitted, Mum and I walked to the Kent & Sussex Hospital, which was located next to St. Augustine's Church along Mount Ephraim. The hospital is still there but the church isn't! The church was subsequently pulled down in the 1950's to allow expansion of the hospital car park!

The formalities were duly completed and I was finally told to go to Ward 11, known as it is to this day, as the Men's Surgical Ward. I was the youngest patient in a large, but very light ward, full of a wide variety of different aged men. I was given a bed about half way along the ward on the right, next to a large window, which gave an excellent view across Molyneaux Park towards Rusthall. With the departure of my mother, the other patient's didn't waste much time in making me feel at home and before I knew where I was, I felt like one of a reasonably happy family and the fears of the impending 'exploratory' operation, fortunately receded.

After a couple of days of varying checks, the Doctor told me that he would be operating the next day. My fellow patients boosted my self confidence at this point and in a way, thanks to them, I wasn't worried about the operation at all and of course the nurses were all very reassuring.

I was pleased to be able to say that the result of the operation, fortunately, was that the 'lumps' were found to be small balls of fat and were not harmful. This proved to be a very great relief to me. We've all been through the traumas of operations so I won't dwell on the subject. What I must say however is that one can never over emphasise the value of the support given by the nursing staff and fellow patients when you are in a situation like that. I guess it was my first exposure to what is an essential ingredient in life, comradeship and team spirit. Both elements of which were to play such an important part later on in my life; particularly in my years after leaving school and during my time in the R.A.F.

In many ways I cannot say that I didn't actually enjoy my time in hospital. Miss Turner was a brick; she arranged for my classmates at Christ Church School to write letters to me, and to send drawings and other school nick-knacks to help keep my morale up. With visits also from Mum, Dad, Trev and Miss Pope, I did pretty well and the two weeks I was to spend there really went fairly quickly. Visiting times were far more limited then than they are nowadays. Unfortunately, whilst in the hospital, I witnessed a very bad aircraft accident. You may indeed ask how someone in hospital can actually watch an aircraft accident?

Well, as I have already said, I had a superb view from my bed space in the ward, looking towards Rusthall, which was probably no more than about a mile from the hospital "as the crow flies". In those days, prior to the post war building programmes, much more open countryside was still surrounding the town. I could see the village of Rusthall and in particular, the local school, very clearly.

I remember it was a lovely clear sunny day when the other patients, and I, heard the sound of a low flying aeroplane. This drew our attention to the windows. Having just emerged from the war it was nice not to have to worry about whether the plane was "one of ours" or not, so we scanned the sky to see what kind of aircraft it was. At the age I was at the time, I was beginning to have quite an interest in aircraft recognition and from my vantage point I could see it was a twin engine aircraft, either a Mosquito or Blenheim, fighter bomber of the Royal Air Force. The pilot was flying extremely low in the area of Rusthall and seemed to be circling the school at about a couple of hundred feet.

The manoeuvre of the aircraft fascinated those who were watching and there were times that the aircraft came very close to the hospital during its circuits, which concerned several of the patients. During one of these circuits, whilst the aircraft was carrying out a very tight turn in the direct vicinity of the school, we saw parts starting to fall off of it. The aircraft appeared to be locked in its turn with the pilot trying to steer the aircraft away from the village when, to our horror, it went into a terminal dive and exploded in a huge fireball as it hit the ground.

The crew didn't have any chance of escaping from the aircraft and apart from that, we were sure from where we were watching that people on the ground must have also been hit as the aircraft fell. It was a sickening sight as the pall of smoke rose skywards; nobody said anything for some time until one of the men said something like "poor buggers".

Suddenly, the lovely sunny day didn't seem so lovely anymore.

I later learned that fortunately, nobody on the ground was hurt in the accident, which surely must have been a miracle. The aircraft crashed into the Rusthall School playing ground and as it was a school holiday, the place was unoccupied at the time.   It appears the pilot, who was a local man, had family relations living in Rusthall.   I guess fate played it's hand in that event but it could have been a total disaster if the 'plane had come down on the village.   In the event, it was just the pilot and his crewman who were the victims; the "poor buggers".   They had made it through the war only to come to grief on their own doorstep during a routine training flight!   Coincidentally, several years later in the mid 'fifties, when I was in the Royal Air Force, a similar incident occurred, in which a Meteor Night Fighter crashed into the centre of the village of Wadhurst, which is also located near to Tunbridge Wells.   Once again, the pilot was a local man and I guess, lost control of the aircraft 'showing off' to his family and friends!   On that occasion, both the pilot and navigator, and several people on the ground, lost their lives.   Additionally many houses were flattened and further lives also lost.   The whole thing was horrific and so wasteful.

I spent about two weeks in the hospital and was glad to get home and to get back with my mates.   Hospitals were able to hang on to their patients for far longer in those early days of the new National Health Service!   The thought of getting back to our camp and our deliberations with the gardeners in the Calverley Ground's, had a strong appeal after my period away from the scene.

It was about this time, just after the war, that the military put on quite a few special Exhibitions and staged manoeuvres in public places to show the people some of the hardware and tactics used in the war.   One of these was a large mock battle, which took place in the Calverley Grounds one summer afternoon towards the end of 1945. The event had been extensively advertised and on the day, was very well supported.   I had never seen so many people in the park before and I doubt if there has ever been as many since.

The 'action' was to take place in the area between the Communal Kitchen and Grove Hill Road and included the Bowling Green and the tennis courts, etc.   The participants were a large contingent of the Royal West Kent Regiment and elements of the Home Guard or the 'Dads Army' as they became affectionately known as!

What made us smile was the fact that our Choirmaster, Mr. Pallant was playing his part in the Home Guard brigade.

He was a very reserved man in his everyday life, except when at choir practice where he had been known to throw the odd projectile in the form of a hymnbook etc, at selected choirboys when he thought they weren't paying attention; so we treated him with a certain amount of respect.

However on this particular day, he was dressed up in his uniform with full webbing, rifle etc. and really looked quite aggressive. This image was further highlighted by the fact that he had blackened his face with boot polish and had implanted leaves and sticks in his helmet! I will never forget the moment we first saw him when we arrived to see the display. We were with my mother walking along to the spectator's area when Mr. Pallant, who was with a group of other men dressed in army uniform, came over to us. The unfortunate thing was that he had the advantage in that he could recognise us but we hadn't got a clue as to who he was because of his camouflage. It was all very embarrassing for a while until he told us it was he. When we realised it was Mr. Pallant, I don't know how we didn't split our sides with laughter, as he really looked as though he had just come out of a 'Boy's Own' comic. When he went on his way to play his part in the display, Mum went into one of her laughing fits and we all joined in. It was one of the funniest things we'd seen for a long while.

After the hilarious start to the afternoon, we were enthralled with the action that then took place. The spectators were located on the banks in the Calverley Grounds, between the bandstand and the Calverley Hotel and therefore had a grandstand view of the event. The object of the demonstration was to show how an attacking force could overcome resistance and obstacles in the path of their advance.

The funny thing to us was the fact that the defenders were played by the Home Guard units and the attacking force were the regular army; in many ways, we thought this an unfair contest but I must say that our choirmaster really put up a great fight before his position was overrun. From where we stood we could see Mr. Pallant having the time of his life as he, and his platoon, threw Thunderflashes and fired off numerous blank bullets at the attackers. It was great fun to watch and many of us youngsters would have given anything to have taken part in it as it reminded us in many ways of the games we would often play in the park; although our ammunition and smoke would be clods of earth and hands full of dirt! As children, we were all very impressed with the display that took place; the loud explosions and heavy smoke effects were most spectacular and we thoroughly enjoyed the event. We were to play simulated games of attackers and defenders in the Calverley Grounds for many weeks after that, although we didn't ask Mr. Pallant to join us!

It was soon after the Army exercise that the Royal Air Force decided to show some of their 'hardware' to the public after the war in Europe had finished. Not actually knowing what was going on, one day we were surprised when an R.A.F. "Queen Mary" arrived in the Calverley Grounds carrying a Mosquito aircraft.   Shortly afterwards, a party of R.A.F. men and a large crane turned up and began unloading the aeroplane from the transporters.

This all took place adjacent to the Communal Kitchen in the main entrance to the park, not far from the location of our camp. Once assembled, and the R.A.F men didn't take long doing it, the aircraft was positioned in the entrance of the park for the public to see. It was a most impressive sight to us youngsters having never seen an aircraft on the ground before, apart from the force landed Walrus! One of the R.A.F. men told us it was going to remain there for a couple of weeks; it was almost as if he was asking us to keep an eye on it! I guess at the end of the war, the Air Force wanted to show people what their tax's had been used for so it was a good way of doing that.

Actually, as soon as they had assembled the aircraft and placed it in the desired position, they loaded up their tools and equipment and drove away leaving the aircraft standing forlornly in the park entrance. What surprised us was the fact that nobody, apart from us, and the grounds men, came anywhere near during the aircraft assembly process and after the men had gone, it still took a considerable time, at least to our way of thinking, before people would go into the park to take a look at it. I guess the problem may have been that the Town Council probably knew about it but didn't tell anyone!

Soon afterward this a sign was erected in the entrance to the Calverley Grounds advising people that the aircraft was indeed there for them to have a look at. I gathered that when the war finished, the R.A.F., along with other Air Forces, had so many aircraft that they did not know what to do with them. So the idea of 'parking' them in public places was a good Public Relations exercise!

Of course, as you can imagine, we all took a personal interest in the 'plane and within a short time, we knew the aircraft intimately, inside and out. What was surprising was the fact that no sort of guard was placed on the aeroplane and it was left unlocked, so really, if you knew how to get into it, you could imagine you were one of the ace pilots of the war! We soon found out the method of gaining access; this was via a ladder that the R.A.F. men conveniently left with the Aircraft which accessed the entrance door which was located under the nose of the aircraft.

The interior was still completely fitted out with all the instruments, controls and electrical switches still in place. Obviously, none of the systems were 'live' so it was safe for people to clamber over, in fact, it was remarkably intact. I guess the Air Force hadn't spent any time taking out components, just the batteries and the oil and fuel.

The aircraft carried a crew of two and we were to have great fun sitting in the crew seats imagining we were flying the aircraft over Germany! I will never forget the strong smell of Aviation Gasoline, Hydraulic Fluid and electric's that hit you the moment one got in or near the aircraft. Of course there was no actual electrical power on the aircraft so we couldn't do any physical harm, like retracting the undercarriage etc.

Possibly, my involvement with this aeroplane really started my 'love affair' with aircraft which would remain with me for the rest of my life. I didn't realise it then of course and it would still be several years before I could actively pursue my interest to the point of it becoming a vocation.

When I look back, I guess in those days we weren't vandals in the sense of what the word means today. We had no inclinations to damage or steal parts of the aircraft or daub graffiti all over it, as would probably be the case with today's youngsters. Our only 'trophy' was that when the aircraft finally left Tunbridge Wells the access ladder found it's way into our camp; thanks to my old friend Jack Warrener!!

It was about this time that the street parties, to celebrate the end of the war in Europe, began. The funny thing was that in our area of Grove Hill Road, there really weren't that many youngsters. I only knew of Brian

Cornford, whose family lived at 7 Mountfield Road, and of David Harris in Mountfield Gardens, who lived the closest to us.   Nadine Tollet, yes, I was beginning to take notice of where the girls were, who was beginning to associate with us, lived just further up the road, opposite Weeks Depository and the Municipal Animal Pound.

We were therefore very fortunate, that the organisers decided to hold the party in Mountfield Road, which was directly opposite our house.   I guess it was a sensible decision to hold it there as the road was a 'no through road', which made it ideal for the venue as it would not affect the flow, or what there was of it, in those days, of traffic in Grove Hill Road. I can remember the day well. All the people in the neighbourhood made a contribution of whatever food or sweets etc. they could spare and this was supported also by the local shops; Garlinge and Scott the fruiters gave a lot of oranges, apples and salad items; Raisewells provided what they could in the way of general groceries and Mr. Lord, who ran the local newsagents and confectionery shop, did what he could in the supply of things like "Smith's Crisps" (theirs were the only brand available in those days) and of what sweets he could give.

Balloons arrived from somewhere and by the time the tables were laid out in the middle of Mountfield Road, it all looked very festive indeed. There were paper streamers spread across the road and most people wore homemade paper hats. I guess the supply of plates and cutlery was by individuals as plastic items weren't available in those days. It was all really very well done though and of course, there was a full turnout of residents of all ages; and especially of the children from neighbouring roads who just turned up.   All our mates from the Grove Hill Cottages and their parents were there, including Wack, Fred Till and Brian Constance and of course, it wasn't long before we were all sitting together as a group with our parents basically leaving us to it as they conversed with other adults. As a group of energetic youngsters, we must have been quite lively; the main thing that probably kept us quiet was the plentiful supply of good things to eat! It had been a long time since any of us could even begin to remember such a spread and I guess we made the most of it!   At the time, the 'spread' was generous by wartime standards, but by comparison with things today, it was miniscule, but still greatly enjoyed.

As the end of war, the street parties took place in the summer and we were blessed with very good weather so the celebrations went on until quite late and of course, were to finish up with the great British sing-song. Not that we knew many of the words but the adults certainly enjoyed it.

It takes an event like that to bring people together, if only for the duration of the party. A classic example of this was the fact that in Mountfield Gardens lived two old Spinsters and one of their brothers. They were to say the least, snobs of the highest order; at least, that was my Dad's description of them.   The man was a Church Warden at Christ Church and the ladies were in things like the Red Cross and other 'establishment' organisations.   My father couldn't stand them!   There would be times when he would expound on the merits, or otherwise, of the hypocritical people who go to Church, and he would use this household to highlight his points.

In hindsight, they were probably very nice people but as children, one can be heavily influenced by what your parents tell you and you therefore form an opinion, which in this case, aligned with that of my Dad. Many would be the time when he would get really steamed up about the Church and out would come things like, "now you take those stuck up individuals in Mountfield Gardens. They wouldn't even wish you good-day if they could avoid it, yet they go to Church every Sunday to tell God how good they've been!" My Dad, who was a very intelligent person, always maintained that there are more 'Christians' outside of Churches than ever go into them. I must say that as I've grown older, I intend to agree with him at times!

Anyway, I've deviated a little from the end of war party. My point was that on that specific day, the Spinsters and their brother were as relaxed and enjoying the party as much as anyone and I can clearly remember my Dad chatting with them as though they were all the best of friends! Trev and I had a chuckle to ourselves about that and didn't let my Dad forget it.

Not that he ever was ever short of opinions whenever the subject of the Church, and it's, in his view, hypocritical aspects came up!!   My Dad called them the "Wiley Wallace Sisters"! Unfortunately, I cannot remember whether that was actually their surname.   Whenever we walked past their house in Mountfield Gardens I could, in my mind's eye, still see them, just watching the world go by as was their way.

The road where they lived, was the main entrance to

the Calverley Grounds from Grove Hill Road so you couldn't help but see them whenever we passed that way.   Several years later, when I used to come home in my R.A.F. uniform, they were amongst many of the older people in the area I had got to know of, mainly through the Church choir, who wanted me to go and see them when I was home on leave. This I did try to do whenever possible. The funny thing was that they had a great respect for my father and would certainly sing his praises whenever they could. I guess it went back to the time in 1950 when he had stood for Parliament. I will be referring to this in more detail later on.

In later years I used to tell my Dad what they had said about him, as it was all very complementary; he would sit in his chair, usually 'twiddling' the corner of one of the cushion's which drove my Mother mad, and have a smile on his face as if to say "your opinion may not be the same as mine and you'll see things differently when you are my age." I guess in many respects, he was right!

But back to the immediate post war years. When I was around ten years of age, I became very much aware of the presence of Uncle Bob. In the years to follow, he would play a very important role in my life in the direction to which I would choose my career.   Bob was probably one of the best engineers I have ever met, although I didn't know that as a child. He was also the perfect 'Gentleman', except when he and my Dad got into one of their 'Political' arguments to which I will refer to later!

At the age of ten, in 1945, it seemed that he had always been around and I guess as children, we didn't ask ourselves the questions as to where he actually fitted into the family structure. The fact that he and my Dad always got on so well together, gave us the impression that he was indeed 'family'. In fact, throughout his very long life, he would always be a key member of our family even though he wasn't actually related to us! He and his wife were childless and he treated us as the children or nephews he had never been fortunate enough to have.

Before our time, Bob had been the personal chauffeur to a Mr. Morley, of 'Morley Foods' fame. These included tinned goods and Christmas puddings, etc. Bob's position disappeared during the war years when his employer died, so he found work in the natural aptitude he had as an engineer. He had learnt all he knew during his time with R.E.M.E. when serving during the first world war. He and his wife lived in a charming semi-detached house near to Woodsgate Corner, in Pembury. It had a large, country garden and was a most peaceful spot.   In all weathers he would cycle backwards and forwards to work on his faithful 'Hercules' pedal cycle. He had installed a wooden box on the rear carrier frame, which gave the cycle a distinctive look. The box was used to carry his lunch amongst other things.   This bicycle was to play another role in my own life in later years.

Bob was working at this time in a small engineering manufacturing company situated next to 'The Star' public house along Mount Ephraim.   I cannot remember the name of the company but I do recall, if we were out for a walk, that we would visit the premises from time to time just to say "hello".   I am not quite sure what type of manufacturing work they carried out there but I do remember that Bob used to complain a lot about the people who ran the place. From the sound of things, they used to take advantage of him a bit, as he was probably one of their best and most knowledgeable workers and extremely conscientious.

It was soon after this that he went and set up his own company, specialising in motorcar repairs. The site of the business was just before the shops located on the left-hand side at the junction of London Road and Mount Ephraim, as you came from the town, and just before the Kent & Sussex Hospital.   A drive led up from the road to a small undercover workshop at the rear; which Bob had converted into a reasonable motor repair facility.

He was a brilliant engineer and made a success of his venture in many ways, but, like a lot of honest businessmen, he was eventually to fall foul of the people who didn't pay their accounts.

My Father
c 1950

My Mother
c 1935

Kent County Constabulary

This is to Certify that

HENRY GARDNER

of the TUNBRIDGE WELLS BOROUGH POLICE FORCE and the KENT COUNTY CONSTABULARY

served in the Police War Reserve from the

_____ 4th _____ *day of* ___ September, ___ 19 39.

to the _____ 25th _____ *day of* _____ August, _____ 19 46,

when RETIRED.

_____

His conduct during the period of his Service was

EXEMPLARY.

_____
J.A. Ferguson
Chief Constable.

25th *day of* _____ August, _____ 19 46.

THIS CERTIFICATE IS GRANTED WITHOUT ERASURE

My fathers police service record.

"Togetherness"
Trevor and I
c1937

**Investigating the 'Mile of Books' at the bottom
Of High Street**

Trevor, on the left, Colin Miles and then myself
C 1943
This photograph was taken by one of the local
Newspapers.

Trevor and I at the Air Training Corps' 'Aircraft Recognition' Exhibition.

Tunbridge Wells Town Hall
c 1944

'Schoolboys'
c1947

My fathers' election circular when he stood as Conservative candidate in Llanelly, South Wales.

c1951

Llanelly Conservative & Unionist Association

8, STATION ROAD,
LLANELLY,
Tel. 3330

Election Agent:
R. S. DE CALMER

Harry Gardner

The Conservative Candidate

Publicity photograph taken by the 'Kent & Sussex Courier' relating to my fathers election aspirations.

These were destroyed by the Luftwaffe during the war.

The Calverley Grounds Bandstand and Pavilion   c 1935

Early picture of Grove Hill Road

My Grandfathers shop was located on the left, just up from Weeks Department Store.

High Street
and Chapel
Place

c1950

Christchurch School is located at the top left hand corner and King Charles School is to be found at lower centre.

Christchurch School showing its proximity to the Central Station. c1950

The school area is now the site of a major supermarket.

Tunbridge
Wells
Central
Station

c1930

Tunbridge Wells Central Station c1950

Mount Pleasant known locally as the "Wells Hill"   c 1950

The High Street showing the Neville Bakery with the tower of Christchurch in the background.

c1950

The scene of a lot of our activities as children.

The entrance to "Birdcage Walk" off the Grove

This picture, dating back to the 1930's, shows a "School Class" locomotive awaiting departure from the Central Station with a train for Hastings. The house immediately above the locomotive tender is in Sutherland Road, where I first lived.

'Grove Junction' c1950

We spent many a happy hour here.

Chapter 9:   Family Ways

At this period of my life Bob's motor repair business continued on at a respectable rate and he employed another mechanic to assist him.   I never really got to know the other chap very well but he was always very pleasant whenever we visited the place.   Trev and I would pop in to see Bob especially during school holidays when one of our areas of activity would be the Tunbridge Wells Common, which was very close to where his garage was located.

There certainly weren't many motor cars on the roads in those days and I seem to recall that Bob really had to struggle to make ends meet but the fact that he was a self employed person, with his own business, raised his own self esteem and his standing within the community.   In my opinion this was thoroughly deserved.

Visits to his garage would invariably find Bob in his overalls, a cap on the back of his head and the inevitable 'Woodbine' cigarette in his mouth. With his characteristic "hello old man, and what brings you up here" welcoming statement, he always made you welcome even if at times he was preoccupied with a job on somebody's car.

Bob used to pop down home to 'number 32' to have his lunch and to tell us all about what sort of a day he was having.   Lunchtime was a very sociable time at home and especially so during the working week when we would all eat together.   During school days, Trev and I would be home until about one twenty five before making our way back to school and my Dad, when he was on afternoon duty in the Police, would be getting ready to start his 'beat' at two o'clock.   Mum would usually serve our main meal of the day at this time although Bob would sit in the corner and eat the sandwiches his wife had prepared for him.

It was all very down to earth but is recalled with fond memories. As children, Trev and I would just sit and enjoy my mother's meal and listen to the adults exchanging their experiences of the day.   Dad and Bob were the best of opposites when it came to the subject of politics and at that particular stage, confined their differing views to verbal disagreements on a relatively low key! (In later years, their verbal exchanges, particularly after we moved to Mountfield Road, were to become very heated and could be heard by the neighbours several houses away!)

One thing always made me smile about Bob's lunch. His wife regularly included a piece of cold battered fish along with the sandwiches and Bob couldn't stand it. We used to wait in anticipation as he opened up the lunch container and with his sense of humour, offered the piece of fish to my mother for us to have with our tea! "I keep telling my gal not to give me fish and she takes no notice of me". He would often say that and even though we expected it, it would always bring a laugh amongst us.

We had a tabby cat in those days which went by the name of 'Tibs'. He was a nice old cat and was fortunate to live a long life with us, possibly due in some ways to having 'had' to eat up Bob's wife's fish! There were days when Bob wouldn't always be able to make it to our house for lunch and the familiar family 'banter' about current affairs would be missed, especially if my Dad was in the mood for one of his 'political' exchanges!

As I have already said, Bob was a very generous person and would always ensure that Trev and I had a few pennies if there was something we considered we really needed to buy. In that respect, it was very noticeable that Bob appeared to be, in our opinions, someone who was reasonably well off compared to my Dad who really didn't have a lot of spending money. (I know now that there were times when my Mum and Dad found the going tough from a financial point of view and considerable juggling had to take place to make ends meet. In those days, just after the war, life wasn't easy for many people, especially with a growing family.) I know there were times that my dear Dad would go down to my Grandfathers shop to seek the odd 'advance' pending receipt of his wages from the police!

I guess the fact that Bob and his wife didn't have a family of their own made their circumstances that much easier and Bob, through his own hard working efforts, had established a very acceptable life style for them both. As I have said, I don't know really how Bob actually came onto the scene as far as my family were concerned. He and my Dad had a very good relationship as dedicated friends, but the main connection between him and us was the special relationship that existed between him and my Mother. In hindsight, I guess they had had, at some time in the past, a soft spot for each other, which was to last for the whole of their lives. This is no criticism of anyone. As it was to transpire, particularly later in life, their tripartite association was to be a great strength to them all and Bob would forever be 'family' to us.

It was about this time that my Mother got me a job as a 'paper boy' as I was coming on to the grand age of eleven years.   This was, at that time, the minimum age for children to be legally allowed to take on a few hours work a week as a paper boy.   The nearest 'paper shop to where we lived was known as 'Lords' and was located just below where we lived on the right hand side of Grove Hill Road.

As it has so happened, the site was destined to always be associated with Newspapers and to this day, has remained so. It is now, or was at the time of writing, a seven day a week 'corner shop' called Masri's, who are Pakistanis, and sells all sorts of things, including 'papers! When I was a lad, it was a relatively small Newspaper shop, which also sold Magazines, Tobacco and Confectionery and the odd paperback book. It was here that, using my paper-round earnings, I bought my first book.

The book was about Ships and Ocean Going Liners in particular and highlighted the luxury of such travel in the pre-war years; I can still remember it's contents very well because in the period after the war, and it was a very austere period, no such luxury existed for anyone I knew.   I guess that was the start of a particular weakness of mine; that of collecting books!   I still cannot refrain from adding to my quite considerable collection and I suspect many of these books may well bore those who follow me!!   I bow to the theory that it takes all sorts.   I do enjoy my books!

Mr. Lord was a jovial type of man, short and on the plump side with a very red face and little hair. I believe that in the early part of the second world war he had been in the Royal Navy but really we didn't get to know him that well; to the best of my memory, he didn't appear to have a wife. Because 'Lord's' wasn't renowned for it's somewhat limited choice of confectionery it was not until I took the paper job that I had really been inside the place very much.   As children, we knew of the shop but that was about all. It was, by modern standards, a small shop and of course in those early days just after the war, it didn't have a tremendous stock of anything; in fact, there were a lot of empty shelves!

As the youngest paper boy on the staff (which totalled all of three, including Mr.Lord!) I was given the 'local round', which was centred in the area adjoining the shop i.e., Grove Hill Road, (lower end) Sutherland Road, Meadow Hill Road, Mountfield Road and Mountfield Gardens.   Once I had got into the swing of things I was able to complete the circuit in less than half an hour!

The paper round gave me the first opportunity to earn some money although, by today's standards, the pay wasn't generous.   It averaged out to about three shillings and sixpence (Seventeen and a half New Pence) per week.   My mother, who herself found it difficult at times to make ends meet, never insisted that I gave her any of my earnings although she did wisely persuade me to open a small but regular National Savings account.   I was however left with a reasonable amount of my earnings still available for me to use as I wished.

It was therefore through my paper round that I was able to start buying a few items towards a model railway collection, although, with limited choice due to the war, it would take some time to accumulate, and money sure wasn't plentiful which didn't help!In those days my model railway collection was based on the '0' Gauge system, primarily 'Hornby' and 'Triang' with the engines being powered by clockwork motors. The more compact '00' gauge equipment, using three rail electric traction, was too expensive for me! This railway collection was made of tinplate which would today be most collectable.   Similar modern pieces tend now to be made of plastic.

Following a lengthy time of anticipation I bought the first locomotive of my collection from 'Huxley's' toyshop in the High Street. It was a Southern Railway 'L' Class 4-4-0 tender locomotive, made, of course, in tin plate with a strong clockwork motor, in the true 'Hornby' tradition. Acquiring this engine took a lot of doing on my meagre earnings and a maximum effort was made to come up with the considerable purchase price of Thirty Shillings. (One pound, Fifty Pence!) I had my eye on the engine as it sat in the front window of the shop and almost every day I would deviate down the High Street to check it was still there!

When I was in the affluent position of being able to put down a deposit on it, as recommended by my Mother, she went with me to see the lady who ran the shop and the engine was finally secured although it would be several more weeks before I would actually have it! Credit in those days was an entirely different thing to what it is today!

Acquiring a 'railway set' did take some doing at the time. My constant visits to 'Huxleys' built a very good relationship with the lady who ran the shop and she always kept me well informed as to what model railway items she was expecting in stock. A lot of the transactions in the shop were in fact frequently related to second hand equipment and that suited my pocket; in fact there were some very good bargains and the lady there always let her 'favourite' customer know what would interest him! She would often summon me into the shop to show me what she had put aside if she thought my pocket could bear the cost. I do recall that Bob was often a great help in acquiring some of the railway items that I just didn't have sufficient cash for.

By this method, my model railway pieces began to accumulate and progressively increased to a workable proportion. One item I acquired highlight's my point about Bob's generosity, which I referred to earlier. One day, the lady told me she had an Engine Shed that would go well with my layout. The price was ten shillings, (Fifty Pence) although not a lot of money for what she was offering, it was more than I could afford at that time with only my paper round earnings as resource. I went home and cautiously raised the subject with Bob, knowing that my mother didn't have any money to spare. Bob, in his usual helpful way pulled out a Ten Shilling note from his wallet and off I rushed to the Toy Shop!

At home, the usual place for setting out and running the railway, was in the front room at number 32. In fact this room was our prime indoor play area as my mother found that two energetic boys in her kitchen was just a little too much and in a three room flat, there really wasn't anywhere else to let Trev and I loose! When I look back, I remember the hard life Trev and I gave the furniture in that room. Mum and Dad had a three piece settee suite, a large oak sideboard, a family table and a long chest of drawers in the room.

We liked the room and it's location at the front of the house gave an excellent view of Grove Hill Road and Mountfield Road, opposite. One could see all the coming's and going's from the vantage point that its elevated position gave and on wet and wintry days it was good to look out of the window and see the people scurrying home from the railway station as we watched from the security of a nice warm room where my Dad invariably had a generous open hearthed fire burning.

As I've already mentioned, the furniture in that room really did go through the mill! We would get up to all manner of boisterous activities either chasing each other around the room and over the settees, which did them the world of good; we were probably imagining ourselves to be Roy Rogers or Errol Flynn in his latest role as some swashbuckling pirate or Musketeer!!

I don't know how my parents coped with Trev and I; particularly on wet days when we couldn't get out to let off steam. As a parent myself, I would have gone hairless (a lot lot earlier than I have!) had my children got up to some of the antics that we did! The settees really took the brunt of our 'unintentional' misuse and even we realised that there was a finite life on things like springs etc, when it became painfully obvious that the comfort of the seat was less than idyllic when you sat in the chair and was greeted with a loud 'twang' as the broken spring therein let one know of it's distress!

The '0' gauge railway, when it was laid out, took up a considerable amount of room and Trev and I used to make full use of running the rails under armchairs etc. which, as far as we were concerned, made perfect tunnels. We particularly liked the early evening period for running simulated 'night time' trains around the place. Strategically placed torches and the glow from the fire, with the other room lights out, gave very realistic effects in our minds and I can still remember the fun we used to have with the railway as we chased the locomotives around the tracks on our hands and knees. Invariably, because the locos were clockwork, it required one of us at each end of the line to 'capture' the train as it reached the end of its run as once the engine set off, there was no way of controlling it apart from physically stopping it. Anyway, it was all good fun and we got a lot of pleasure from it!

I have many happy memories of the front room at number 32. As I've already said, the view from this room was particularly good. The fact that cars were few and far between allowed for unobstructed views as far as the railway bridge when looking towards the large 'Courier' newspaper building and Weeks and, in the opposite direction, up Grove Hill Road, the animal pound.

In those days the resurfacing of the road surface was not the mechanical operation it is today.   One of my favourite memories was the use of steam road rollers and the lovely smell of Tar when Grove Hill Road was resurfaced which must have been roughly every couple of years. At that time, they didn't burn off the top surface as they do today and the lack of modern labour saving equipment resulted in a lot of hard work.   The magnificent 'Invicta' steam road rollers belonged to the Tunbridge Wells Borough and Kent County Council's.

They usually they operated in pairs with their magnificent chuffing exhaust and the smell of hot oil, coal and steam and this, coupled with the smell of the hot tar, made them a sight to remember. At least in those days the lack of motor vehicles made the road workers job that much easier.   I wouldn't like to think of doing that job today with the congestion of motor vehicles that accumulate in Grove Hill now!

One interest I had at about that time was the fascination of the Cinema Projector and the Cinema in general.   With the location of our camp in the Calverley Grounds being at the rear of the Great Hall Cinema, we couldn't fail to be aware of the function of the Cinema so close to hand. From our vantage point almost next door to the theatre, we would hear all the sound tracks of the popular movies of the day, particularly during the summer when the projectionist would leave the door of his projection cabin open to get some fresh air in the place.   One of the operators was quite a friendly bloke and would sometimes allow us to have a quick look at the movie from the vantage point of his projection room.

This didn't happen that often, as the management obviously didn't look favourably on youngsters cluttering up the place! What was interesting in those days, was that the film material, not being as durable as the materials of today, would often break, usually resulting in cries of anguish from the audience. When the projectionist spliced the film back together he would usually cut quite a section out of the film to ensure that he had sound material.   This resulted in varying lengths of film littering the floor of the projection room and as they were only fit for the rubbish, I'd grab a couple of lengths out of interest.

I guess the unreliability of the film materials used in those days gave me quite a collection of these filmstrips. In hindsight though, they were of little or no use but at my age, I didn't really think about that.

I perused what I could actually do with these strips of celluloid and eventually came up with a Heath Robinson idea for a home-made projector which as it's power source used a cycle lamp. Hardly the thing to project a very bright image! The operating theory of this contraption was that by fitting a cardboard tube around the light housing and installing a slot adjacent to the light itself, one could view the film slide by drawing the film across the face of the lamp and view the subject. In many respects, it was the old 'magic lantern' in reverse.

The climax of Mike Gardner Productions was a performance, on a winter evening, to Mum and Dad, Granddad and Trevor in the front room when it was well and truly dark. To supplement the filmstrips, I made up some very rudimentary 'slides' of my own, drawn on tracing paper. The theme of this element of the programme was local shops!   In fact it was a form of free advertising; for example, 'Buy your Sprouts at Garlinge & Scot's',   'R. Septimus Gardner for all your Taxidermy and Furs', 'Get 'Cracker's' at Raisewell's' (a suitable reference to the Manager of the shop my Mum called Cracker's!) etc.

The chosen audience assembled, the lights were switched off and the performance began. To say it was an anticlimax is an understatement!   Before the programme had been running more than a couple of minutes, there were exclamations from the audience that they couldn't see anything. The principle of my 'projector' wasn't to throw an image onto a screen but to use the theory of back lighting the subjects by passing the 'slides' across the lens of the cycle lamp. Well, as you can imagine, the performance really wasn't a success, only the operator could understand what was going on and unless the audience sat about twelve inches away from the 'projector', they would have had difficulty in making out what the projected images were! This was definitely 'low tech' equipment and that particular show was to be the only one! At least the (captive) audience didn't ask for their money back. Of course when I look back now, I realise just what an ineffective system I was using but at the time, it did give some inspiration at least and my audience were very 'understanding'.

As you look back on these rather silly things we did as young people, it meant something to us at the time. We were exploring ideas and I probably grained a sense of achieving something. With material things being so few for us, we had so little of in those days, the adaptation of what few things we did have, albeit carried out in an amateurish fashion, did at least give the satisfaction of doing it yourself! I often think of instances like the one just described, when my children and now my Grandchildren, do similar things to impress their elders. Children haven't changed at all really; all that has changed is the different circumstances in which the scenario takes place.

Chapter 10: Farewell to Christchurch School

July 1946 and the end of the Summer Term at Christchurch School was also to be the end of my years at that school. The thought of progression to Secondary School at the end of the summer holidays was quite a sobering thought as the last few days of attending Miss. Turner's class, slowly passed by.

My last term at Christchurch School was quite eventful. I must have taken on a 'macho' role at that time which, really wasn't in my character, as one day, I took it upon myself to 'sort out' the school bully! The boy concerned was a lad with a chequered past with a history of bullying. He was in the class below me at Christchurch but his name was known at all levels in the school and the teachers had a job controlling him. Most of the other pupils usually gave him a wide berth.

He lived somewhere at the top of the town in the area near the Opera House. His family had a bad name in the town and from what my father said, some members of the family were serving prison terms in Maidstone Jail. The incident whereby he and I came to blows was started when he started pushing around a puny little lad called Willie, who Trev and I both knew quite well. (He lived in Mount Zion and was the youngest member of quite a large family who always appeared to be on hard times. Sadly he was to eventually become one of life's victims)

On the day in question, at morning playtime in the school playground, the bully, who had always taken the opportunity to have a go at Willie for the slightest provocation, really let into him on this occasion. I can't remember what we were doing at the time but we were some way away from where the bully and Willie were so it was only when we heard the commotion that we went to investigate. Now the bully was a strapping lad compared to Willie who was really a very frail individual so there was no way it was going to be a fair fight!   I guess that for the first time in my life at that point I saw red.

What possessed me to intervene really was the unfair way in which this lad was laying into the smaller guy. I distinctly remember pushing my way through the ring of spectators, grabbing hold of the bully and dragging him away from Willie. He didn't take kindly to this and before we knew where we were, we were thumping each other for all we were worth with the surrounding children shouting and actually almost encouraging us on.

Of course, the commotion brought out the teachers to find out what was going on. With two strong sturdy lads knocking the living daylights out of each other even the persuasive power of Miss. Turner and Mrs. Ritchins still took a few minutes to separate the warring factions! He and I were immediately taken into Miss. Turners classroom whilst the other children were kept outside. What, she wanted to know, was the reason for such behaviour; I had a feeling that after hearing what we had to say, she probably wanted to support the action I had taken but she couldn't officially take that line and we were both subjected to the same punishment. Six lashes of the cane were followed by he and I having to stand in opposite corners of the classroom with our faces to the wall for the remainder of the school day. . I distinctly remember that at school assembly, the following morning, Miss Turner made us stand at the front of the assembled school whilst she read the 'riot act' about what she would do in the event of any repetition of such behaviour!

Funnily enough, after that incident, the bully kept well away from me and as I was virtually at the end of my time at that school, our paths did not cross again.   At the time, he also left Willie alone but this was not to last. As I've already mentioned, there was to be a tragic sequel to this event so I'll leap ahead a little here. Soon after I had started at King Charles School, there was another confrontation between the bully and Willie. This time it was to happen out of school hours on the Tunbridge Wells Common. Apparently, Willie and some of his mates were playing on the 'Common' after school, when this bully and a couple of others came across them.   I never did really understand why this lad had loathing of Willie and he certainly couldn't have seen him as a threat as he would have made two of him! However, on this occasion, the resulting fight between them left Willie with a brain haemorrhage caused by a heavy blow over the right ear. Willie died three days later.   The bully was placed in Juvenile Custody; we never saw him again.

In my last term at Christchurch School, I did fairly well in Geography, a subject that I really quite enjoyed and as a prize I received a book on the British Empire. The award was made in the last few days before I left the school and was part of the end of term celebrations.

I still have the book to this day and I can remember how much this award meant to me at the time of my receiving it.   It is probably hopelessly out of date now with the complete change in the role of Great Britain in the world and with the alterations to boundary lines and changes of names of several countries. It was with a certain amount of remorse that I bid farewell to the school. In many respects, the first school you attend makes a huge impression on you and when I looked back, having spent the war years there, I was sorry to say farewell to Miss. Turner, Mrs. Ritchins and the rest of the staff.   It was probably the thought of going on to King Charles School, where the teachers were all male that made me realise that it certainly wasn't going to be the same as the time I'd spent at Christchurch school.

One consolation, however, was the fact that several of my classmates were also going on to King Charles School with me and this included the fact that my best mate, Jackie Warrener who was a little older than me, was already there. Anyway, before the new term could start there was the thought of a six week summer break; which would be a fun time.

It was about this time that Trev and I had our first visit to the sea. The war had been over more than a year at this time and people were starting to venture to certain coastal resorts where sea defences had been, or were in the process of being removed.

Bob had bought a little car, it was an Austin Eight Saloon and I can still remember the registration, EOD 502. It was a black, two doors, four seat saloon with real leather seats.   To the best of my memory what cars there were about, in those days, were primarily painted black.   Soon after he acquired it, he offered to run Mum, Trev and I to the seaside one afternoon. This was a real thrill as we had never been in a car; not that there were very many about in those days.   Our journey took us to Rye and Hastings. It was great driving along the deserted roads and through little towns and villages we had never seen before knowing we were to see the sea for the very first time. Our excitement was a little deflated when we first arrived at Rye, which we thought was a really lovely old place. Bob parked the car fairly near to the beach and after a short walk, there was the sea.   No problem with parking then nor the need to pay to park the car!   Unfortunately, we were not able to get down as far as the water as there was still barbed wire running along the entire length of the beach. Actually the place was completely deserted apart from us and although the sun was shining, it wasn't particularly warm.   The absence of other people probably made the place seem unwelcoming and the disappointment of not actually being able to get to the water did not alleviate this feeling.

We were able to sit on the pebbles and listened to the sound of the surf whilst looking out at the expanse of open sea in front of us. Mum had made a few sandwiches and a flask of tea, which we all needed to warm us up; after all, this was an English summer day Bob sensed our disappointment at not at least being able to have a paddle and decided to drive on to Hastings to see if the situation was any better there. As it turned out; it was to be exactly the same. I think the barbed wire and sea defences ran the full length of the British Isles. Although there were a few more people at Hastings, there were no seaside activities as we know them today and we couldn't even get an ice cream!   After the war there was quite a long period of time when Britain went through what became known as the 'austerity' period. We later found out that the reason why people were not allowed to get near to the sea was because of the fear of unexploded military ordnance and mines being washed on to the beaches, which could prove to be rather dangerous!

It would take a considerable time for the seaside resorts to become anything remotely similar to what they are today. Another couple of years would pass before many beaches would be declared fit for people to use. What we have to remember is that at the end of the war, Britain, along with just about every other country in Europe was financially on the rocks. The fact that the defeated country, Germany, was to forge ahead, financially, well ahead of Britain in the years to come was not a cheering thought.

What Government spending there was would be limited to trying to put the country back on to its feet. Leisure certainly wasn't the industry then as it is today and was considered a low priority when it came to allocating funds.

Our first motorcar journey may have been a little disappointing in relation to its outcome, but nevertheless, it was a memory I will never forget. In many ways, we take modern travel for granted. Although we only went about thirty miles in each direction, it was a significant journey which was probably aggravated by the fact that the roads weren't as good as now; cars were not as fast and travel took that much longer.   In some respects, the fact that there were so few cars on the roads in those days allowed the road system as it existed then, to cope well with demand.

By this time, Trevor and I were fully fledged participants in the Christ Church choir and Mr. Pallant, the Grove Hill Road Barber, was the Choirmaster.   In hindsight, I must say he had his hands full with youngsters like us and with one or two others in the junior section of the choir.   Funnily enough, I really cannot remember many of the other youngsters by name.   Our associations with them were only during choir practices.

In the summer, after church services or after Sunday Evensong, we would all go racing out of church, and through the Grove to Little Mount Zion, where there was an 'Off Licence' which was run by the Lisney family.   What pocket money we had in those days was usually sufficient to allow us to treat ourselves to a bottle of the latest 'pop' after church.   We would all sit outside the shop downing the contents as the local parishioners passed us on their way home with looks on their faces as if to say, "we thought we saw you lot in Church a few minutes ago!"

The visit to 'Lisney's' after church really became something of a ritual on those warm summer Sunday evening's.   Mr. Lisney would always let us know what the latest pop drink flavours were on our arrival at his shop; brands like 'Ice Cream Soda', 'Tizer' 'Cydrax' etc, come readily to mind when I look back and I can clearly remember how much we looked forward to our visits.   It was at this time, after the war years, that soft drinks companies were beginning to introduce various flavours in the soft drinks and expand the choices for their customers.   To us, it seemed as though there was a different flavour drink introduction virtually every week!   However, I don't think we generated our thirsts by the amount of singing we did, more by the exertion of running hell for leather from the church, through the Grove to the 'Off Licence', to see who could get his order in first!   We were good runners in those days.

In general Trev and I were good participants and attendees in the choir. I accept that Mr. Pallant's patience at times was to be well tested but he couldn't complain about us not turning up for Church services; Mum made sure if that!

Trev and I still have a chuckle about some of the antics we used to get up to in Church. As you can imagine, the sermon was always the most difficult part of the service for us to really understand and therefore, it was the time when things happened to relieve the monotony. Favourite 'sermon boredom alleviation's' included the game of 'Battleships', 'Noughts and Crosses' and the daring pursuit of shooting paper bullets across the Chancel at choir members on the opposite side! Who would have believed that boy's dressed as little angels could be capable of such goings on.

Of all the sermon activities the paper bullets were the favourite but at some risk to the 'shooter', particularly if Mr. Pallant saw you doing it. The key to one's success in this game was to ensure you went in to the service with plenty of ammunition.

The method of firing the paper bullet was that you placed the projectile on the palm of your hand and at a suitable point in the sermon when the Vicar was in full verbal onslaught. Firing commenced by 'flicking' the missile with the finger of the other hand. It was quite effective.   Mr. Pallant, who was also the organist, would sit at the organ and continually scan the choir via a large mirror that was located on the organ above his head. It gave a panoramic view of the choir stalls so if one was sitting facing him you had to judge the right time to fire if you didn't want him to see you. On one occasion, when most of the choir boy's were engaged in this activity, Mr.Pallant lost his temper and grabbing a hymn book, he threw it across the chancel intending to hit one of the boy's but unfortunately, missed. The hymn book hit one of the male members of the choir who was rudely awakened from a session of 'forty winks'. The startled chorister must have wondered what on earth was going on and quite a commotion took place, which probably woke up some of the congregation as well.

Mr. Pallant was furious, the vicar was embarrassed and the male members of the choir were ready to wring the necks of the junior choir!   The riot act was read to all of us at the end of the service by both the vicar and Mr. Pallant. After that incident he checked our pockets to ensure that we never carried 'ammunition' into church again although we did manage to sometimes fool him on that!   All in all, I think we enjoyed our involvement in the Christ Church choir and were part of it for over six years although we never aspired to becoming soloists. Compared to church choirs today, we were large in numbers both in the boy's section and the men's and virtually never missed either the morning or evensong services.   The congregations were also much larger and it is a sad comparison to the sizes of congregation you see in many a church today.

Another 'character' in the choir was Reg Manktelow. He was a very serious type of person and rarely smiled; his duty was to lead the choir into the church carrying the cross. He certainly was the ideal candidate for that job and really took it all extremely seriously. Actually, when I was older and was able to get to know him a little better I was to discover that he really was a decent sort of person.   Reg Manktelow and his wife Janie lived in Mountfield Road, not far from the house my folk's would eventually live in. They had a daughter and in general, life wasn't destined to treat them very well. I cannot remember their daughter's name now but she was a very frail child and was to die of Tuberculoses whilst only just in her teen's. (Their tragic circumstances were to continue when Reg died in early middle age of a heart attack. This was to happen whilst I was in the R.A.F.)

As kid's we thought Reg was a weird sort of person mainly because he was very much a loner and only seemed to be happy when he was associated with church functions. I think that from his viewpoint, he must have thought that we were real scallywags and didn't accept the fact that we were really only having fun; usually at nobodies expense but our own. When I was a few years older I came to accept Reg as he was, accepting the fact that people are all different. Unfortunately that kind of analysis only comes from maturity and experience, something, that as young choirboy's, we didn't have at that time.

Mum was a regular churchgoer virtually for the whole time Trev and I were in the choir. She would usually go to the church with Miss Pope, taking up their usual position at the rear of the church on the pulpit side. Christ Church appeared to be a huge building to us when we were kids although when I looked at it in later life, it was really just a normal town church. Its location, almost next to the 'Central Station and the main London to Hastings railway line, meant that when inside the church you could surprisingly still hear the activities of the railway clearly. In fact the chancel area backed on to the railway tunnel, which carried the railway under the Grove and towards Grove Junction. With folks in London beginning to get away, mainly by rail, to the coast on summer Sunday's, the railway was very busy and the heavily laden trains really made the church shake as they hauled their payload's to the sea-side.   As train enthusiasts we didn't mind, but there were times when it made it difficult for the vicar to be heard in the middle of his sermon.

Just after the war the Reverent Smith was the vicar at Christ Church.   He had been a clergyman in the Royal Air Force during the war before he and his family came to Tunbridge Wells and I remember he wore the emblem of the R.A.F. on his cassock and surplus.   I guess that by any standard's he was a very handsome man; tall, slim and dark haired. Mum thought he was wonderful and really had a soft spot for him. There were times back home, after the service, that she would go on about him, much to the annoyance of my Dad who would usually counter with his arguments about the pro's and con's of religion. It certainly made the Sunday lunch entertaining! I wonder whether Mum would have gone to church as regularly as she did if the vicar had been an old fogey?

One of my Dad's favourite subjects was the merits of those who went regularly to church only to lead a life that was less than what the gospel apparently preached.   The subject of the 'Wiley Wallaces from Mountfield Gardens would probably be brought up for the umpteenth time. He had reason to believe they were habitually highly critical of other churchgoers and of folk in our vicinity in general. Mum would be saying things like "Dod's, (my mothers name for my father) you have got it wrong", but it was always to no avail.

From the best of my recollections, the Wallaces lived at number six Mountfield Gardens. My Dad referred to them as the 'Wiley Wallace Brigade'.   At the time I was a lad, they were all in their sixties and you would see them going off to church for morning and evensong to the point where you could almost set a watch by them. The source of my Dad's argument was that these people looked down their noses at just about everyone around them. They wouldn't grant you the time of day if you passed them in the street and gave the impression to all and sundry that they were of some superior race.

I can still hear my Dad saying "there they go again those b----- hypocrites. They think that going to church twice every Sunday makes them Christians; well I've got news for them, there are more Christians outside the door's of the church, than ever went through them". I can remember that particular statement of my Dad's so clearly; in many respects it is probably one of the truest statement's he ever made. My Dad was typical of many people who were not actual church goers. He never set foot inside a church in his life, other than for weddings, christenings and funerals, as far as I can gather, but a more 'Christian' person, in the way he conducted his life, never walked this earth.

I know at the time my mother enlisted our participation in the church choir, we were not at all impressed. However, being in the choir did have its reward's. In those day's of very little entertainment, the cinema was about the only outlet really and in the period I am referring to, I certainly wasn't a cinemagoer; that was to come a little later. There were a lot of out of church activities held in the Christ Church Hall, which stood next to the church. We, being so involved, got to know of most of these well in advance. The vicar would announce such events at the Sunday Service. In particular, these were the days of slide presentations and talks, given in the Hall by Missionary Societies and various church organisations, etc. These were always early evening functions, usually starting about seven o'clock and even at my young age, I found them to be very interesting and we became regular attendees.

These evening activities mainly took place in the winter. Like most church halls in those days, the heating left a lot to be desired and the audience relied very much on their heavy outdoor coats to prevent them from freezing to death as they watched scenes from foreign lands of natives living in the dust and blazing heat of their homeland. Quite a difference to the English winter's as they were then! The attendees at these presentations comprised quite a few of the regular congregation from the church plus a few others who I guess really wanted to pass an interesting and sociable evening.

Television was practically unheard of at that time and nobody we knew had television set; plus in those day's, there were only a couple of radio stations, the 'Light Programme' and the 'Home Service', on offer from the BBC. Therefore home entertainment as we now know it was virtually nil. Because I was a 'regular' I soon became a general helper in the functions run in the church hall. I used to get involved in the preparation of the 'hall and assisted in serving refreshments during the interludes. Mum and Miss Pope used to go to some of the events and would always join in with the clearing up afterwards.

With my involvement in the Church Hall events and my newspaper round, I got to know a lot of people in the area of which we lived. I can remember several occasions when old ladies would ask Trev and I to help them sort out old jumble and things they didn't need any more at their homes saying that if we'd like any of the stuff ourselves, we were very welcome to it. The remainder would then be sent to the jumble sales held from time to time in the 'hall'. Actually, we got hold of several rather useful things that way and really enjoyed doing it. It was to us, surprising what some of these people would dispose of in those days.

One really useful thing that was going to be destined for the jumble, before I retrieved it, was a 'Cats Whisker Crystal Radio Set'. We were helping a lady who lived in one of the large houses at the top of Grove Hill Road where it joins Camden Park. When I first saw it I couldn't figure out what this thing was and it was only when the lady said that I'd find it an interesting thing to use that she told me it was a means of picking up radio signals. To those who, like me at the time, did not know what a Crystal Radio Set was I will try to explain.

From the best of my memory it consisted of a wire coil mounted on a hardboard base of about nine inches square. The coil was wired at one end to a small receptacle which contained a crystal, about a quarter of an inch in diameter. A pivoted arm, with a short piece of sturdy wire was used to make contact with the crystal; in fact this was the power source for the unit and was in fact the part known as the 'Cats Whisker' from whence it got the name. The other end of this arm was wired to the coil. A variable slider, which moved along the coil, was used to vary the wavelength and a pair of headphones plugged into the baseboard, completed the unit.

I spent hours playing with this contraption in the kitchen of number 32. I would tuck myself away in the corner of the room of an evening, which was the best time to pick up the radio signals and by patiently prodding the crystal whilst varying the resistance, it was amazing what Radio Stations I picked up. To mind, I can recall a lot of foreign language stations but as a rule I could usually pick up Hilversen, in Holland, which broadcast in English. The hours of enjoyment I obtained from the radio set was incredible; when I was absorbed with it, my mother never knew I was in the room; it was a fascinating way of passing the time and I think my parent's thought it was worth it's weight in gold.

On the whole, Trev and I really got on very well together but sometimes, as often happens with youngsters, a slight disagreement could end in quite a punch-up!

I'll never forget one night in the kitchen of number 32, Trev and I really had a go at each other. I haven't a clue, now, as to what started it but before we knew where we were, we were going at it hammer and tong's and thumping each other in probably the worst fight we were ever to have. I don't think my Dad was there at the time and my mother couldn't break us up herself so she had to call on the assistance of Miss. Pope, in the flat above. Not that she had much of an idea as to what to do; being a spinster. I can still remember my mother's words at the time, saying out loud, "let them kill each other for all I care". I know she didn't mean it but I guess she was at desperation point at that stage not knowing what to do. We really were a handful at times for her!

One of my very good friend's from Christchurch School was Cedric Gibbons, whose family were also friends with my Mum and Dad, and they all lived in Church Road, opposite the Holy Trinity Church, in a basement flat. Cedric's Dad was a very tall thin man and Cedric was almost a replica of him. At about this time, Cedric's Dad took up a job as the live-in caretaker of the Tunbridge Wells Clinic, which was located in Crescent Road; almost next door to the Police Station.

The Clinic was located in one of the most attractive building's I'd ever seen. It was a three/four storey Victorian building with a basement with countless room's, ideal for its role. Cedric's family moved into the flat which was located in the top floor of the building. The Gibbons family always made me very welcome both at their flat in Church Road and after they moved to the Clinic. Cedric's sister, a vivacious type of girl was several years older than him and in the latter part of the war, she fell for a Canadian soldier who was stationed near to the town. They were to get married after the war was over.

The Clinic, in my opinion, was always a creepy sort of a place. During the day it was a hive of activity with countless numbers of people going there for all sorts of treatment. There was also a Dentist on the premises for as I've already said, it was a large building and clinical activities took place on several floors including the basement. I went there on a couple of occasions mainly to see the Dentist, but it was after the people had gone home that Cedric and I, usually with some of our mates, would have the free run of the place. One of our favourite games, bearing in mind the size of the place, was to play 'hide and seek'; the variety and choice of 'hideaways' were countless which made the finding of people, extremely difficult.

Cedric's parents were probably glad that we had the space to run wild as it certainly gave them some peace and quiet as their small flat was hardly ideal for a group of young lad's to let off steam in.. What was interesting was the fact that the clinical areas were not locked up outside of business hours. Some of the boy's didn't like going down in the basement as it was always very dark down there and, to say the least, a lot more creepy than the rest of the building.

I must say that it gave me the creeps especially when you went down there when it was getting dusk. The rooms in this part of the building were used for laboratory testing in support of the clinic's patients; fortunately, at our age we didn't really know what all the equipment there was for but in hindsight, I don't think we should have been permitted access to this area at least. Inquisitive youngsters could have caused chaos; or even caught the dreaded berry-berry or something of similar ilk the way we used to play the fool in the facilities!

On one occasion, Cedric and I planned to give our mates something of a shock. We decided that when it was our turn to 'hide', we would go down to the basement, giving each other moral support to actually go into that area, and don a surgical gown each, which in those days were white. It was a particularly dull and dismal sort of day ideal for the purpose we had in mind. Having gone to the basement, we dressed up in these white gowns in a room at the end of the corridor, and awaited the arrival of the 'seekers'. It took them a few minutes to get to our area, having to check the rooms above as they made their way down. We knew they would come in a group as nobody liked going down to the basement on their own so they would only go there in numbers! The plan worked perfectly as our mates entered and crept along the corridor towards us, Cedric and I emerged from the room we were in to confront our friend's. You have never heard such a commotion in all your life; I guess we were lucky that nobody had a heart attack. Our mates ran literally petrified from the basement as fast as their legs would carry them falling over each other as they went.

Cedric's father heard this commotion from the top of the building and came rushing down to find out what had happened. He was almost flattened on his way to the basement by an avalanche of our mates going hell for leather in the opposite direction!   When he found out what had caused the fracas he was less than impressed. Cedric and I had the riot act read to us (again) and after that the basement was strictly out of bounds to us all.   That was probably a good decision as there was a lot of research equipment there which really could have been damaged accidentally if we were not careful. In hindsight, it certainly wasn't the place to play the fool like we did!

Actually I was glad it was put out of bounds as it was one of the creepiest places I have ever encountered. (it would have made a good set for a 'Hammer movie' that would come around in the sixties!)   There was an Alec Guinness film in the 1950's called 'Green for Danger' and that film always reminded of the Tunbridge Wells Clinic building; especially the basement.   This was yet another example of the hard life we gave our parents. Unfortunately Cedric and I were to lose track of each other as we got older which was probably associated with the fact that he went on to Skinners School after Christchurch and I went to King Charles where we would ultimately make new friends and associates.

Chapter 11: King Charles School

The summer holidays between leaving Christchurch and moving on to King Charles School were, as always, much enjoyed. As far as I can recall summers in those days were always fairly predictable weather wise and more settled than now or so it seemed.   As youngsters we really enjoyed ourselves.   Material things didn't matter so much to us at that time as we could always keep ourselves entertained with our group of friends.

These were in many ways the austerity days. The war was over but food rationing was still in place, public moneys were allocated to rebuilding the damages of nearly six years of war and people led quite a Spartan way of life. On the whole though, and this is only my opinion, people seemed happy enough but I may have only been seeing it from a youngsters point of view and did not appreciate really how people's attitudes actually were. The signs of affluence were still a long way off in 1946.

We even had 'austerity buses'! These were introduced during the war years as cost effective but paid little attention to the comfort of the passengers as they had wooden seats. Public transport had been allowed to decline during the war as money was needed for more important things. Most of the buses on the road at this time had been built in the pre-war years so updated replacements became a priority as the people began to start getting out again. The family car really didn't exist; only the well off could even think about owning one, so the bus companies and the railways began to do very well as the people ventured out into the country and seaside again.

As I have mentioned already, Bob had his little Austin saloon and we got to go out in it once in a while. However, our main outings were still the 'ride there and walk back' trip's with my mother and Miss Pope. It was on one of these outings that we had our first trip on one of the austerity buses.   These were double deckers built by the Bristol Omnibus Company and were operated by the Maidstone & District Omnibus Company. The main difference between these vehicles and the pre-war buses was that they had wooden slat type seats, which really made journeys of any length a bit of an endurance test. Every single bump the vehicle went over, and there were plenty of potholes around in those days, really was painful and people would usually give these buses a miss if one turned up on any but an 'in-town' route.

Fortunately, the bus company relegated these particular busses to 'in-town' only work in the end in an attempt to keep the customers happy.   On the occasions when Mum took us on one of her ride and walk outings and there was an austerity bus on the route, we were glad to walk back.

My Dad was still in the Police Force at this time and as we grew older, if he had to go in to make a report or something, he would sometimes take us to the Police Station when he was off duty. That way we got to know quite a few of the policemen and they us which we didn't always think was a good thing when we considered some of the thing's we got up to.

It was about this time that we, and our mates, started to venture a little further from home in our activities. One of our favourite areas was around the 'High Rocks' about two miles away from the centre of town.   The area between Tunbridge Wells and High Rocks was a superb environment for us lads, encompassing the 'Common as you left the town and wooded countryside running parallel to the railway line from the 'West Station, between the town and High Rocks. The railway carried the mainline from Tunbridge Wells West to Brighton, Eastbourne and London Victoria, and in those days was extremely active. Of course the proximity of the railway added to the other attractions of the area, really made this one of our favourite activity areas.

Another attraction was the stream that ran along the whole length of the distance between the two places following the track of the railway line. My mother had equipped Trev and I with Wellington boots for use on wet days to save our other footwear. However we didn't have to be told twice to wear our 'Wellies' when we made off towards High Rocks as there was a lot of fun to be had wading through the water which was better than walking along the road. A landmark that exists now in that area is the Ramslye Estate; fortunately this was only in the early stages of construction at the time I refer to so, for us lads, the place was virtually unspoilt. It could get quite lonely out there at times, particularly on cloudy days, but to us it was a youngster's paradise. We could explore the stream virtually along its whole length as the water was very rarely deeper that about ten inches, it was great fun!

Which now leads me to the further association's we had with the Police!

One thing I can remember during the war and certainly afterwards, were the signs around the place telling people to beware of unexploded bombs and ammunition. I guess it stuck in our minds particularly as we ventured further off the beaten track and therefore, our imagination could run a little wild at time's. One day we were wading our way towards High Rocks in a part of the stream we hadn't tried before. We always took notice of the things around us and especially on the bed of the stream hoping I suppose, to find something like a gold coin or other valuable treasure. As we progressed along we came across a cylindrical tapered object, dark green in colour, laying half submerged in the sandy bed. There was some embossed lettering on the body of this thing, which didn't make any sense to us; there was no doubt about it, in our opinion, this was definitely an unexploded German bomb, or at least a shell! We decided there and then that the majority of the lads would stand guard over this thing whilst a couple of us went back to the Police Station in the Town and reported what we had found.

We eventually got to the Police Station and made our report that we had found this suspicious looking object. The desk Sergeant took it all very seriously and decided that he would send one of the police patrol cars to the scene to investigate. In those days the police operated a limited fleet of cars which in the main, comprised of Wolesley saloon's and M.G. sports cars. The local police constables mainly managed with bicycles or walked. We had always fancied a ride in one of the M.G's, although they were basically a two seater. As a Wolesley wasn't available it was to be our good luck to ride in an M.G.

We squeezed into the rear of the little sports car and off we went with two policemen towards High Rocks. Well, the car journey was definitely worth the walk we'd had to the Police Station and we seemed to fly to the site where our friends were waiting with the unexploded object. The policemen made us all get away from the adjacent area and they went off to investigate while we waited with the M.G. It wasn't long before the policemen returned holding an old green bottle! I can't remember what they said but I don't think it was very complementary; aggravated by the fact that in the retrieval of the bottle, one of the policemen had slipped into the water and his boots were full of water!

We thought we had been responsible in reporting what we'd found but all we got from the policeman with the wet feet was "I'll be speaking to your Dad when I see him". The funny thing was that a few days afterwards, we found another mysterious object not far from where the 'bottle' had been reported. It was during another of our outings to the area and was virtually a repeat performance. On this occasion the object in question was a black cylinder, parallel in shape and very ominous in appearance. Again, there were letters stamped on the body of the thing which was about three feet long and the language certainly wasn't in English; we were convinced that this time we had really found a genuine piece of German ordnance. The problem was that nobody wanted to report the 'find' to the police, bearing in mind the previous incident.

Well one of the other lads and I put on a brave face and departed for the Police Station. When we got there fortunately the same policeman was not on desk duty as before. That was a relief to us. We thought it would make our job of convincing him of the facts that much easier.

As soon as we began to tell him of our discovery he said, "are you the lads who reported the unexploded bomb the other day?" Assuring him that yes we were, he immediately started lecturing us that he hoped this wasn't going to be another waste of valuable 'Police time'. "Your Dad will get to hear about this if this is one of your pranks," he said. We assured him that it certainly wasn't our intention to waste anyone's time but that we were sure we had in fact found something very sinister.

Anyway we convinced him that there was good cause to send out a patrol car to check things out and before we knew where we were off we went in another M.G. Sports car speeding towards the High Rocks. Our mates didn't know whether we'd convince the Police or not so until the time we arrived back with the policemen they were hedging their bets that the police wouldn't believe us! As soon as we'd shown the police the object they knew that at least, this time, their journey hadn't entirely been in vain.

What we'd found was a piece of an aircraft, probably German, although having been half submerged in the water it was not instantly recognisable as such. Anyway the policemen had some idea as to what it was and weren't too concerned as they pulled it out of its resting place. They reckoned it was part of an undercarriage door, semicircular in shape and would have closely resembled something more deadly as it protruded through the water.

At least this time we hadn't entirely wasted valuable police resources; they assured us, as they made their way back to their car; the object was worth retrieving. In hindsight, I guess the corny phrase "don't call us, we'll call you", would be an appropriate ending to this part of the story.

It was about this time that we were able to buy ice cream once again. One of the first purveyors of ice cream into Tunbridge Wells was George DiMashio, who daily travelled up from Hastings, by train, bringing his ice cream barrow. He would arrive on the mid day train travelling in the guard's van. A group of us would wait for his train to arrive. He would get off and push his old wooden barrow to a place outside of the railway station. The brightly painted barrow contained two metal tubs of ice cream which were immersed in a reservoir of ice and Mr DiMashio would dispense cornets and wafers as required. My favourite was a three penny wafer! The barrow looked as if it might have been a relic of the Victorian age. If any ice cream remained the barrow would then be pushed to a good position outside of the Christchurch School! Within one hour all the ice cream would usually be sold. The Italian salesman would then return to Hastings on the next available train.

The ice cream sales were so successful that a few years on in my early teens, Mr DiMashio established an ice cream parlour in his name in Bazenhall Lane, Tunbridge Wells. He became very well known indeed around Tunbridge Wells, for his ice cream and apart from the shop he also owned a brightly painted veteran Austin 18 van which he would station either in the Calverley Grounds or on the Higher Cricket Ground to make his sales from. A second ice cream van joined his business in due course and was driven to the surrounding suburban areas which became further means of selling his delicious product. Unfortunately the Bazenhall Lane area no longer exists due to massive development of the Victoria Shopping Mall. The name of Di Mashio, as an ice cream vendor, has long since disappeared. However, in the mid nineteen nineties when we went to watch the annual London to Brighton Commercial Vehicle run, we were astounded and delighted to see DiMashio's veteran Austin ice cream van taking part.

Soon after the arrival of the barrow of ice cream becoming a regular feature in the town a little café opposite Christ Church in the High Street, began to sell iced fruit lollies. These were called 'Liklaps'. Many a summer evening after church, and before heading towards Lisney's for a bottle of pop, we would go to the café, which was still open then, in order to buy a 'Liklap' each! This was before 'Wall's Ice Cream' became established and would be sold virtually everywhere.

'Andrews Funfair' regularly took up residence on the Lower Cricket Ground and either 'Chipperfields' or 'Billy Smarts Circus' would always pay us a summer visit and raise their 'Big Top' there. For us youngsters the highlight of the circus was the parade of Elephants which took place at the lower end of the town. The animals would be transported to Tunbridge Wells West station by train. When unloaded by their handlers, they formed a parade that took them from the station area, past King Charles Church and up the High Street returning to the Lower Cricket Ground by way of Vale Road.

Having never seen live Elephants before, the sight of these magnificent animals parading through the town was fascinating for us. One thing that made us smile was the size of the droppings they produced! To actually get to see the circus we offered our services to the circus people for odd jobs during the assembly and preparation and in the final clearing up of the site at the end. It was a means to an end for us but my mother thought the whole concept of a circus was a cruel event but for us it was one of the highlights of the summer.

My father was always interested in British politics and had a great understanding of the subject. In pre-war days he attended a speaker's college sponsored by the Conservative Party and became one of their best speakers.
In 1946 the first General Election after the war took place and I can remember my Dad going off to several meetings both in the town and in London.

The 'Tories at that stage were still led by Winston Churchill and their leadership included many of the politicians whose names had become household words during the war years. Anthony Eden & Rab Butler were two names that readily spring to mind, whilst in the opposition Labour Party, Clement Attlee and Stafford Cripps are names that would eventually take their place in history.

I really didn't know very much about the political scene but I think at some point in a young person's life they will take a directly opposite stance to that of their parents. It's part of growing up I guess and in some respect's, is done to register to the parents that their children also have an opinion of their own which doesn't always have to conform to that of their elders. With this in mind I took on a distinctly strong Labour supportive role, much to the annoyance of my Dad in particular. My mother had her own views on the subject and would not allow herself to be swayed by other people's opinions. However she usually went in the same direction as my Dad!

With the economy in ruins after the war, the main issues were how to get the country back on its feet again. (It sounds very similar to the scenario we have today All pretty much ongoing I suspect) Joking apart, things were pretty grim at that time and some drastic action was definitely needed.

After Winston Churchill's magnificent leadership of the country through the dark days of the war, it seemed to me with my limited knowledge of the political scene that Winston Churchill could easily walk away with the election. When I 'ribbed' my Dad that Labour would be the victor I really didn't have the courage of my own convictions but, cussedly, I had to make the point just to rile my Dad! When the outcome of the election was a strong win for the Labour Party I simply could not resist the temptation to tease my Dad at every opportunity. He used to get so mad at me and promised that he would "knock my block off" if I didn't keep throwing the name of Clement Attlee at him. I think both Trev and I kept on having a go at him, mainly out of fun, but I suppose you can have too much of a good thing. However, we didn't let my Dad forget the demise of the Tories!

During the summer of 1946 my first day at King Charles, Church of England secondary School, loomed ever closer. My good friend Wack, who was slightly older than me, had already had a couple of terms at the school and he kept those of my mates and I, who would soon be joining after the holidays, briefed as to what we could expect. My Mum, bless her, had done her pre-school shopping to ensure I would be in a presentable condition when I went to the new school. With her Clothing Coupons and spending limitations, she set me up with my first pair of long trousers and blazer and, as much as I hated them, the inevitable flannel shirts. As winter would be coming on she bought me a pair of black boots as she reckoned I'd need them walking, in all weathers, 'to' and 'thro' to the Chapel Place part of Tunbridge Wells where the school was situated.

I remember the first morning of my Secondary School term. I called for Wack, who lived in Grove Hill Cottages, behind my Grandfather's shop, and off we went; with a strong feeling of trepidation. Apart from the other teachers at the school, the name of 'Clacker Clark', in particular, was one that we'd heard a lot about and the thought of meeting this stern disciplinarian didn't inspire me with confidence as we waited in the play area for the first assembly.

King Charles School didn't have a large playground area; the paved area between the school buildings and the Church Hall was the only space that could be considered to be the 'playground' and it was an insufficient space really to accommodate everyone. When all of the pupils were present it was extremely cramped, as it was to be on that first morning of the new academic year.

It was a beautiful late summer morning as the Church Clock peeled the hour of nine o'clock. The teachers came out of the school building and into the yard to address the assembled pupils; including all the 'new boys'. The fact that we were now to be taught by male teachers, including the notorious 'Clacker Clark', really made us jump to attention that first morning and certainly concentrated out thoughts.

We stood in the yard outside of the Church Hall and the teachers faced us standing at the top of the step's that led into the hall, to give themselves a good view of the assembled school and in particular, their first look at the newcomers. No familiarisation visit during the previous term had even been considered.   The Headmaster was a Mr. Bradman, a tall quiet sort of man who made us feel more relaxed as he addressed the pupils.

Our relief was however short lived as he pronounced that this was to be his last academic year as he was about to retire.   We were to automatically assume that 'Clacker' would be the prime choice to take over and in those fleeting moments, feared the worst for the time ahead.   To be honest, at this point we were very unfair to Mr. Clark as he had yet to open his mouth.

Mr. Bradman then introduced the rest of the teachers to

us. Firstly, Mr. Tommy Mann, a short, ginger haired man who, to our great relief we were told, would be taking over as Headmaster 'very shortly'. Next to be introduced was Mr. Clark; a bespectacled broadly built Yorkshire man who said that he reckoned that if his pupils worked hard, they would all have a happy and productive relationship. He was a stocky man with very thin grey hair combed close to the scalp and we were to never see him without his wire framed glasses and he always wore a dark blue suit. Although he gave the appearance that he was going to be a strict disciplinarian, we were later to discover he had a very human side to him as well and that would become more apparent when, in my final years at the school, he was my class master.

We were next introduced to a Mr. Short who was younger than the previous teachers and he immediately gave an air of being a lot more casual in his approach than either Mr. Mann or Mr. Clark. He told us that when we got to his classes, in the second and third years, swimming lessons at the Monson Bath's would be mandatory for all pupils. As this was to be a new experience for just about everybody there, it was something we would look forward to with eager anticipation. (Sadly, quite quickly, we were to give him the nickname of "Wanker Short". Familiarity had bred contempt in us youngsters. May I emphasise that at our young age, in the 1940's, we had no idea exactly what 'Wanker' meant! The media had not spread its precocity around in those days and most youngsters were very ignorant and even immature then by more modern standards.) But it sounded about right, as far as we boys were concerned!

The last teacher to be introduced to us was a Mr. Richardson who would soon be known as Dick; at least behind his back. He was the youngest of the team of teachers and was a very tall man with dark curly hair and a moustache. To us he was the tallest person I had ever seen and was like a walking lamppost as he was very thin. We were to later learn that he was in fact six feet, six inches in height which was quite unusually tall then. When he addressed us he had a very pleasant attitude towards us and it was very reassuring when he said that he would be our class master for what would be the lowest form at the school. Right away this news made me feel a lot better. What was strange in some respects was the fact that this was a Boys Secondary School. Initially the absence of girls seemed odd, we actually missed them, but we would soon begin to appreciate that in those days, before the 'coeducational' schools were introduced, it wasn't to be a bad thing. Our school building certainly wasn't large enough to accommodate the large numbers of pupil's that the later type of system would require. None of the local schools were and the new ones would need to be designed specially and built much larger for the coeducational requirements. The 'Girls' equivalent to King Charles was 'Murray House School', and this could be located close by in Mount Zion. There was however, very little in the way of direct relationships between the two schools. I think in those day's the powers that be thought it better to keep boys and girls apart. I wonder why!

When we settled into the academic life of the school it was immediately apparent that things were to be much changed from how things had been done at Christchurch School. Not only would we be studying things in greater depth but additional, to us, new subjects would join the curriculum. I really began to settle in quickly to my life with the Secondary School way of doing things. Many of the newly introduced subjects, i.e. Science, Higher Level Mathematics and History, were to become some of my favourites at the new school and during my time there I would do quite well at them. My life in Class 1 was to be a new experience in many ways. In the very early days of the new term, we were introduced to the Shakespeare Classics in the form of 'Macbeth'. Dick Richardson considered this to be essential reading. One of the very first 'home–work' sessions he gave us was to read Polonious's Speech and to memorise it. I am unable to remember much of it now but one part still remains in my mind;

> 'Neither borrower or lender be,
> For 'oft loses both himself and friend'.

This example did, for me, highlight the relevance of classical literature to the modern day. After some suitable period of home study, we all had to read the 'speech' out aloud in the classroom. Unfortunately, I had a particular 'hang–up' when I was young about speech confidence, in fact, it lasted well beyond the time I got married and it took a long time to finally get the problem out of my system.

In later years my wife Leila was a great help in reassuring me that there wasn't a physical problem but that it was more down to my suffering from a lack of self confidence. It took time, my wife's help and some small successes to improve my level of self confidence   Anyway when the time came for me to do my thing in Class 1 and to read aloud, I was a bag of nerves.

Dick Richardson did give me a lot of reassurance, it was obvious to him that I really did believe I had a problem and in his introduction to my piece, I remember him saying to the class that "Mike doesn't like reading out aloud, but let's give him our support."   However it didn't really help much because as I stood up I can still remember some of my class mates whispering to each other, "He stutter's."   In the event, it didn't go too badly.   I got stuck on a couple of lines but eventually worked my way around them.   At the end however, I felt completely drained; the adrenaline required to carry it out had exhausted me.

I know that at the time this really was a big problem to me but which improved with adult experiences and small successes. I became adept at finding alternatives to the kind of words that might cause me a problem. An example of this was the reading of the School Register in the classroom following morning assembly. The way they did it at King Charles, was for the pupils to shout out their names in alphabetical order and as it went around the class, the teacher would mark the record accordingly. I had a real problem with this; when it got to 'Gardner', I often couldn't get the word out. It was really embarrassing.   I never did overcome this no matter how much I tried to sequence the preparation of my name, which, if I can remember, followed a lad named Fox. This was most apparent when I reached 'Clacker Clarks' class but 'Clacker' really did understand, and for the first time permitted the boy sitting next to me to come to my aid, and for him to shout out my name when the time came.   For this little alteration to the usual system I was really grateful to 'Clacker' and for his foresight.

I'm not sure what age I was when I realised that I did have a problem; it probably became more apparent when I went to 'King Charles' where one was expected to be much more outgoing than we were at Primary School. I know that my parents would confirm that as a youngster it really was a concern. Trev would also remember some of the occasions when this problem let me down as it happened as frequently in out of school activities as it did in the classroom. Fortunately my family and friends were very loyal and never made me feel embarrassed about it.   It was to continue to be something that was always in the back of my mind as one did one's best to counter the problem. In later years I truly sympathised with others suffering from similar speech problems.

One of the main disadvantages of King Charles was the fact that the school, in common with many others, never had a dedicated sports field or, in fact, any sports facilities at all. Just after the war it was the norm' for Secondary Schools not to have these amenities; and it was the premise of the Grammar Schools to offer such attraction's and, I guess, to coerce pupils on to better things. As far as K.C.S. was concerned any sporting activities must take place on the nearby Common. As a result of all this the school really didn't place a high value on sports; certainly not as much as they do today. I suppose it went back to lack of funds and that children used to leave school a lot earlier in those days. In fact when I first started at KCS, the school leaving age had only just gone up from fourteen to fifteen years of age.

With lack of space the Secondary Schools had to make the most of what they had easy access to; in our case, the location of the Common being just across the road was advantageous but no alternative for the real thing! The closer 'Fair Ground' area of the Common, which would have been well suited as a sports field, due to its proximity to the school, still bore the results of having been used as an Army parking lot during the war years. We therefore couldn't make use of it and had to rely on the piece of ground opposite the Pantiles, which lay between 'Major Yorks Road' and what is now, the Public Conveniences.

If you can picture the area today you would agree with me that it was totally unsuitable for any sort of dedicated sports activities. When the teacher's took us over there for 'Sports' it was nothing more than one big giggle and the sports session turned out to be nothing more than a period in the fresh air with the nearest thing to sport being exercises and, if you were lucky, a few minutes spent in kicking a ball about. I do regret the fact that we didn't have the chance to seriously partake in a sport; I really enjoyed and fancied playing cricket but this was limited to a group of us playing in the Calverley Grounds and with debatable rules. The opportunity for proper involvement in games would have been wonderful.

However, the school did place a high value on its achievement's in swimming. Mandatory weekly sessions at the Monson Baths ensured participation. It was thus easy for our ability to be noted if one had any. I had never been to a Swimming Bath up until the time I went to 'King Charles and I don't think one ever forgets the smell of the chlorine as you enter the place and the echoing voices amplified by the high roof of the building.

In the junior classes, Tuesday afternoon straight after lunch was the period allocated for swimming. One had to have a very good excuse not to take part in the activity. The alternative was going back to school and sitting in on one of the other teacher's lessons which really wasn't that productive. Usually I elected to go swimming and in many ways I'm glad that I did. At least I managed to learn to swim. I would never excel at it but the main thing was that it was an opportunity not to be missed. The teachers used a method of instruction which was that after showing you how to actually keep yourself afloat the pupil would be hauled across the width of the pool at the end of a long rope with a ring, which the boy placed around the body. The problem was that as the teacher dragged you across the pool, you never knew when he was going to let go of the rope; in theory anyway, that was the when you were to begin swimming.

Well to the uninitiated this certainly wasn't an enjoyable experience and there were to be one or two incidents which were examples of panic, followed by urgent rescue by the attendant 'swimming instructor'. The first time I did it, when I felt the rope suddenly slacken, I did everything as I had been instructed and immediately sank like a brick! When you find yourself sinking and see bubbles venting to the surface you really does start to panic. So it was back to the practising in the very shallow end of the pool where the majority of the class appeared to be; natural swimmers seemed to be in short supply.

My mate Wack, although in the class above mine, was in the same group as I for swimming. In those days, the water wasn't Wack's natural habitat either. I don't know what the opposite phrase to 'a fish out of water' is but Wack was more like the condemned man being led to the gallows when it was his turn to 'take the rope'. Fortunately I was able to master this method of learning to swim after only a few sessions and could then progress to the 'deep end' of the pool. However poor old Wack just couldn't get to grips with it at all. After a time, the majority of the class had been successful in at least keeping themselves afloat which did put a lot of pressure on those who hadn't; Wack being one of them.

Kids will be kids and can be quite cruel. As often happens those who had in fact mastered the basic swimming technique took great pleasure in having a laugh at those who hadn't. At one session in particular, most of us were standing on the side watching the lads who were still 'roping it' across the pool. It came to poor old Wack's turn; he was in a state of panic as he saw all his mates standing on the side watching him do his thing. That certainly didn't help his confidence because when he was about half way across the pool the teacher let go of the rope, and Wack, of course, sank immediately. I will never forget the sight of his feet vanishing beneath the surface as he vainly tried to find the right way up. He went under for what seemed a long time before one of the instructors pulled him upright and into the fresh air. Wack was always rosy in his features but on this occasion, he was like a Belisha Beacon! I felt so sorry for him and the experience was to really shake his self confidence for many years where swimming was concerned.

Please don't think I was a natural in the water, I certainly wasn't. In my opinion Trev was a far better swimmer than I and went on to achieve his competency certificates, including the 'Half Mile' award. My only mark of success was the 'Fifty Yard's' basic certificate. It meant a lot to me however and I felt was a real mark of achievement. At least, if I were to find myself in a position of danger from drowning, I could swim enough to hopefully save my life. As for Wack, it was only when I met up with him a few years ago and the subject of swimming came up in our conversation's, that I learned that he only learned to swim properly when he was in his late forties! This enabled him to enjoyably encourage his young grandson to swim and to be happy doing so. He regularly swims nowadays at the newer swimming baths which were built a little out of town and close to his home. I guess that this proves that "while there is life, there's hope".

Chapter 12: Towards My 'Teen's'

In many ways, life at King Charles school wasn't that bad. I won't say that I actually looked forward to going to school but I found a lot of the subject matter absorbing and had some good friends so all in all life was pretty much all right during those years as I approached my 'teen's'.

By this time Tommy Mann was the new Headmaster at the school. We discovered that he was a man of great integrity and he would go to almost any lengths to improve the welfare of his pupils. He taught English to most of the classes at the various levels required and he had a good way of getting the most out of the boys. In other words, he was a born teacher of the old fashioned kind. He was also a particularly sensitive person of whom one normally would know very little of other than relating to his school time affairs. But unfortunately during the war, he lost his son who was a pilot in the R.A.F. His son flew Mosquito Fighter Bombers and was lost during the R.A.F. raids on Arnhem in 1944, during operations to support the Allied Airborne Forces who had parachuted into the area to capture bridges across the Rhine, held by the German's.

It became obvious to us all that Mr. Mann had thought the world of his son and what caused him considerable anguish was the fact that the remains of his son had never been found. We did know that Tommy and his wife, in an attempt to find their son's grave, paid annual visits to Arnhem in the years immediately after the war. When he felt like telling the class about his efforts to find out what had happened, we all listened with keen interest and we all hoped that one day he would be able to tell us that the grave had been found.

Eventually, I'm pleased to say that he was able to tell us that they'd heard from the War Graves Commission to confirm that his son's grave had been found and that the remains were to be transferred to the British Military Cemetery in Arnhem. It must have been a tremendous relief for Tommy and his wife. I can recall that although they had been dealt a cruel blow, sadly along with many others, the knowledge that they could now go and visit the resting place of their sons remains, helped them enormously.

At about this time I developed a severe skin infection

around my toes. We never did find out what actually caused it but it proved to be one of those ailments that would really take some shifting.   This incident goes to show just how considerate a man was our headmaster. When the infection first started my mother took me to the Clinic for the usual analysis and treatment and I really didn't worry too much about it.   However it was persistent and no matter what the clinic gave me to get rid of it as nothing seemed to work. Soon I was unable to wear proper footwear and had to rely on plimsoles which were the only footwear I could get onto my feet.

Being very active as youngsters this was a real problem for me as any restriction upon one's activities had far reaching effects. In particular my paper round seemed to take twice as long as normal when the problem imposed limitations on how far or fast I could walk.   When the Clinic couldn't get to the root of the problem they directed me, further afield to the Kent & Sussex Hospital as an outpatient. This produced its own set of problems as the only time they would treat me was in the mornings and of course, this arrangement clashed with school.   To be required to attend the hospital on a daily basis, for some length of time, caused many problems.   Not least because I could only walk rather slowly and the hospital lay up steep hills and was higher up in the town than where we lived.   Eventually, however, Mr Mann heard of the difficulties my mother and I were experiencing and he came to the rescue.   Such a personal interest in one of his pupils was so typical of Mr Mann.

Mr. Mann had a little car, I believe it was a Morris Minor but it turned out to be a real 'Godsend'. He would collect me every morning from home at half past eight, take me to the hospital, wait whilst they treated me and then drive me straight to school. If he had an early class he would leave me there and then come back for me as soon as he could. This really was a tremendous help and I usually got to the school in time for the morning break which wasn't bad going.   This arrangement went on for the duration of the treatment and I will always be grateful for his help.   It took several weeks to get the problem fixed, the final solution was that I had to go into the hospital for a day where they had to remove several of my toe nails, including the big ones, as it appeared that the source of the infection was in fact being generated under the nails. It was probably one of those illnesses, which would now be treated by antibiotics in a fraction of the time.   We had continued to use a tin bath in the kitchen for regular more thorough ablutions.   With the best will in the world hygiene was not as easily maintained then so I am surprised that I was the only member of our family to suffer from the infection.

My Dad had left the Police Force by this time and was working as a caretaker / barman at the Grove Bowling Club which was located in Grove Hill Gardens. We would often go up to the club to see him whenever we were playing in the 'Grove as it wasn't far away.

However whenever there was a match on, as a sensible precaution, he always made us stay well out of the way as it would have been considered a sacrilege to disturb the players during a match.   At my young age I was of the opinion that many of the players took the game too seriously.

At this time I can well remember that my parents were often at loggerheads with each other. With Dad leaving the police there had been a considerable change in their life style and this seemed to put some strain upon their relationship. Sometimes the arguments, between them became very heated and it did spoil our previously harmonious family life. As I got older, in hindsight, I realised that my Mum and Dad were almost certainly no worse than anybody else in not always agreeing with each other.   It was just that as a youngster one expected things to be as perfect as possible for all of the time and a disagreement between one's parents is not what one wishes for or can understand. As a parent myself I now know that one needn't always take such situations too seriously as, from time to time, differences of opinion between two adults will occur and will require sorting out – hopefully amicably!   Unfortunately, youngsters do not have the experience to comprehend these things at the time.

One morning my mother and father had a row just before I went to school. I remember my Dad storming out the door to go to work and the parting words of my mother as I left the house were, "I'm fed up with Dad, if I'm not home when you come home for lunch, then I've left him! If that happens, I'll let you know where to send the striking clock that sits on the mantelpiece as that was given to me by my Mum and Dad when I got married". I'll always remember those words; fortunately my Mum was there with our lunch when we came home from school and the subject never came up again. Comparing notes with others it appears that similar family dramas happen to everybody at some time or another.

I remember one Christmas in particular when my folks had a real bust up. The people in the top floor flat had changed not long before Christmas 1948. The Longley's left and Joyce and Sid Freeman then moved in. They were to stay at number thirty two for many years. Sid was in the mobile side of the Police Force and had known Dad during his time as a Special Constable so they were good friends. At about this time I was very interested in art and drawing and one of my favourite shops was Saltmarshes, which was located in Vale Road opposite Christchurch School. The shop was run by the Saltmarsh sisters, a couple of spinsters, and specialised in Artist's Equipment and the sale of their works. I loved going to the shop and spending what I could afford from my paper round or choir money, on drawing materials; one of my loves being sketching. On one of my visits to the shop, one of the Miss Saltmarshes showed me a really nice Wooden Paint Box which, as she said, "With Christmas coming, somebody might get it for you if I dropped a hint".

Well, when I saw the price, I really considered it beyond the likely contents of my parent's purse. It was Twenty Eight Shillings, (One Pound and Forty Pence in modern currency.) This was a considerable amount of money in those days and I thought my chances of getting it was pretty slim. It was roughly almost a week's wages for a young person just starting out at work in those days. Anyway, Mum got out of me what I would like for Christmas and of course when I mentioned the paint box, I also told her that it was very expensive and so not to worry about it. My mother was the sort of person who would give her family exactly what they wanted if she could possibly afford to do so.

So in a way I wasn't really surprised when, on Christmas Day, the paint box appeared as the star gift amongst my small selection Christmas presents. I do recall her carefully saving small items of cash throughout the year, in containers stored around the house; the contents being for the payment of regular bills and also for unexpected contingencies such as my expensive gift. I was over the moon about this and couldn't thank Mum and Dad enough.

My Dad always popped down the road to see my Grandparents on Christmas Day, after we had opened our presents leaving us to enjoy what we had been fortunate enough to receive. It did not cross my mind to wonder that we did not accompany him on these Christmas Day visits to the grandparents on our father's side.   On the day in question Dad was gone for about an hour and returned to find Joyce and Sid with us as they had a little something they wanted to give us. When my Dad got back he was not in a very good mood, I think Mum jumped the gun and accused him of having too much to drink at his mothers. Anyway, before we knew where we were, a big row broke out between my Dad and my Mum. Poor old Joyce and Sid didn't know what to say or do and we felt very embarrassed about what was going on in front of them on this day of peace and goodwill. This was the only time I ever saw my parent's have such a verbal fight. What had upset my Dad I will never know but to vent his anger at whatever was at the root of the row, he grabbed the nice wooden paint box I had been given and threw it against the wall which did it no good at all.

You can imagine as to what happened next. Mum was absolutely furious, I guess I started crying at seeing my nice present broken up and poor old Sid felt he had to try and calm my Dad down. It was all so embarrassing. Fortunately Miss Pope was away for Christmas, with friends at Etchingham, so the only occupant's of number thirty two were all present at the time of the disturbance. I think my Dad realised that he'd gone too far with the throwing of the paint box and with Sid trying to mediate felt it would be better if he went off out again, which he did. Probably back to my Grandparents.

When my Dad came back later he was very apologetic and really tried to make up for what had happened; fortunately Sid was a bit of a 'Mr Fixit' type, and had been able to repair the paint box so things weren't as bad as they might have been. My folks made their peace from that point onwards Christmas could be enjoyed. As to the reason, well we never found out and I, accepting Dad as he was, did not bear him any ill will knowing there had been nothing personal towards myself in his action.

It was one of those storms in a tea cup which at the time seemed to be the end of the world. The truth is that there are more family upsets at Christmas than at any other time of the year, and that's a fact. Buried resentments seem to surface at what has always been quite a stressful time of the year. Additionally there were most probably anxieties over money in our home at that time. At the time I did not realise any of this.

With food and clothing still on the ration, any extras for

Christmas were not easy to come by. I believe the Government did give some little additions to the ration for Christmas, things like a small increase in the meat and sugar allowances on a one off basis which made things just that bit more bearable for the festive season but those day's could not even begin minutely to match what is the norm' these day's; times certainly have changed and of course, so has the value of presents that people give each other compared to during my childhood and growing years. With a recession on at the time of my birth I can see that my parents had known little else but hardship during the whole of their marriage.

One of our friend's was a frail little lad, an only child, who lived at 4 Sutherland Road. His name was Peter Burden. Although he was younger than both Trev and I, we got to know him mainly due to the proximity of the passages that ran along the rear of the houses we lived in. Living in Grove Hill Road, as we did, the passage at the back of our house joined into the passage at the rear of the houses on the left hand side of nearby Sutherland Road. These were good play areas for us and it wasn't long before Peter joined in with us. His mother was also a good friend of my mother's so there was an affiliation between us. I think Peter used Trev and I as examples of what he wanted to be like when he was a little older. (God help him!) Trev, who was still at Christchurch at this time, used to take Peter back and forth to the school as his mother appeared to be the sort who worried about him when in the company of other children than ourselves.

Unfortunately we weren't to know that Peter was suffering from the then totally incurable disease, Leukaemia. I guess it should have been apparent to us that Peter was suffering from a serious health problem with Peter but at the age we were, you didn't think of those sort of things. The fact that Peter's parents wanted him to play with us as much as he could was in a way letting him make the most of what, unfortunately, would only be a short life. In those days, there wasn't the sort of medication available that there is now. Therefore from the time Peter's complaint was diagnosed, he would try to live as normal a life as he could at home until he got too weak to go out anymore.

So it was that one day, when Trev and I came home for our lunch from school, Mum broke the news to us that Peter had died at home earlier that same morning. As I have said, he wasn't one of our inner circle of friends, mainly because of the age difference, but he was still a good friend of ours, and when we heard the news we were shattered by it.   We couldn't believe it, in our mind's, only old people or those in accidents died; not young children!

Peter's parents wanted Trev and I to see Peter and I remember my mother offering to go round to his house with us. We both seemed to wish to go to say farewell to our friend. But we both declined having Mum to accompany us and went to the house individually. For us it felt better that way. It was the first time I saw a dead person and I was extremely apprehensive as to how I would react. Peter's mother took me into the front room of their house where Peter was laid to rest. The curtains were drawn although there was still enough light to see Peter was in an open coffin, on pedestals, in the centre of the room and when his mother led me over to him, he just seemed to be asleep.

In the half light of the room I felt he looked as though he would suddenly wake up and ask if we were going out to play. For some time it was hard to appreciate that we would never play together again but gradually the finality of the situation deepened and we became able to accept the situation.

I knew then how much we would all miss his devilish little face and the way he seemed to look up to us as his older friends. The first time you see a person who has died is something of shock and it certainly was in our case. It hurt even more when I realised that he'd had such a short life. Death is so final and I remembered all of the things I had wanted to say to him but now would not have the chance to do so.

One thing I remember so clearly was the winter of 1947. History will identify that particular winter as one of the worst, in Great Britain, during the twentieth century.   I suppose that when one looks back to the period, the fact that this severe winter came at a time when life was still trying to return to some sort of normality after the war, made it seem that much worse.

The problem was compounded also by the fact that heating of all premises was a pretty haphazard affair compared to the universally available heating systems of today. With coal mining still being undertaken those were the days of coal or coke being used, and of the side effects of polluted air mixing with freezing fog. Fog was a common occurrence when I was growing up and on many occasions life used to literally grind to a halt. The amount of coal dust in the air used to leave a black deposit over everything. Health problems escalated whenever periods of 'Smog', as it became known, were prevailing. The people most at risk were those who suffered with respiratory problems, especially the old folk, and many people used to wear 'Smog Masks' to ease the problem.

My Dad always kept a good fire burning in the Kitchener, even if at times his enthusiasm required the Fire Brigade to put out the chimney fire which to the best of my recollections, seemed to happen with uncanny regularity! My Dad was the only person to ever attempt to sweep the chimney as far up as he was able to reach. This was all a bit inadequate really. To conserve what supplies of coal and coke my parents could get hold of we only had a fire alight in the kitchen and never used the front room fireplace so the remainder of the flat was, of course, an absolute icehouse. Especially so was the toilet which was outside the back door! The fact that the kitchen was the warmest place determined that it was the only room we would use, apart from when we went to bed which was almost painful with the temperature change from the kitchen being colossal. Trev and I used to get changed into our pyjamas in the kitchen and then made a run for it into the bedroom and each made a dive into what seemed like our iceboxes and prayed that the temperature would increase before we got frostbite anywhere. OK, that is an exaggeration I know, but the cold did take some getting used to. Chilblains, which itched when you finally did get warm, were a real nuisance to many people at that time and it was understandable why.

I can not remember when the snows of that particular winter started but it seemed to go on forever and the snow remained on the ground throughout the winter months. The weather curtailed a lot of our activities outside of school but we and our mates were to find that the snow opened up a lot of fun for us, and we could do things we hadn't done before. My Dad made Trev and I a really excellent sledge. It was large enough to carry at least four people and in many respects it became one of the best sources of fun we ever had. Our favourite 'sledging run' was in the Calverley Grounds as it was near to home and our mates, which meant that you could always pop home for a quick warm up, or in the worst case, a change of wet clothes!

The hills in the Calverley' made it ideal for sledging and we would spend hours there having the time of our lives. We didn't tire of making the most of the snow and our sledging activities used to go on well past the time of darkness. Darkness descended so early that the only solution was to install cycle lamps on the sledges and it all added to the fun; I can still remember hurtling down the sledge runs in the dark just as fast as we could go. It was exhilarating and we certainly didn't feel the cold then!

Another of our favourite sledge runs was on an area of the Common known as the 'Donkey Stands' between Mount Ephraim and London Road. I believe the name came about from the horse drawn carriage days, quite a bit before my time, when the horses were rested and refreshed as they made their way through the town. What association this had with Donkeys, I don't know unless perhaps, it was an area popular with travelling gypsies and their donkeys. However it was certainly a very good place for sledging as the 'run' started on Mount Ephraim (not far from the Kent and Sussex Hospital) and you literally flew down the hill over some bumps, which, if you didn't remember were there, would throw you completely off the sledge, and you finished up, if you were lucky, at London Road near to where the old General Post Office stood before being pulled down for apartments to be built opposite Emmanual Church. Quite a few bods came to grief at this place and there were one or two who finished up in the aforementioned hospital with broken limb's! Fortunately, that didn't happen to our group but there were some very near misses. There was no doubt about it we really enjoyed ourselves in those days. My mother didn't have to worry about us not sleeping in the cold bed room as we were usually exhausted and simply crashed out after our activities. If it had not have been for the need to go to school, my mother wouldn't have seen us except for when we came home starving hungry and a tired out after being in the fresh air for so long.

During that seemingly never ending winter transport almost came to a standstill and especially so did the buses trying to negotiate the railway bridge in Vale Road and the 'Wells Hill as Mount Pleasant was known as. At one point the authorities banned all buses from going up or down the hill as it was considered too dangerous and at that time a temporary alternative route was used. We used to watch the buses trying to get up the hill. It would be very exciting for us to watch, especially as when they got about half way up they could go no further before they gradually slipped all the way down to the bottom of the hill. Fortunately there were very few motor cars around so the chances of a collision were fairly remote. The bus company would re-routed them via London Road and along Church Road in both directions until conditions eventually improved.

The railway managed to retain as near a normal service as it could, mainly due to the fact that they used de-icing trains along the route which did help. Our fascination with the railway certainly hadn't diminished, in fact by this time, it was becoming quite an obsession with us and the Winter activities on the line made it all the more interesting. Most of the railway staff at both the West and Central Stations knew us and they usually let us have the run of the place when we went to either station.

One thing we liked was that the station rooms always had lovely big open fires burning. I guess they obtained a lot of their coal from the passing locomotives; I can still remember seeing station staff coming away from the engines with coal in buckets as the train stood in the station. As far as I can recall the buckets they used to collect the coal were the buckets used to hold sand in case there was a premises fire. Well for sure, the buckets certainly came in useful.

We also knew many of the engine crews on the line and so we were often offered to get up onto the foot-plate of the engine. This enabled us to have a welcome warm up whilst the train stood in the station. That was the place to be, it was like being at the heart of a living thing and the roaring fire and the smell of hot oil and steam really was a wonderful experience. Don't get me wrong, we realised that being part of a locomotive crew was hard work and we didn't under estimate the heavy work involved in crewing and running the locomotive. Some of the engines, used in our area, were very old, ranging anywhere between thirty to seventy years of age and that made a lot of them darned hard work. A lot of the older engines, especially the old tender locomotives, didn't have closed in cabs and relied on a tarpaulin draped from the roof of the driving cab to a point at the front end of the tender. This system only really kept out the rain; it didn't make for the most comfortable environment in which to drive the thing, especially when the weather was bad, as little heat could be kept in.

From our vantage point at the bottom of Grove Hill Road, where we used to watch the trains, I can still remember the lower part of the town in the area of the station, heavily snowed in and hardly a soul about. One winter evening in particular I remember waiting for a goods train to come through the station. The temperature was well below freezing and there was a beautiful sunset where the sky had turned a brilliant red and orange in colour. There was hardly anybody about and there was quite an eerie silence as I waited for the train to come. Suddenly there was a huge roar as heavy snow, laying on the sloping sides of the Central Station roof, came cascading down onto the sidewalk below where today, taxis would be parked. Fortunately there weren't any taxis there at that time and nobody else was in the area. If anyone had been underneath at the time there would have been some possibly fatal injuries. After seeing this incident I made a point of walking in the middle of the road whenever I had the opportunity.   With little traffic, then, one could do that in comparative safety.

There was always something of interest for railway enthusiasts to observe. The Labour Government, as part of their Socialist policies, pushed legislation through Parliament to 'Nationalise' the railway system in the United Kingdom. Up to this point in time various areas of the country were served by one of the 'Big Four' railway companies.

These companies were, the Southern Railway, Great Western Railway, London North Eastern Railway and the London Midland & Scottish Railway. The 'Big Four' were the results of amalgamations carried out in the twenties and thirties whereby the numerous private railways were brought together to improve the quality and service to the travelling public. That was the theory at least.

It was therefore seen that to 'Nationalise' these railways would improve still further the product offered to the traveller and introduce sufficient funding for the modernisation of the system which through the war years had, like so many other industries suffered through lack of investment.   That was the argument for introducing this particular legislation. At the time there were many sceptics and a lot of people really didn't think it would work. (it is odd to realise that in effect, the railway system now has had to go back to the 'area' railway idea of the pre 1948 vintage, and is now controlled by a large number of railway operating companies in larger numbers than ever before)   To us though the idea was very exciting. People talked about the fact that there would be a certain amount of locomotive exchanges and some trains would run from the North of England right through to the South. Tunbridge Wells would see classic locomotives that we had previously only read about, operating right on our doorstep. It really did seem as though it would be a railway enthusiasts dream.

In reality it didn't work out like that at all. Yes, there were strange locomotives operating from Tonbridge and Tunbridge Wells West, but they were few and far between and were mainly Tank Engines. Our old favourites were still bearing the brunt of the work on the lines around the town, locomotive classes like the E1, A1X, L1, D, D1, N, U, H, P, Schools and Q class engines were destined to be the stalwarts of the 'Southern at that time. I think my cousin Peter was one of the most disappointed as he had assured us that we would see all the famous classes of engine in our area once nationalisation had been in place awhile

About this time Mr. Lord sold his little newspaper shop to a family by the name of Tuppen. Mr. Tuppen was an ex Royal Navy man and we immediately took a liking to him. It was obvious that he had a lot of ideas that would change the shop out of all proportion to what it had been when Mr. Lord had owned and run it. One of the first things he did was to carry out some limited enlargement of the premises to open up what space was available in order to lay things out better and to hopefully encourage more people into the place. These were the days before the multi purpose 'corner shops' came into existence. Mr Tuppen was then limited by what he could actually find had been produced that he could purchase in order to sell. Being primarily a 'Newspaper Shop' the law at that time also enforced that he stuck to that line of business only. By opening up the premises it certainly did begin to attract more customers. Some of these were probably commuters on their way to the station which was very close.

Under Mr Tuppen the newspaper business really began to take off. People who never used the shop when Mr. Lord ran it began to come in and before we knew where we were the paper round activity doubled. With the offer of a pay rise from Mr. Tuppen, I took on a new and longer paper round which would start at the top of Grove Hill Road and take in the roads leading to, and the whole of Camden Park and Prospect Road, including the road's leading off from it right along to the area known as St. Peters.

It was quite a long round but fortunately I was offered the use of a Tradesman's bicycle which had a carrier on the front to carry the heavy paper bag. Papers then did not additionally include the numerous magazines and pieces of advertising which weigh them down far more than when I was a paper boy.   I really enjoyed this 'round as it took me well out of the town and with the use of the bike I didn't find the task too difficult to achieve before going to school.   As there was then considerable open countryside on the route it became something of a real pleasure to do the 'round and see the changing scenes as the seasons of the year progressed.

My mother used to get me up by 0630 and I was usually at the shop within ten minutes before setting out at about a quarter to seven.   The hardest part was at the start with my pushing the cycle whilst it was loaded to its maximum, up to the top of Grove Hill Road where the deliveries began.   However, once you started it began to get a lot easier as the load lightened.   The Camden Park section of the 'round was particularly attractive as there were some very exclusive houses in that part of the town with a lot of trees around which gave them maximum privacy.   Places like 'Oaklands House', 'Oaklands Cottage', 'Hollyshaw' and 'Charnwood' readily spring to mind when I look back.   The disadvantage of this 'round was that in winter it was extremely quiet and dark until well after I had finished that section.   It was decidedly spooky in some places especially in the bottom end of the Park where the houses had long private drives, as "Hollyshaw" and "Charnwood House" had in particular.   I used to cycle as hard as I could between these places, so fast sometimes that if anything had got in my way I'd have flattened them, as I wouldn't have been able to stop!

In the summer however it was a different story.   The pleasant summer mornings with the sound of bird song and the smell of the countryside were memorable and I didn't rush like a mad thing then.   I felt it really started my day on a very good note and put you in a good frame of mind for my studies at school later.   I couldn't always say that though as some days I got soaked to the skin and when I got home, I would need a full change of clothing before I could go on to school.   My poor mother would be left with the problem of how to get my things dry other than by draping them around our kitchen.   Modern conveniences such as airing cupboards and clothes dryers were still things of the distant future.

My mother already had all the regular items of wash to get dry before my lot turned up.   One other good thing about being a 'paper boy' was when you got back home after all that good fresh air you had a really big appetite.   How my mother found the food to keep Trev and I satisfied I'll never know but breakfast was certainly a favourite meal of mine in those days and, I guess, it still is.

I got on really well with Mr. Tuppen. He treated me as his senior paperboy as I was by then, about the oldest and (without being big headed) he knew he could count on me. There were times when if one or other of his boys let him down, I'd set off and do some or all of the other lads 'rounds for him. On days when that happened it did make it a little tight in getting to school on time but fortunately, it didn't happen too often.

Mr. Tuppen always saw me 'all right' and my pay went up to Ten Shillings a week for doing the largest 'round. I used to go into the shop to give him a hand after school some days and particularly at Christmas time or when there was a need to do a lot of preparation such as marking up magazines for the following morning. I really enjoyed my association with the Newspaper shop and it gave me an incentive that one day I would have a similar shop myself. I didn't know then that the 'Newspaper Shop' as I knew it would change totally in character in later years to the sort of 'Corner Shop' they are today where they sell just about everything; including newspapers.

In the late nineteen forties things were slowly returning to some sort of normality after the war. Although most things were still rationed some things, like magazines, were beginning to increase in numbers and interests. Being in the business so to speak, I would get the opportunity to see most magazines of the day as I distributed them during the preparation and circulation of my paper round. Actually I got addicted to magazines and would spend a fair proportion of my paper round earnings on a huge variety of them.

Such magazines as 'Navy News' and 'The Railway Magazine' were high on my list of 'regulars' and others like, 'Picturegoer', 'Picture Post', and 'Motor Cycle' were amongst those I found hard not to acquire. My mother used to go on at me about spending so much on magazines but never used to complain about it in the evenings when she wouldn't hear much of me as I sat absorbed in the subjects the magazines covered. Children's Comics were becoming popular again about this time and several new one's were coming onto the market. Amongst them was the 'Eagle'. Being in the business so to speak, Mr. Tuppen had kept me in the picture, through the advance publicity he had received, about this new comic well before the first issue was released, and it really whetted my appetite. By modern standards the advance publicity may have been considered rather low key, but in 1948 it was something of a sensation. (even without Commercial Television!)

I won't forget the first time I was to read about Dan Dare and his confrontations with the Mekon and the men from other Planets. It was captivating stuff and the weeks could not come around quick enough in order to read the next episode. In its day the 'Eagle' was a revolution in the comic paper business. It was so far removed from the 'opposition' with its large format presentation and the mixture of fact and fantasy that it was in a class of its own.

One of the features I particularly liked was the centre fold where they would display a sectional drawing of feats of mechanical engineering. It was excellent and became the most popular boy's magazine of the day.

.

Chapter 13: The Swan Hotel

Life at King Charles School went on apace and I progressed from Mr. Richardson's class through that of Mr. Mann's and eventually into Class 3 with Mr. Short who had the unfortunate nickname of 'Wanker'. We kept in touch with the other teachers who still covered specialist subjects but our predominant teacher was 'Wanker'. Actually he really wasn't a bad sort of bloke and although he gave the impression of being a disciplinarian, he was in fact fairly easy going. Class 3 was located right next to the top Class, number four where the teacher was 'Clacker Clark'; 'Clacker's' name was spoken of in an air of trepidation as his reputation was one of strict discipline.

Being located next door to 'Clacker's' class, which was separated from our class by a wood and glass folding set of doors which allowed the whole area to be opened up as one, certainly didn't ease our concerns for the day when we would eventually find ourselves his pupils. It seemed a regular occurrence to hear the sound of Mr. Clark screaming at some poor unfortunate in his class and the impact of book hitting wall as it missed the culprit he had aimed at.

'Clacker' was a staunch Yorkshireman in the true sense of the word and had a very strong accent. He was a man of medium height with thin grey hair; his appearance was rendered all the more imposing by the wire framed glasses he wore which had very thick lenses. He always wore a dark suit which was contrary to the other teachers who seemed to prefer 'separates'. My first impression of 'Clacker' was that he would put the fear of God into you if you didn't do as you were told in the event, I, and many others were to be proved totally wrong when the time came to become one of his class pupils; but more about that later!

It was whilst I was in Mr. Short's class that the King Charles School 'Marathon' run took place. This was the first to be held since they had ceased for the war and had not been restarted until now.   At the time I had no great enthusiasm for sport and so I really didn't know what the difference was between a 'Marathon' and a 'Cross Country Run'.

Up to this time my education had been fairly comprehensive, within the limits available at a primary school, but had a huge gap in it where sports activities or sporting instruction were concerned. And for the life of me I cannot recall how I got lumbered with having anything to do with our school 'Marathon' run which would be of almost four somewhat hilly miles in distance. My name can only have been pulled out of the 'hat' for me to have been one of the participants; there were sixteen pupils chosen from each school house, and the inclusion of me cannot have been based on 'form'. I found myself as a nominated 'runner' for the event along with fifty nine others. I had been selected to represent the house of Rupert. The other houses were entitled Ormonde, Falkland and Montrose. Apparently these men were all supporters of King Charles 1st.

It wasn't as though participants had a lot of choice as to whether they took part or not, once your name was drawn, you were in it. Maybe it was a case of if you could walk, you could run. What made the whole thing so ridiculous and very much a hit and miss affair was that due to King Charles School totally lacking in sports facilities, all such activities took place on the 'Common directly opposite the Church or in the Church Hall; hardly a good grounding for aspiring athletes!

Actually Trev and I together with most of the Grove Hill Road Gang were in fact pretty good runners (having obtained a good track record in running away from the grounds men in the Calverley Grounds or, once in a while, from the men in blue!) The disadvantage I had when it came to the school run was that I really didn't have the right kit, and in particular, I didn't own a pair of running shoes or suitable plimsoles. If you recall, it was at this time that I was getting over the foot infection that had plagued me for some considerable time and soft footwear (we hadn't heard of 'trainers' in those days!) was strictly taboo as far as the medical people were concerned, so the only footwear that I possessed at that time was, would you believe it, a pair of Army boots!

I guess that had I made my case to the teachers I would have been allowed to drop out of the run because of the foot problem but I suppose I did not want to be seen as 'letting the side down' or to be seen as a bit of a 'wimp'. Anyway the day came for the great event. Two o'clock was the time fixed for a mass start from the Lower Cricket Ground on the 'Common. This overlooked the 'Swan Hotel'. It was a damp drizzly sort of day for the big occasion as we all made our way there. I must have looked the perfect long distance runner dressed in a white vest, black PT shorts and army boots! All the school had strict instructions to be there, or else, so it was well supported. I seem to recollect that there were some of the girls from Murray House School there to add a little 'glamour' to the event.

The routing for the race was directly across the 'Common, past the 'Brighton Lake' and on towards High Rocks, running parallel with the railway line, until you reached the 'High Rocks Hotel' where the runners were 'logged' by one of the teachers as they turned for the return leg home which was run along the same route they had taken on the way out. The only difference on the return route was that you went towards Major Yorks Road as you approached the Common and then turned for the start and finish point opposite the Pantiles. I suppose it was a run of about four to five miles, which really does not sound much but when faced with it all to do it was quite a daunting task, especially as although I was very active I was not really the athletic type. As a youngster I was tall and fairly slim but with quite a large frame.

As two o'clock loomed the 'athletes' assembled in line abreast on the start line. There were exactly sixty participants and the start was designed so that nobody had a particular advantage as we stood huddled shoulder to shoulder waiting for the starter's gun to go off. "On your marks, get set, Go!" shouted Tommy Mann as he fired the start gun and the field streamed off across the 'Common as though we'd been shot from guns. Don't get the wrong impression, peak speed was only achieved for about one hundred yards as the throng funnelled into a single track and a lot of jostling took place before taking a more leisurely pace; the restriction in the width of the path dictated that those in the lead at that point stayed there for a time until the route opened up a little about a half mile ahead.

It actually was a case of survival of the fittest at this point as one needed to be something of a 'couldn't care less' type to press on, if necessary, trampling others underfoot as you went, to maintain your position! Pacing yourself was not really heard of then. It didn't really make a lot of difference to me though as I was some way towards the middle of the pack at this point and after the initial burst of speed, was trying to get into a more comfortable pace with quite a long way to go. I could see considerable manoeuvring for position ahead of me as we jockeyed for position and whilst still in the middle section the group was not quite as competitive.

By the time we were half way towards High Rocks I was beginning to ask myself 'was it all worth it?' However on we went and the leaders were beginning to draw out a considerable advantage; I was starting to fall back a bit as running in my army boots was beginning to feel like running with ballast in them. This definitely slowed me down. By the time I got to the turning point I was probably in the last ten and the pace was becoming painful. The ironic thing was that as we approached the High Rocks we were passed by the leading pack of runners who were already on their way back, and that really rubbed it in. After that it became hard to keep motivated.

After turning at the hotel it was obvious to me that I really wasn't a natural at this kind of sport and I had the distinct feeling that it was going to need a superhuman effort on my part to even get to the finishing line. With that ignominious thought in mind I pressed on together with a group of fellow 'sufferers'. As we headed for the finish line climbing the hill which led towards Major Yorks Road, it was, for me, like climbing Mount Everest. At least when I reached the main road it would all be downhill back to the Lower Cricket Ground; but my legs really didn't get that message.

What was fact, at this point, was that I was certainly towards the end of the field and I had the ominous feeling that I could actually be the last man. Some confirmation of this was that as I pressed on over the 'Common towards the finish line, I passed a group of people out walking; and as I passed them, they gave me words of encouragement which I remember to this day, "press on mate, the others have all gone home for tea". That really made my day but I guess inspired me at least to motivate myself to reach the finish line.

As I painfully continued the finish line came into sight and the good thing was that the rest of the runners hadn't "gone home for tea" and many were shouting words of support to me as I limped towards the line. When I flagged across the finish line there were words of encouragement from the assembled crowd and of course the inevitable "last but not least" phrases. The main thing to me was that I felt good that I had actually finished, albeit, at number sixty of sixty but it still gave a sense of achievement in many respects as I had at least completed the course. With the race over we made our way back to the school to change and Tommy declared school over for the day and I went home to a high tea of Bloaters (one of my favourites) that Mum laid on as a special treat for me. Both Mum and Dad thought that to finish the race was the most important thing and didn't worry about where I had come in the field so I felt pretty good about that.

The following morning at school all the pupils were assembled for the official ceremony to recognise the winners of the school cross-country race. The winner and runners up were duly acclaimed by their fellow pupils and each received their prize from the head master. At the conclusion of the winner's ceremony Tommy Mann then referred to the lad who had come in last. Me! I couldn't believe my ears when he started to air that in his opinion, and not taking anything away from the winners, he was extremely proud of the lad who came in at number sixty; and that was me. In Mr. Mann's mind, he really felt that the lad he was referring to had made a sterling effort to enter (I don't remember having a choice) and then actually to finish a race that would have been an impossible task a few months earlier because of the medical problems that he'd had with his feet. Also, in his opinion, to run the race wearing a pair of army boots was a very worthy effort. He then beckoned me to come to the front of the assembly and stand there whilst a round of applause was forthcoming from the rest of the school.

Frankly I found it all a little embarrassing but Tommy meant what he said and he wanted the school to understand that in life it isn't always the winning that's important but staying and finishing the course. Probably at the time I really didn't understand the full meaning of what he was trying to get across but I must say, in many respects, in ones life there is probably no truer statement. It meant a lot to me that he took the time to say what he did and it was a great 'consolation' prize.

As far as school was concerned I was getting on reasonably well and all in all quite enjoyed it. By now I was starting to collect the odd prize for the subjects I had excelled in and end of term award time usually saw me obtaining a couple of books to add to my growing collection.

It was about this time that Bob took out a lease on the Garage associated with the Swan Hotel, at the 'Pantiles' end of Major Yorks Road, next to the Fair Ground. The garage (the building still remains at this time) was located directly opposite the hotel with a small parking area in front for the use of those of the guests who were car owners. The majority of the guests were still using rail or bus transport at that time.

I cannot remember the circumstances leading up to his decision to close down the place he had at Mount Ephraim; I can only surmise that the probable reason was to reduce costs as the Swan Hotel Garage was a lot smaller than the other place and Bob could run the place on his own and not employ another man. You have to remember that in those days there still were very few cars on the road and those that did run were limited by petrol rationing which was still in place long after the war years. The motor repair business wasn't therefore the most lucrative business to be in.

At about this time I was coming up to the grand old age of fourteen and my folks and Bob were keen that I should be thinking about what I would do when I left school in a year's time; should I not go on to further education. I certainly had a strong interest in mechanical things and motor vehicles in particular so there was a consensus of opinion that I ought seriously to consider learning the motor trade.

Bob, in his wisdom, offered to take me on under his wing when I eventually came to leave school and would teach me the trade through an Apprenticeship. However he thought that to give me the opportunity to see if I'd like the type of work, he would let me work at the garage with him on Saturday mornings and during school holidays. This really did seem an excellent idea. In the beginning I began to look forward to my Saturday mornings working with Bob in his garage and getting a feel of the motor repair business.

As I have already said there really wasn't a lot of motor work about at that time and business certainly wasn't booming. Bob had some regular customers he'd brought with him from Mount Ephraim including a one man taxi company belonging to a man by the name of George, who operated a single Standard Twelve saloon. This man was ultimately, through his failure to pay Bob for the work carried out on his car and of other cars, belonging to various of his 'friends' to bring Bob to the verge of bankruptcy.

Another of Bob's customers who was well known to me was a fairly well off lady by the name of Mrs. Horne. She was a widow who lived at the back of the Wellington Hotel on Mount Ephraim in an exclusive apartment block. She had one or two motorcars of her own and sent these and those of her associates to Bob for maintenance. In fact her Austin Seven

'Ruby' Saloon seemed to be permanently at the garage. At this time and with this kind of clientele, there were good reasons for Bob to at least make a reasonable income from the garage business and for a time it all really worked quite well. As I joined Bob in his garage I was soon conversant with the terms of 'reboring', 'decoking', 'valve seats and overlaps' etc., I soon became his 'able assistant' during my spare time.

On looking back I can remember exactly how the 'Swan Garage' looked in those days. The building is still standing and the covered portion and hard standing are still used for the cars of people visiting the hotel. I wouldn't be surprised if the wire mesh screen that Bob eventually installed, to secure his repair half of the garage, is still in place today. Initially Bob utilised the whole building with the end nearest Major Yorks Road being the workshop and repair area and the remainder used for parking cars. It wasn't a very large building but certainly adequate for the purpose he wanted it for and the number of customers he had. I guess it would probably hold around ten cars allowing for working space. There was a loft area over the workshop and this was used to store a lot of Bob's odds and end's; in other words it was a bit of a dumping ground for things that one day would come in 'useful'. (Whenever I have gone pass the old garage in recent years, I have often thought 'I bet there are still some of Bob's old 'useful' things laying up in that loft' as the garage appears not to have changed one bit from the days when he was there!)

Once Bob had got himself established whenever I would be there, he seemed to have a fairly regular line of work with several vehicles usually in the shop. With the close proximity of the school I would go there most days straight from school. Bearing in mind he was a one man band so to speak, some of the cars would be in pieces for some considerable time because when they required spares, he would start another one and so on.

In those days spares support from the manufacturers was a very longwinded process and you could wait weeks sometimes for even the simplest of items. These were the days before the 'Do It Yourself' craze and motorists discount stores. ('Halfords' were in business at that time but only in the bicycle trade)

I got to know the names of the different types of motor cars, suppliers and agents such as 'Tunbridges' for Austin parts and 'Caffyns' and 'Stormont's' for Rootes Group and Ford respectively and I was really beginning to enjoy my activity in the 'motor trade'.

As soon as he was able, Bob separated his workshop area from the rest of the garage by installing a wire mesh screen which ran the full length of the garage allowing him to secure his tools and equipment in the 'workshop' half of the building. This came about because one night, somebody got into his workshop and stole a number of his tools and lubricants. The Police were involved but it was like trying to find a needle in a haystack and in the end it was better to secure the area which he used predominantly for carrying out the major repairs.

It was about this time that I drove my first motorcar! (totally illegal at the age I was) Actually it was only on the forecourt of the garage but it was to be my first experience of 'man and machine' so to speak. Mrs Horne's long resident Austin Seven 'Ruby' Saloon never appeared to be used by her. The only running it got was out to the front of the garage, around the forecourt and back in again.

It was a really lovely little car. Often when there wasn't much to do I would sit in it inside the garage and pretend that I was driving the thing, reproducing aural car and gear change noises as I 'drove along an imaginary road'. I can remember it as though it was only yesterday; the smell of the leather interior and the stale air inside of a vehicle that rarely went anywhere. When Bob asked me if I would like to drive it I really didn't take him seriously and thought he was only joking. However one morning he decided to put some of the cars he had in the shop outside to allow him to have a good clean up. Up until this point, I had only been allowed to run the engine of the Austin (he gave me good instruction about ensuring it was out of gear before I did so) about once a week. After we'd cleaned the shop he, in his inimitable fashion came up to me saying "come on old man, you can drive the Ruby back into the garage." Fortunately, he said he'd sit next to me!

One characteristic of Austin Seven motorcars was the very fierce clutch operation. The clutch appeared to only have a travel range of about one inch before the engine took over and you were on your way. For a first timer they were not the ideal vehicle to learn in and not having any experience of the correct clutch operation and things like the biting point. My first 'drive' was more like a short journey to the moon from the way we leaped forward as I attempted to move the car forward. You could say this was my first experience of the term 'Kangaroo Petrol'.

My problem was that the forecourt went uphill into the garage and this made for good 'clutch control' essential. Hardly the best place for a first timer. Anyway, I am pleased to say we did get the car back into the garage in one piece and avoided extending Bob's workshop area. This was mainly thanks to Bob's involvement in the short journey. I was a bag of nerves. It was quite an experience. I was to repeat the exercise several times again but increasingly successfully.

These good days of working with Bob were, unfortunately, to be relatively short lived. I can remember the day when, after some discussion on the subject, Mum and Bob took me to one side to say that as the business really wasn't doing very well. They thought it would be unwise for me take up an apprenticeship with Bob when I eventually left school. Although I still had just under a year remaining of my school days we could see the possible risks in my pursuing that particular career path and sadly especially not with Bob. Bob stressed that he would always welcome me to at garage and I could still help him but at the same time it was obvious it wasn't a viable long time idea. I was really upset at the prospect of not working with Bob. I guess it was because I began to realise that when the day came to leave school I would not now have the assurance of still being in a more or less family environment but would really be setting out in the big, wide world.

Primarily Bob's business wasn't going as well as it should because there were a lot of customers who proved to be 'difficult' when it came to their paying their bills. Apart from Mrs. Horne, the majority of the other customers seemed to come into this category. In particular I can remember the name of George as being a poor payer. He was the man who ran the one man, one car Taxi firm. I guess it's easy to be wise after the event but Bob was a very kind hearted person and not the type of man who would, or could, pressurise people who owed him money, to pay up. He really wasn't a real businessman in the proper sense of the word; he was just too nice a person really. Unfortunately, from my observations, they are often the people who do come a cropper in life. It was obvious too that several of those who owed Bob money could usually be found propping up the bar in the 'Swan at lunchtimes.

George certainly wasn't the only one who contributed to Bob's business problems. I cannot recall the actual names of most of the poor payers but high on that list was the owner of the 'Swan Hotel' itself who was to prove to be a real mixed kind of personality. I quite liked the man but only as a passing acquaintance until one day, he really turned out to be a 'Good Samaritan' to my mates and I at least.

One of the great enjoyments my mates and I had were the days when we'd make an early start for a day out in the High Rocks area. This lay just beyond the High Rocks Hotel, on the road towards Groombridge, where it dips down to cross a water outlet, there was (and probably still is) a path that wends its way to a railway bridge across the same water. Surrounding bushes and undergrowth made it an ideal camping area with the bonus of our being able to see many trains passing by. Over a period of time we were to build ourselves a pretty decent 'camp' there. Those were the days before any of us owned a bicycle so the journey was by foot; sometimes I would persuade Mr. Tuppen to loan me the tradesman's bike used for the paper round. This was the ideal tool for the job because of its carrying capacity; yes, we travelled heavy even in those days!

We would go off for the day well 'provisioned' by our parents and with the odd tin of soup or Baked Beans we'd managed to purloin from some source or other, so we were usually well laden. Of course, no good 'camp' would be complete without the campfire so we always ensured that our little group carried suitable fire lighting materials etc.

This responsibility was usually in the capable hands of Trev.

As I've already said most times we went to High Rocks on foot so were quite used to the longish walk. The walk mostly alongside the railway line, always kept our interest. On the day in question Trev and I, along with the rest of our happy band, about half a dozen in total, were at the campsite. One of the reasons why we enjoyed this particular place was that apart from being 'away from civilisation', it was located right next to the main railway line from Tunbridge Wells West to both London (Victoria) Lewes, Brighton and Eastbourne etc. so it was a very busy place to be in those days. High Rocks Halt, which was about a hundred yards away from our camp, was a 'Request' stop for the use of the very few passengers who lived in that area. Most trains were unscheduled to stop there but some local trains, not going as far as to London or to Brighton or to Eastbourne, would stop for beckoning passengers. If you wanted the train to stop you had to signal the driver as the train approached the Halt and, hopefully, the train would then stop to pick you up.

On the day our Good Samaritan helped us out we were still gathering more twigs for our newly lit small 'camp fire', as part of our preparations for lunch when the rain began. It was one of days when it became obvious that the weather was not going to improve for us. The rain didn't relent and the fire was soon washed out and reduced to nothing; it wasn't our day really so the decision was made cut our losses, pack up and head back home. As you can imagine, we were not really dressed for a three mile walk in the rain and we were soon pretty well soaked through soon after starting our return journey.

We had gone about half a mile and must have looked a really sorry bunch as we plodded our way back to civilisation. A car came along the road heading towards Tunbridge Wells and was about to pass us when it slowed down and stopped. Cars were not very frequent then and I thought I recognised the car and was proved right when the owner of the Swan Hotel got out and came over to us. It was purely by chance that he had stopped as he could not have recognised me. In an attempt to keep out the rain, most of us were walking under a groundsheet which we held between us so from the rear, must have looked more like a large 'blob on the landscape' with legs!

We really were a bedraggled bunch and were therefore all the more surprised when he offered to give us a lift to the town. Fortunately it was a fairly large car and we all squeezed in with a sigh of relief. The man knew me from my sessions of working with Bob so I suppose that helped. But what really surprised us was when he asked us whether we'd eaten. On telling him we had not he immediately offered us the opportunity to visit the kitchen of the Swan Hotel on our arrival, and there, he said, we would be very welcome to have any 'leftovers' from the mid-day lunch menu. When we got to the Hotel the car disgorged its bedraggled bunch of passengers, and we filed straight into the hotel through the front door.

As we entered the hotel I noticed Bob was sitting in the bar, as we went through the lobby, and on seeing us he nearly fell off his bar stool. His immediate reaction was "what have you lot been up to"?   The hotel owner quickly reassured Bob (and other curious guests) that we were his guests for lunch, albeit, in the kitchen. However I will never forget the expression on Bob's face.   It was a picture!   I guess we were a very scruffy bunch of 'guests'. I will always remember our lunch in the hotel kitchen. The owner gave instructions to the chief chef that we were to be given anything we wanted that was left over from the lunch. Even back in those days when food was still on the ration, we were amazed at how much food, particularly meat, there was available in the hotel.   In fact, what was actually 'left over' was more food than any of us had ever seen in our lives. We tucked into roast pork and beef with all the trimmings and finished up helping ourselves to fruit salad and ice cream; it was a banquet and I think none of us would ever forget it. A day out 'camping' at the High Rocks would never seem the same again!

When we related the day's events to my mother and father they didn't know what to say and probably thought we were stretching the tale a bit far until Bob himself confirmed he had seen us all actually inside the 'Swan'!

Chapter 14: Family Happening's

Although my aspirations to work with Bob, in his garage, and to pursue an apprenticeship with him were not to be fulfilled, I still had a strong desire to be an Engineer when I eventually left school. You may wonder why it was that with my love of railways I did not wish to follow a career connected in some way with rail transport. I have often asked myself that question and as far as I could see from my youthful viewpoint that no proper training was available for youngsters interested in trains. It all sounded a bit 'hit and miss' to me. And later on in life, as steam began to disappear, the nostalgic memories of associations with railway engines would resurface and it was then that my love of them would start all over again. I do not regret the fact that I followed my desire to become primarily and initially an aircraft engineer; but that was all still to be well on in the future.

In particular the memories are still with me of our visits to the engine sheds at the 'West. Sunday afternoons were a good time to visit the sheds as activity in the area was a lot less than during the week and shed staff were preparing the locomotives for their Monday morning tasks. Engines used to be parked in a ready for service condition adjacent to the shed and access was very easy for us. The shed staff never stopped us entering the property, apart from days when an 'inspector' was on site, so we had good access to the engine footplates, providing we didn't touch anything. I have always seen engines as living things and really respected them. We never did anything to jeopardise our being allowed onto the site. It was the same when we went into the shed itself. Being at rail level, as you entered the shed, you were met with the huge driving wheels of the locomotives parked there. To us youngsters they were huge and there was always the wonderful smell of the 'sleeping engines'; these are memories which remain with me to this day.

Apart from steam engines, really and truly, I had an interest in all things mechanical. It was about this time that we became avid 'Bus Spotters'! But I'll tell you more about that later on.

So with our never ending pursuance of all things steam, we would often talk to the railwaymen, particularly at the Tunbridge Wells West sheds where we knew a lot of the staff, about life on the railway. Most of the enginemen were career railwaymen and had worked most of their lives on the railway. They would tell us all about the days when they were young lads, straight out of school, and working all the hours God made for an absolute pittance; it appeared they had all started out as Cleaners and eventually worked their way up through the ranks of the Firemen to become Engine Drivers.

I think one of the problems with taking up a career on the railways was the fact that there was no actual 'apprenticeship' as such and that at the age of eighteen years, you would be drafted into National Service in the military and one would then probably review ones career path based on what you did in the services. Personally I felt that, on leaving school, a proper apprenticeship would be the preferred way to go, as that would at least mean I would have to complete an apprenticeship before going into National Service. However, with some months of school days still ahead my leisure time could continue to be related to the trains I loved as a boy.

But it was roughly at this time that I decided to try and get a Saturday and holiday job. The newspaper round was still going well and I used to do a lot of out of hours tasks for Mr. Tuppen at the paper shop. But, by now, I was ready for and wanted a bit of a change. Actually there really wasn't a lot of choice with things still being depressed after the war. Many people were trying to find full time employment so my chances were not particularly hopeful. I went to all sorts of places trying to find something but didn't even get near to an offer. I did however take up an offer from Bert, the 'John Browns Dairies' milkman whose round included Grove Hill Road and all the side roads in the area, to help him on Saturdays and Sundays when he was at his busiest. He was one of the first to use the new type of electric milk float, which had a tiller control handle at the front by which you controlled the drive, speed and direction of the unit.

I was to work with Bert for a couple of years, on and off, and really enjoyed it. Believe me, it didn't pay well; Bert used to give me sixpence (two and a half new pence today) every time I helped him which was worth having in those days. There were no laws about minimum wages then; as far as I knew at least.   But I did not expect anymore, as I knew that whatever he gave me came from his own pocket. Actually I enjoyed helping him and I was always finished at the latest by eleven o'clock so it was worth it as there was still a lot of the day remaining to do other things.

As I still had my paper round to do before I joined the milk round, I usually met Bert at the top of Grove Hill Road. He would always greet me with a smile and we would simply flash round the rest of his deliveries. He once told me that it was worth sixpence to him as the early finish allowed him to get back to the Dairy promptly. This put him in line for the opportunity for 'overtime' which suited him. Bert used to let me 'drive' the milk float on quiet mornings and as I have said, it was the type that you walked in front of using a tiller with a twist grip that controlled the steering and electric motor throttle control. It was quite easy to operate and I enjoyed having a go at it. One day however I got distracted and forgot to apply the brakes in good time and the milk float ran into me. I finished up with a deep gouge on the inside of my left leg above the ankle and I still have the scar to this day.   It caused a minor panic at the time but fortunately didn't require hospital treatment; that may have been a little difficult to explain, so I was lucky.

In the pursuance of additional income from jobs Wack and I finally resorted to standing outside the gates of the Tunbridge Wells Goods Yard, situated at the bottom of Goods Station Road to await an opportunity to chat up one of the delivery wagon drivers as to whether he needed a 'helper'. I guess this line of attack could be considered a last resort but in the end it turned out to be a good move as the guy who accepted my offer of assistance became a really good friend and I was to work with him for several years even after I started work.

The guy I met up with was Herb Morely. He was a ginger haired man of about thirty five years of age and there was an immediate rapport between us; from the start we really got on well together. I think at the start of our relationship he was a little apprehensive as he was actually breaking the rules of the railway by a) allowing non railway employees ride in the vehicle and b) using me as an 'assistant' which certainly wasn't condoned by his employers. To reduce the chance of his getting caught, we always used to meet up well outside of the railway premises and he told me that in the event of him having another passenger in the cab when I was due to meet him, to ignore each other as it may have been a railway supervisor or the like.

This did in fact happen several times and I would then follow the vehicle on foot to a point where the 'passenger' took his leave of the vehicle. Herb's delivery round usually started at the bottom of the 'Wells Hill' (Mount Pleasant) and I would meet up with him there at a prearranged time. This arrangement worked very well and I can still recall the many times I waited at the bottom of Grove Hill Road waiting for Herb's wagon to appear at the traffic lights at the top of Mount Pleasant.

In those days the railways in almost all regions of the country used Scammell articulated units for their delivery services. This comprised a three-wheeled 'tractor' unit with a removable trailer, which allowed quick changing of the empty trailer for a loaded one when the unit returned to the goods yard. To the best of my recollections, they used to carry up to five tons in cargo so shifting the goods was very labour intensive. Everything had to be loaded and unloaded physically; not the luxury of hydraulic lifts as they have these days.

I can still recall the registration number of Herb's 'Scammell'. It was HGC 381 and apart from times when he would have another unit, due to his own requiring attention, it was always HGC 381 that he drove. I became quite attached to it and it was like an old friend. The reason why the tractor unit had been designed with three wheels was that it allowed a fantastic ability to turn in the smallest of areas; maybe that's where the expression "it would turn on a sixpence" came from?

Herb's delivery round concentrated on the lower part of the town, an area I knew like 'the back of my hand'. He would have many 'regular customers' so to speak and soon they got to know me as well as him. Places like the 'Neville Bakery' and 'Godkins' the chemists, at the top end of the High Street were typical of his 'regulars'. But there were many others and often they'd welcome us when we turned up and often we would get the odd cup of tea to help us on our way. I really enjoyed working with Herb; he was a really nice guy. Many of our deliveries were to the Eridge Show Ground area where several light industries had started up after the war.

The Eridge Show Ground, as it was called was an area behind the 'West Station which, in the pre war years, had been where the Agricultural Shows had been held and it had retained its name. During the war it was used by the military as an equipment storage area and also sported a brace of Anti-Aircraft guns. I believe that one Agricultural Show was actually held there in the immediate post war years but the area was soon allocated to housing and the Ramslye Estate sprung up.

At the time there were several well known industries there, such as 'The Baltic Saw Mills', 'Charltons Nurseries', 'Elders and Fyffes Bananas' and 'Romary's Biscuits', so there was a need for regular deliveries to this part of the town. It was in this area that Herb let me have my first drive of the Scammell. The 'Show Grounds' site was indeed, after the army pulled out, a very large open area of waste land. The distance of the track which led from the road, to where some of our customers were located, was probably half a mile across a safe open space; this was ideal for a learner driver.

This chance of a drive was to become a regular occurrence whenever we went there and I really enjoyed it. Fortunately the Scammell was very user friendly so I am very pleased to say that there weren't any mishaps. To give credit to Herb, he was certainly a patient soul and must have winced a few times as I let out the clutch in less than the smoothest fashion. The Scammell was a very forgiving vehicle and it wasn't long before Herb could relax a little as I drove on. After a while whenever we had a delivery to this area, Herb would stop at the entrance and with a "she's all yours" statement, we'd swap over positions in the cab and off I'd go. Compared to the need to pay for modern and expensive driving lessons I was fortunate to be getting this driving experience so young.

Like all good British workers we didn't go without our cup of tea for long and Herb would usually schedule his round to include a stop at 'Jack's Café' in London Road for the customary mug of tea and slices of hot buttered toast. It was a real down to earth 'truck drivers' venue and always appeared very busy. Because it was such a popular place, there was usually a problem with us finding a seat but we got by. It was a great place to go, particularly in the winter where the warmth and the smell of good hearty snacks always made it extremely difficult to leave.

'Jack's Café' was located in London Road at the back of the 'The White Bear' public house facing Rawson's Garage, as it was then. It was a small place and had probably once been a private house. It was as though the premises which had originally comprised of a sitting and a dining room had been opened up to provide the space for the Café and it was very successful. 'Jack' was a burly ex Army man and really got on well with his customers; I guess he knew all too well that all they wanted was a good value snack and the British 'cuppa. I know the first time I went into the cafe with Herb, Jack's immediate reaction to Herb was the statement "I didn't know the Railway was employing school boys". Herb countered that by saying that, in his opinion, I worked as hard as an adult and we were good mates; with that said I never heard any further remarks from Jack. After that I was always treated as part of the 'trucking family'; maybe the fact that I was, by then, nearly as big as Herb helped.

As I have already said, Herb Morely really became a very good friend both to me and to my Mum and Dad, whom he also gradually became acquainted with. Herb, his wife and children all lived in Southborough when I first started working with him and I would visit them on many a Saturday afternoon. In winter we would often go to watch Tunbridge Wells Rangers football club play at Down Farm, which was situated along St. John's Road; within walking distance from where Herb lived. They would also ask me to their house whenever it was someone's birthday and also at Christmas when other members of the Morely family would be there and we all got on so well together.

Herb was a bit of a 'do-it- yourself' man and often made the presents he would give to me at Christmas. I can clearly remember him giving me an electric question and answer board game that he made. When I consider the amount of work he put into making this thing it certainly was a very generous gift. This game was made up by a base board with about twenty four numbered lights mounted in four lines, six abreast. Along the bottom of the board was a pack of questions covering various subjects ranging from History to Travel etc. The question pack had an interconnection to the main baseboard whereby, when one answered the question correctly, the respective light would illuminate. It was a fascinating game, the type of game I really liked and when I considered Herb had made it himself, it was quite an achievement.

In these days of sophisticated computer games I guess that game was a little antique but at the time it was really something and I got a lot of pleasure out of it. I guess we all used to place more value on things made by hand and the quiz game that Herb made for me meant a lot. In many respects, he was like Bob who also had a wonderful flair for making things out of virtually nothing in fact I have never met anyone quite like Bob with the capability to either repair the impossible or, to coin a phrase, to ' make a silk purse out of a sow's ear'.

(Soon after I left school, Herb and his family were eventually to move from Southborough to seventy seven St. James Road. There, from time to time, I would visit them. Even after I joined the Air Force I would pop in to see them but when I went to Aden for a couple of years and started working away from home, I regret to say that I eventually lost track of the Morely family which, in hindsight, was a great shame. I have often regretted that as they were very good friends to me.)

But I am digressing and moving forward too fast. By this time I was in my final school year in Class Four at King Charles School and under the control of the notorious 'Clacker Clark'. All my premature fears about him, shared with most of my mates may I say, were to be proved groundless. Yes, he was a hard taskmaster and didn't stand for being mucked about but if you put your best into the lessons and made a conscious effort to be a good pupil, he was to prove to be the best teacher I ever had.

Bearing in mind that for the majority of the lads he was to be the last teacher they would have before entering the world of employment; his methods and way of making us wake up to the real world were to put many a pupil on the right road. 'Clacker' couldn't stand anyone who didn't return the loyalty to him that he believed he deserved. What was very obvious was the way there appeared to be an automatic bond between the students and 'Clacker' and this became apparent quite soon after you joined his class.

What I liked about him was that he would go out of his way in assisting the slow learners and had a wonderful sense of pride in his pupils and especially in his 'old boys'. He had a special place in his life for his 'old boys' and when I was to visit the school after joining the RAF, he would almost put you on a pedestal in front of the class, especially if you were wearing uniform.

There were group photographs of bygone classes hanging all round the classroom and there in each one would be 'Clacker' in the front row with that proud look on his face as if to say these are "my boys". He would often reminisce about the boys of the years gone by and give examples to us of those who were to be exceptions, not always because of academic achievements but some just because they were good human beings. I noted at those times, a glint of a tear would show in his eyes when he recalled some of his 'Old Boys' who went off to the war and didn't come back. It was because of his sincere commitment to his pupils that I think most of us made a promise to him that when we left to go into the world, we would return at some point to visit, as he had created within us a genuine desire to please the man; it really did mean so much to him.

One of the best periods in the lives of most children at school is the period which leads up to Christmas. Lessons began to take a less important role as the festive season approached and that time was enjoyed by teachers and pupils alike. King Charles School was no exception and I believe that 'Clacker' was a great exponent of bringing the Christmas message to life. His top favourite, and soon to be mine, was Charles Dickens 'A Christmas Carol'. Until I went into his class I really hadn't heard much about it; although the book was available in Libraries. It really wasn't the kind of reading I would normally pursue, preferring instead, books on railways and the like.

We had heard from previous pupils about 'Clackers' Christmas celebrations and a key part of this was, in the days leading up to the start of the Christmas holidays, his reading out loud to the class the whole of 'A Christmas Carol'. His renderings of the story would captivate all of us and he had a wonderful way of bringing the story to life.

Listening to 'Clacker' we could easily visualise the characters of Scrooge, the Cratchet family and the Ghosts of Christmas past. In some ways 'Clacker' made us think he was the epitome of Ebenezer Scrooge from all that we had heard about him before we became his class and it was good to be proved wrong. Since those days 'A Christmas Carol' has been one of my favourite books and that was all due to 'Clacker'. I've never forgotten it and it is as good to read today as it was then. This is surely the hallmark of a true 'Classic'. He had succeeded in opening my eyes to just a glimmer of the fascinating world of classical literature.

Those were to be very special times indeed thanks to the efforts of people like him, especially during the austerity years after the war. Another thing he did was to bring many of his own games and toys into the school. I guess these may well have been some that he had had as a youngster. Looking back I realise that many of those things would be considered to be antiques. At the time all he was interested in was that we would get some enjoyment from the games.

He also introduced a scheme whereby we would all buy each other small Christmas presents. This worked by drawing the names out of a hat in pairs with the two names each buying the other a present which would be given out on the last day of term. He fixed an arbitrary sum of Two Shillings and Sixpence (Twelve and a half new pence today) as the limit as nobody had much spare cash.

It all added up to a very memorable time for all of us but I wondered what sort of Christmas 'Clacker' would have himself; I believe his Christmas really took place at the school with his pupils. I am pleased to recall that we boys at least had the foresight to jointly buy 'Clacker' a small gift from 'the boys'. He always appeared to be a very lonely person. We knew he was an unmarried man and also looked after his invalid mother on whom he really seemed to dote. As we went away from school to look forward to a family Christmas, we would have pangs of remorse for him as he made his way home and hoped he would have a nice time but secretly knew that the best of his Christmas had probably been and gone by then.

My newspaper round, as it so happened, included Cambridge Gardens, off Prospect Road, where 'Clacker' lived although I didn't actually have to deliver a paper to his house. I would often see his Wolesley Sixteen motorcar, always in pristine condition, standing outside of the house and knew how much he loved that vehicle. I must say it was a magnificent car and always kept in an immaculate condition, particularly when you consider that he did not have a garage. In those days all the cars seemed to be black in colour and the paintwork was always gleaming.

It was a vehicle built on very stately lines and in some ways was reminiscent of the kind of car still used by Undertakers to this day. 'Clacker', like Bob and a lot of men in those days, always wore a Trilby hat, and gloves, when he went out and this was a distinctive feature when he drove his car because, even in the car, he wore the hat, which I thought was most unusual but looked very smart indeed. Although school lessons and subjects were time consuming with homework, I still kept busy with the paper rounds and helping Mr. Tuppen when his work load required it which seemed to be quite frequent. His shop was doing very well and he relied on help after school whenever I could spare the time. He would always give me additional wages whenever that occurred and I used to enjoy working with him. He had a son, John Tuppen, but John didn't seem to take much interest in the activities of the shop so I think that was the reason why Mr. Tuppen used to get me to help out. The fact that I lived almost next door too was an advantage.

What with my working with Herb on the railway wagon Saturday mornings and during school holidays, helping Bert with his milk round on Sundays, my paper round every day and assisting in the Newspaper Shop after school quite frequently, I was kept fairly busy which I guess pleased my Mum and Dad as at least it kept me out of mischief!

However, I did enjoy the paper round and got to know many of the customers. Of course, you always tried a little harder at Christmas time and hoped the customers would recognise one's efforts with generous 'Christmas Boxes'. I realise that is a very mercenary thing to say but to be honest, I always tried to make sure that newspapers and magazines arrived in good condition so felt a little 'thank you' at Christmas wouldn't come amiss. With a relatively large round I really did very well and would accumulate quite a few pounds by the time Christmas came which really helped with buying presents and other seasonal goodies that were available! One lady in particular, who lived in Calverley Park, was very generous to me not only at Christmas, but throughout the year. Her name was Mrs. Manser and to the best of my memory, she lived with her husband, a Doctor Manser at number nineteen.

She really was a very pleasant and genuine person and she would regularly leave a box of eggs or fruit on the doorstep for me to take home. There were times when she had a clean out and then I'd find a sweater or scarf or the like with the customary note hoping they would be of use to me. A few years later, when I was in the R.A.F, whenever I was home on leave. I would be asked by Mrs. Manser to meet her at the Cadena Cafe' for morning coffee. Later, after I had met Leila, who was nursing at the Kent & Sussex Hospital, she could easily recall actually nursing Dr. Manser in the hospital where he had once been a Consultant. He was one of her favourite patients too. It was a coincidence in many respects but I guess that at times life has a way of steering people towards each other.

My only regret was the fact that when, in later years, I worked far away from home, I was to lose contact with the by then widowed Mrs. Manser; there was always something else to do I'm afraid and I have regretted that many times.   My Dad used to see her in the town and she would always want to know where I was and how things were going and say that it would be much appreciated if I was to contact her when I came home on leave.   I was to spend over two years away from home in Aden, as part of my Air Force service and that didn't help with keeping up with friends.   It was after I met Leila that I learned that the Manser's had lost their only son in the R.A.F. during the war. Lacking some of the facts and with a hectic young life of my own I just didn't appreciate that at the time. As I say I do really regret that, it is a shame that you can't put old heads on young shoulders. As an adult I can now see that she was really looking for a substitute for her son.

Hindsight is a wonderful thing, twenty/twenty vision. The realities of life become more important as you get older and one tends to take more notice of people accordingly. Maybe with experience comes more understanding. One of my classmates at King Charles was a lad by the name of Rodney. He was always something of a mystery character and gave an outward impression somewhat similar to that of a lowly character out of a Dickens classic. This opinion was shared with my other classmates as he never joined in with the rest of us either during, or in out of school activities. He was a real 'loner' and wasn't someone who you could make friends with very easily, although several of us tried. Actually we had empathy for him but it was difficult to get our feelings over in the hope that he would feel we cared about him.

Rodney lived near Groombridge, not far from the Tunbridge Wells West to Groombridge railway line. From the way he dressed, he appeared to come from a poor family as he often had a very unkempt look about him.   Some of the lads thought he came from a family of gypsies; this was however untrue as we later learned that his father worked on a farm near the Sewage Works which were located between High Rocks and Groombridge. One of the most noticeable things about him was his long unruly hair, which in those days was the exception to the rule and always gave the impression it could do with a good wash!   I really don't mean to be unnecessarily unkind, maybe he thought the same about some of the rest of us but it was part of his appearance that made him seem different to the rest of us. The feeling of foreboding that one associated with Rodney was to unfortunately come true in a shocking way.

One day he failed to turn up for school, not that that was a very unusual occurrence for him, but around mid morning the Police arrived at the school and 'Clacker' was summoned from the classroom to talk to them. This intrigued us and for a while there was considerable speculation as to what the Police wanted with 'Clacker' as, at the time, we didn't associate the non appearance of Rodney with their visit. 'Clacker' returned to the classroom in a very sombre mood and told us he had some distressing news to tell us. He came straight to the point and told us that Rodney had unfortunately met with a serious accident and would never come to school again. Without giving any details he simply told us that Rodney was killed late the previous evening.

We were totally taken aback at the news and an air of extreme sadness descended on the classroom. At that point we were dismissed for an early lunch break whilst the teachers conferred on the situation and we were left to talk amongst ourselves as to what had actually happened to Rodney. It would be some little time later that we learned the truth of the incident and that made us all feel a lot worse about it. Rodney had simply left his house late one night; had walked to the railway line where he laid his head on the line to await the passing of the last train from Brighton to Tunbridge Wells West.

His body was found the following morning by a group of workmen. The shock to his family must have been tremendous considering the way he had died and it had a severe impact on the boys in the class although, as I have said, it would be several days before we knew the full details. I don't think the question of 'why' was ever really resolved; I guess that Rodney was destined to be one of life's tragedies.

It was on March 10th 1948, to be precise, that Trev and I were to experience one of the greatest surprises in our life. On that day, we were presented with the news from my Dad that we had a brother!

I had got up to do my paper round and was surprised to find that my Dad was already up; a most unusual thing as he was a great one for staying as long as possible in his bed and it usually took considerable rousing on the part of my mother to get him up for work, so you can imagine my surprise when he greeted me as I was about to leave the house. He met me in the hallway and told me to look in on Mum who was using the front room as her bedroom. Having not heard a thing during the night as neither had Trev it appeared, I couldn't believe my eyes when I saw a baby laying asleep in a cot at the side of my mothers bed!

At the time this was probably the biggest surprise I had ever had in my life, as could also be said by my younger brother Trevor. Neither of us had an inkling that such an event was about to occur. We didn't have any idea about it and for some reason or other, and I never did get a satisfactory answer from my Mum; why they never told us anything about it beforehand. This always remained a mystery to us. Sex education was definitely not taught at school and neither of our parents could ever bring themselves to raise the subject. We did not ask questions and merely gleaned further information over the coming years as best we could. Haven't times changed.

Anyway, as much as we found it hard to believe, Trev and I had a brother and I can remember telling Mr. Tuppen of the news when I got to the paper shop that morning and a look of disbelief passed across his face. I think he thought I was pulling his leg. I must say that in many respects, coming to terms with the arrival of another member of the family really took some doing. When I told my friends at school about our 'new brother', I got a similar reaction to that of Mr. Tuppen so I guess it was a shock to more than just us. The arrival of Robert, in our home at number thirty two, was to have a significant effect on the accommodation situation in the flat. We were now a five person family living in three rooms with only basic amenities. The flat didn't have a bathroom and our only toilet facility was in the brick outhouse where there was no electricity and the water supply regularly froze up in the winter. We really didn't know anything better and it didn't make us envious of other people's houses. I suppose such things were not considered as important then.

The kitchen was the focal point of the flat and our life centered on it. The room wasn't large and I can remember the layout so very clearly to this day. My Dad had a large comfortable old chair in the corner, opposite the door from the hall, right next to the Kitchener range and he would rarely move out of it when evening came around. Particularly so during the winter when he'd ensure there would always be a really good fire in the grate.

The kitchen table took up the space opposite the Kitchener and the sink was in the far corner next to the larder; and between that and my Dad's chair was the door into the back garden/yard area that led to the outside toilet. The cooker was located on the right as you entered the kitchen and a large sideboard was located along the wall on the left hand side of the door as you entered from the hall. Robert's arrival confined us to this room, which as I've said, was an extremely cosy environment in the winter and made going to the bedroom a shock to the system as the temperature change was unbelievable. I think Trev and I would have broken world records for the time we took to change into our pyjamas once we got into the bedroom.

Frankly the living accommodation for a family of our size really wasn't generous and some form of additional space was therefore very necessary. Our upstairs neighbours at that time were Miss Pope, living in the flat directly above us, and Mr. and Mrs. Freeman in the top flat. My parents came to an agreement with Miss Pope to rent a small spare bedroom in her flat at the front of the house which she had no need for. I was given this room and it was such a wonderful feeling to have one's own room for the first time, something I had never had before and I really couldn't believe my luck. My moving out of the main bedroom which my Dad, Trev and I had shared, allowed Robert, when he got a little older, to move into that room as well; during our remaining time at number thirty two, Mum would retain the use of the front room as her bedroom throughout.

Personal toilet requirements for us all had to utilise the sink in the kitchen as the flat had no bathroom. The only bath in the whole house was located in the top floor flat, and therefore was the domain of the Freeman's so we were to use it rarely. Actually, the bath was of a kind known as a 'foot bath'. It was a bath in which you sat in as opposed to laying in. The days of having a bath in the old tin one, which had been the stalwart of the family for so long, were gone as we were now big lads. The solution came in us going to the Municipal Baths in Monson Road once a week to 'swim the ocean' as my mother used to put it. Actually, they were a godsend for a lot of people in those days as not many had the luxury of their own bathroom and some of those who did have the facility, couldn't afford the cost of heating the water as coal was still rationed and not all had gas.

As the years passed local grants were made available to assist with the cost of homeowners adding on a new bathroom to their existing home or to convert a small bedroom into one. Actually we enjoyed our visits to the 'Slipper Baths' as they were known and they were very popular with a lot of people. The individual baths, just as you would have at home, if you were lucky enough, were each in their own cubicle and the bath was filled with suitable quantities of hot and cold water, and soap and towels supplied by an attendant all for a small cost. Unfortunately you couldn't add additional hot water if you needed it as all the taps were operated by using the attendants key and he also was controlling how long you stayed in the bath. I remember, during busy periods, the attendant would come and bang on the door and tell you to "get out". This was usually after a period of about twenty minutes. When I look back it was surprising just how many people stayed at home and merely used the old tin baths which would hang outside on the wall from 'bath night' to 'bath night' which was normally a weekly ritual. Apart from us, both our Grandparents had them to our knowledge. Actually my Dad continued to choose to use the tin bath at number thirty two right up until the time when the family moved to 7 Mountfield Road in 1957.

It is funny in many ways, looking back to those days, the standards of living were so different to those of today yet we never queried it; it was the way of life as far as we were concerned and I guess it was a reflection of the statement that 'what you never have, you don't miss'.

It was in 1948 that the Stringer family, (the ones on my mother's side), decided to have a 'reunion'. With the war over and travel becoming a lot easier, Uncle Jack and his wife Gerda, who lived in New York, were planning to visit England and the whole of the family would get together in Tunbridge Wells. Uncle Jack had left England in the nineteen twenties to begin a life in the U.S.A. and this was going to be his first visit back to the old country since well before the war. There was a lot of excitement about this and plans were made to hold a get together of all the family at the home of Frank, one of my mother's brothers and his family who lived in Hawkenbury, not far from my Grandparents. This was to be quite an event and it even made the local newspapers. Uncle Jack, his wife and their young daughter, Ellen, duly arrived in England after their Trans-Atlantic journey which they made by sea on one of the "Queens". Air travel wasn't

as available or affordable then as it is now so the majority of
ordinary people used the sea route, which took about five
days.

I must say that we took a real liking to the couple when
they visited us at number 32 and my Dad, not the most
enthusiastic supporter of the Stringer family, also got on
with them very well which was a relief for my Mum!

Uncle Jack gave me an American book on Red Indians
which I treasured for many years. In fact I believe I still have
it tucked away in one of our 'storage' areas! Jack had
become a typical American and had quite a distinctive accent
which I found fascinating. The day for the 'reunion' duly
arrived and we all assembled at my Uncle Frank's house,
funnily enough I cannot remember whether my Dad actually
went; he had such a reluctance to socialise in family circles,
especially where my mother's family were concerned, so I
think it may have been doubtful. I believe my Dad had a
distinct impression that they really didn't approve of him and
this was a view, made by my mother when talking with her
about family relationships many years later. I don't know
why that was to be because, in my opinion, my Dad was
equal to, if not better than any of the Stringer men folk.
Anyway, Mum, Trev, Robert [in pram] and I, did our familiar
walk through Camden Park to Hawkenbury to attend the
reunion.

I recall it was a really beautiful day and that allowed the
function to be held out of doors in the garden of my Uncle
Frank's home. As youngsters we enjoyed the get together
but I don't really remember that much about it apart from
that there were a lot of family around and many of them we
were meeting for the first time as my mother's family were
well spread out, coming from places like Coventry,
Lemington Spa, Eastbourne, London and, of course, the
U.S.A. The function went off with a swing and all had a
good time.

Unfortunately that was to be the only time the whole
family would manage to get together and on the demise of
my Grandparents, the Stringer family appeared to fragment
somewhat. I felt that there had always been an 'us and
them' situation in the relationship between what were the
Hawkenbury relatives, and most of the rest. It certainly
wasn't anything to do with any 'family politics' concerning
my Dad but I believe it was induced by the attitude of my
mothers oldest brother Fred who seemed to have the opinion

that he and his sons were the heirs apparent to the Stringer dynasty. Of course, my Dad didn't want to get involved in this situation and was happy to let the others sort it out amongst themselves. This didn't happen and the 'at loggerheads' situation was to remain until most of the original family members had passed away.

At this particular time my Dad was going through changes in his job situations. The war now having been over now for more than two years, meant that the Police reduced the number of Special Constables and consequently, my Dad was one of the first to be released from the service. He had taken a job at the Grove Bowling Club as Barman and general factotum after leaving the police, which I am not certain really suited him. In the pre war years, and probably up to the time that he met Mum, my Dad had been a Radio Officer on Clan Line merchant ships, his parents having paid for him to attend qualifying school to achieve this position. At some point, probably, just before I was born, he took up full time speaking for the Conservative Party and often gave presentations at their staff colleges.

The presentations were in addition to the public speaking engagements he carried out. The war years obviously stopped most of that and his Police activities put paid to anything other than his duties. However in 1948 there was to be a General Election and Dad was selected by the Conservative Party to stand as a Member of Parliament for Llannelly, in South Wales. The Labour opposition for this seat was indeed formidable as is was none other than Jim Griffiths, a miners selected candidate and a member of Labours National Committee. My Dad really didn't have a great chance to take this safe seat from Labour but he was to give it a darn good try.

Before he left Tunbridge Wells to go to South Wales there was a considerable amount of local Press involvement in producing articles about him and his family and apart from the local newspapers, others such as the 'Kent Messenger' and 'The Evening Argus' also did news items about him; I guess they were fascinated to meet a man who could be seen as entering the lions den to take on the miners champion. I remember coming home from school one day to find Mum scurrying around number thirty two to make it look its best and telling Trev and I to change into our best clothes as the press were en route to meet Dad and take 'family' photographs. Fortunately we still have a copy of one of Dad's press handouts with the photograph of the family; it was unfortunate that they took the picture at the back of the house right next to the coal cellar but I guess it was at least a true indication to our way of life.

As it turned out the Labour Party under Clement Attlee were to romp home substantial winners in the election and my Dad never got the Llannelly seat away from them for the Conservatives. He had made an excellent effort and given it his best but it was like trying to move a mountain. I am led to believe that by his efforts he made quite an indentation in the majority held by Griffiths so there was at least, poetic justice to a point. I can remember the Conservative Party being very pleased about his efforts and he did receive a letter from the Chairman of the party thanking him for his hard work.

With the election out of the way Dad really didn't have a full time job. A good friend of his, George Coker, who ran a sports business opposite the Central Station and had a large house at the top of Grove Hill Road, number seventy four, offered him work looking after the gardens of the house and other odd jobs. We rather liked Dad working there as we were able to go and 'help' him from time to time. We really enjoyed assisting with the lawn mowing and bonfires and particularly when the apples and pears were in crop; quite a few 'windfalls' made their way home with us.

I have no doubt that Dad received considerable financial help for the family from his parents as I really can't see how my parents made ends meet otherwise with three sons to bring up. I also believe that Bob used to contribute when he could as well but he was going through the doldrums with his garage business at this time so his resources were indeed limited. George Coker was instrumental in helping my Dad get the job as Barman and odd job man at the Grove Bowling Club, which was located in Birdcage Walk, just up from the Grove. Unfortunately, this job had its seasonal limitations so really wasn't the final solution but I guess coupled with the speaking dates he got on a regular basis and the work he did for George Coker, my parents were able to make ends meet as best they could.

The 'Grove' as it is today.
The old bandstand has long gone and the park resembles little of how it was when we were young.

The Caverley Grounds today.
The communal kitchen, used during the war years, was located in the area between the footpath and the buildings in the background.

The Calverley Grounds Bandstand today.

The Caverley Grounds Bandstand today.
A shadow of its former self!

Modern housing built on the site of 'Wells Depository' in Grove Hill Road with the 'animal pound' on the right.

The 'animal pound' today.
When my father was in the police, he would often round up stray horses and secure them in this place.

The 'Ritz' cinema.

Our home as children in Grove Hill Road.

Mountfield Road, where we moved to in 1957.

Chapel Place.

The plaque recalling this building was once 'King Charles School'

KING CHARLES SCHOOL
FOUNDED IN THE CHURCH
OF KING CHARLES THE
MARTYR IN 1698
OCCUPIED THIS BUILDING
FROM 1848 TO 1960.
SANS PEUR ET SANS REPROCHE

The site of 'King Charles School' today– It is now a restaurant!

The site of 'King Charles School' today– It is now a restaurant!

The Pantiles.

The Pantiles.

The Pantiles.

Tunbridge Wells West Station.
The building is now a restaurant.

The 'Swan' garage site where Bob introduced me to the motor business.

Tunbridge Wells Town Hall

Chapter 15: School Days Draw To A Close

Fireworks were beginning to reappear after the war
years and Trev and I were to spend considerable amounts of
our hard earned moneys in celebrating the Fifth of November
with fireworks displays, which usually took place in the
Calverley Grounds at the back of the Great Hall Cinema. I
can't actually remember exactly how and when we first got to
set up our Fireworks and Bonfire celebrations in the
'Calverley but it was to become something of a ritual over a
few years and I can remember it brought a lot of fun to a lot
of people in the Grove Hill Road area, at a time when there
really wasn't a lot of fun about.

Probably the original idea started with Trev and his
fascination for fires. Anyway, our 'gang' would make
strenuous efforts in the weeks leading up to Bonfire Day in
acquiring fireworks and as much in the way of combustible
materials as we could manhandle to the allotted bonfire site
which was a piece of waste ground not far from some
derelict 'Courier' buildings. We took turns going to people's
houses asking if they had any suitable rubbish for the
bonfire and at the same time inviting them to the actual
event. Our main supplier of fireworks was Mr. Tuppen who
had a very good stock of the things and was prepared to sell
them to us a little below their normal sale price.
Fortunately, in those days, we didn't have a law that
prevented the sale of fireworks to people under the age of
sixteen, so the only limiting factor was how much we could
afford.

All of our friends played their part and in particular,
Richard Ticehurst and his sister Maureen, whose father ran
the 'Clarendon' public house opposite the Central Station,
were good contributors as they always seemed to have a
reasonable supply of pocket money. However, it really was a
team effort and it was quite amazing just how much stock
we were able to accumulate prior to the big day. At the
same time it was a maximum effort to build the bonfire and
we were very successful in this; as the bonfire was built on
some old hard standing once used as a car park when the
'Calverley was in its prime before the war, it was a relatively
safe venue. The only anxiety was the combustible material
which was the surrounding trees so we made sure we were
well away from them.

Even the grounds men in the park who we were by now on much better terms with, gave us some help with all of this. The Guy and the fireworks, unbeknown to my Dad, were kept in safe custody at number thirty two until the evening of the event. When I look back at this, I must say it was a real safety hazard for us in having all those fireworks in the house and the fact that we didn't 'let on' to my Dad was a little irresponsible of us. I guess one could say that it didn't strike us as dangerous at the time and my parents were really a very understanding and tolerant pair by now.

One of our main concerns was that some mischief makers would wreck or set fire to the bonfire in the period leading up to the Guy Fawkes night and I can remember that we would mount 'guard' rosters during our free time in the days leading up to the event. Fortunately our 'camp' was adjacent to the site of the bonfire so at least we weren't sitting out in the open and I'm glad to say that nobody did try to wreck all our hard work. We didn't really enjoy sitting in our camp on those dark cold evenings but it did ensure that the bonfire would still be in one piece for the fifth. Once, however, I can remember a gale going through the day before and it was a case of all hands on deck to put to rights the effects of the storm, so that proved to be a close call but, fortunately it had no real detrimental effect on the actual night.

On the night of the event the procedure was that the show would get on the road around six thirty p.m. with a torchlight procession starting from our house and then proceeding to the park via Mountfield Gardens. Bob was a great help in the manufacture of the torches as he had what seemed to be a limitless supply of old engine oil in his garage. Rags secured to short poles, soaked in this old oil, made really good torches and would normally last until the procession had made its way to the site of the bonfire as we paraded Guy Fawkes to his fate.

It was amazing how many people seemed to turn up for this event even though the weather did have a dampening effect sometimes but that was all part of the fun in many ways. For some reason or other we never seemed to run into problems with the law at these events and I can't remember ever seeing a Policeman coming around to find out what was going on. We did try to make sure that the bonfire would go ahead with the minimum of disruption and I recall that those folks who attended really did enjoy it. In those days we were able to get hold of some really effective 'bangers' and there was no law in effect which limited the 'bang' these things could make compared to rules and regulations of modern times. These were not large fireworks and had a very slow burning fuse made out of string; so one had to be little patient with them as they seemed to take an eternity to explode but the wait was well worth it. They went off like gunfire and certainly weren't for the faint hearted especially if one happened to go off near you. These things were actually made in the U.S.A. and were very cheap to buy so you got plenty of 'bang' for your money.

Funnily enough we never questioned how much we all spent on the fireworks for these occasions. The thing about money never really came into it as we all looked forward to the event and the only thought was that it would all go well on the day, which I'm glad to say it normally did. No one even thought about us passing a bucket around for coins to be thrown into by those watching the fun!

I have already mentioned Richard and Maureen Ticehurst from the 'Clarendon'. Going to their home at the pub was always an experience and I suppose the fact that the 'Clarendon' was the first pub I had ever been in probably had something to do with it as well. The 'Clarendon' was a big old Victorian building and the living accommodation was spread over four floor levels plus a big old basement which they used as a kitchen and general living room, not unlike number thirty two. Maybe one of the reasons I liked going there was the fact that they always had food in preparation and usually gave us lads some of the odds and ends which pleased us.

They employed a funny sort of chap to run the kitchen and do all the heavy jobs around the place, his name was Harry and was the sort of person that when you met him for the first time, had a distinctly sinister appearance. He was a unique sort of person, dedicated to the job he did, in fact I can't remember ever going there and he not being there so I don't know when he ever had a day off. What was striking about him was the way he dressed. He always wore black and we got to nickname him 'Black Harry'. His usual dress was a striped collarless shirt and waistcoat, black trousers and knee length gaiters; he really was like something out of Dickens. I never saw him without a long leather apron which reached almost to his feet. Another thing about him was the fact they he always wore boots, this coupled with the gaiters really made his appearance very striking as you could hear his footsteps on the stone floors well be before he actually appeared; sometimes that was to be a good thing if we were, with the connivance of Richard, raiding the larder. Today one would really classify him as Victorian; possibly someone out of a Bronte novel.

'Black Harry' certainly wasn't one of natures beauties; a long thin face and hair plastered flat on his head probably with a generous helping of 'Brylcream', which was all the rage in those days, certainly would have made him stand out in a crowd. Actually his appearance didn't give a true description of the individual as when you got to know him, he was a very lonely sort of person and his life centered around the 'Clarendon' and the Ticehurst family. He would have been a lost soul without them; I guess it was a reciprocal arrangement as with the running of the pub, Mr. and Mrs. Ticehurst had to leave a lot of the mundane jobs to him to carry out.

Trev and I always made the most of going to Richard's home and it wasn't unknown for the odd small bottle of cider to find its way to where we were playing in the building; of course, it had to be kept out of sight of Richard's Dad who would certainly have 'blown his top' if he'd found out. Don't get the wrong impression, we didn't do things like that very often and when we did it was more of a dare than the need to consume the cider itself. I can remember on one occasion, there really was a real bust up with Mr. Ticehurst when he discovered a number of packets of cigarettes missing from his stock room. The first we knew about it was when he came to our house to see Dad and virtually accused Trev and I of taking them.

This was one time that we really weren't guilty and fortunately my Dad did believe it when we told him that we didn't know anything about it. It later transpired that it was actually his son Richard who had taken them. I have no idea what he did with them as he never brought the cigarettes to our camp as he'd actually done previously when he'd 'acquired' the odd cigarette or two from the pub.

Our love of all things railway hadn't diminished and we were as active as ever with our train spotting activities. Visits to the locomotive sheds at Tunbridge Wells West and Tonbridge were our favourite haunts and we always still were often given the odd footplate ride when the engines were manoeuvring around the shed facility. It was about this time that Trev and I got friendly with some of the crews operating the London to Hastings trains. It all came about by chance really. One day on one of our many visits to Tonbridge after which we would make our way back to the 'Wells by rail we would allow for sufficient time to say hello to the engine driver and his mate before boarding the train.

Just by luck one day we were talking to the driver of our train home when, to our great surprise, he asked us if we'd like to ride on the footplate. This was an offer we really couldn't refuse and we literally leapt up onto the locomotive. The only rule that the crew laid down was that we must keep out of sight as the train passed the large signal box, which was located on the right-hand side of the track as the train pulled out under the bridge at Tonbridge Station. There wasn't a great choice of places to hide on a locomotive footplate but we used to get close to the cab side nearest the signal box and by squatting down, probably were not visible to the signal-man as we passed. The regular locomotives on the London to Hastings trains were of the Maunsell 'Schools' class; 4-4-0 tender engines which were amongst the most powerful 4-4-0's ever built. They were magnificent engines and the thrill of riding in the cab for the first time was an experience I will never forget.

As the train left Tonbridge for Tunbridge Wells Central it had to cross the London-Dover main line and with a heavy train this usually resulted in considerable 'wheel slip' as the engine crossed the other tracks hauling its train up a quite considerable incline as it headed past the locomotive sheds towards the tunnel, about 3/4 mile from the station. The locomotive had to work really hard at this point and it was a full time job for the crew to keep headway. (There are many instances of trains stalling on this section of line and had to resort to assistance from one of the shed locomotives at Tonbridge, to make it up the gradient by getting a push at the rear.)

The first time you experience, at close quarters, a hard working locomotive hauling its heavy train into the mouth of a tunnel is something you never forget. The sense of sheer power coupled with the resounding noise as the exhaust of the locomotive rebounds off the tunnel roof immersing the cab of the engine in extremely hot smoke and steam, is an experience that will live with me forever. Initially, the experience is one of complete terror and it feels as though you will never emerge from what is a very claustrophobic situation, so the moment the engine exits into the sunshine at the other end of the tunnel gave you the feeling of the dawning of a new day.

Once through the tunnel the train gathers speed and the real thrill of travelling at speed with steam, on what is nothing more than an iron horse without the comfortable suspension of the motorcar, really becomes apparent. Across High Brooms viaduct, with the farm animals scattered below, usually running away from the train, the engine draws into High Brooms Station.   Another hard pull faces the engine as it slowly leaves the 'Brooms passing the Gas Works on the left, with the associated smell of sulphur and heads towards the recreation grounds in the Grosvenor area; wheel slip again being one of the main hazards at this point and requiring considerable skill from the crew to keep going.

Tunbridge Wells Central is reached via the tunnel that runs practically under the centre of the town.   The locomotive roars into the station making boarding passengers stand well back as it decreases speed and stops at the far end of the platform only yards from the mouth of the Grove Tunnel. I don't think our feet touched the ground as we made our way back home to tell our parents of the fun we'd just had. We were very lucky in as much that we were able to repeat this experience on several occasions; some of the crews made a point of letting us know when they would be operating on the route so that if we were in the right place at the right time, they would offer to pick us up if there wasn't an inspector on the train.   One such crew was Jack Hoathly and Alf Waghorn who were based at St. Leonards, Hastings.

We had made their acquaintance on the line and they knew us as regular enthusiasts but it still came as a big surprise one day when they asked us if we'd like the opportunity to ride the footplate from Tonbridge to St. Leonards on a particular Saturday. This was to be quite an exercise in logistics as we had to be at Tonbridge at a certain time to meet up with them which meant going to Tonbridge only to travel back down the line a little while later; it was to prove well worth it.

As it so happened, all went according to plan. They had told us that they were scheduled to operate one of the morning 'semi-fast' London (Charing Cross) to Hastings trains which had limited stops so was perfect for what we all had in mind. Trev and I duly made our way to Tonbridge and awaited the arrival of the train we wanted, all we thought of was the hope that it would all go as planned.

The train arrived in Tonbridge hauled by Schools Class locomotive, 30906, 'Sherbourne'. Alf, who was the driver and located on the platform side of the engine, made sure the coast was clear and then beckoned us up onto the footplate where Jack told us to get under a tarpaulin until the train had left the station. The Schools Class locomotives, as with many of their contemporaries, did not have the enclosed cab which became common with the Standard Class of locomotives; had it had, it certainly would have made hiding Trev and I a lot easier. Hence the need for us to get under the tarpaulin as it was quite an open space between the footplate and the tender and the engine crew were keen on not letting anyone know they had additional people on the footplate and didn't want the staff in the Signal Box outside of Tonbridge Station, to see anything. There was no doubt about it, they were really taking a chance by letting us onto the engine footplate, especially as the train was operating a semi-fast service so they felt it necessary to take certain precautions to ensure they weren't caught. We virtually held our breath until we heard the whistle from the guard to signal the 'all clear'. I think all of us gave a huge sigh of relief as the train began its journey out of the station.

As soon as we were clear of the Tonbridge railway depot, Alf and Jack told us all was clear and we were able to begin to really enjoy the experience that lay before us. As a semi-fast the train did not stop at High Brooms and it was a great thrill as we raced through the station with the engine working hard to handle the gradient past the Gas Works. The thrill of being on the engine footplate as it emerged from the tunnel into Tunbridge Wells Central, is something I will never forget. Having only ever been an enthusiastic spectator watching trains come roaring into the station from the mouth of the tunnel, actually being on the footplate myself was a very exciting moment. The trains used to enter the station at considerable speed and heavy brake application was needed to stop the train at the end of the platform between the road bridge and the Grove Tunnel.

The 'Central had very long platforms with tunnels at each end, a pretty unique layout really and being only a two track station, passengers on either platform were in close proximity of trains in either direction so all appeared to take a step backwards when a train came into the station with considerable noise, smoke and steam. It was always a vision of 'raw motive power'.

Having only ever watched trains as they left the 'Central

and headed towards Hastings, the thought of actually being on the footplate ourselves, was one of tremendous excitement and anticipation.   This particular train was scheduled to run fast from Tunbridge Wells Central to Crowhurst, a distance of over twenty miles non stop, and it was to be an experience we would never forget.   The 'Schools' locomotives of the Southern region of British Railways, were of a class of locomotive which were immensely powerful and much liked by their crews.   They were capable of considerable speed and 'Sherbourne' was a very good example of her class and an excellent performer. Alf wound off the brake and opened the regulator, blowing the whistle in the process and we were on our way out of the 'Central, next stop Crowhurst.   Climbing out of the Grove Tunnel we passed the Signal Box on our right and with a wave to the signal-man, 'Sherbourne' made easy going of the up hill section towards Hawkenbury and Forest Road and the short tunnel which ran underneath it.

I guess it was then that the real thrill of riding on the footplate of a steam locomotive, really got to us.   To Alf and Jack it was every day business, but to us it was the epitome of all that we could ever have hoped for as train enthusiasts. The train was now going faster than I had previously experienced and the reality of the brute force of driving and firing a steam locomotive, which was working flat out really came to us.   The passion we had always had for all things steam railway, was fully realised as we sped along at speeds between sixty and seventy miles an hour.   This was probably faster than we had ever travelled at that time in our lives so you couldn't help but be impressed as we sped on through such places as Frant, Wadhurst, Stonegate and Etchingham etc.   It certainly had to be experienced to be fully appreciated as the engine rocked from side to side, vibrating and shaking as it traversed the rail joints and the points on the track.   The lack of soft suspension went right through you to the point where you had to really hold on to something to prevent ones self being thrown around the cab. The engine crew were obviously used to it; the driver had a seat on the left side of the cab as he perused the line ahead and the fireman was fully occupied satisfying the unquenchable appetite of the firebox.

Amazingly they were actually able to brew and pour a cup of tea from the proverbial white enamel 'Billy Can' that hung just above the firebox doors; a vantage point to ensure that the contents always kept hot!   At speed passing another train coming in the opposite direction was an unbelievable experience; the air pressure generated as the two locomotives met, created an almost explosive reaction. The first time we passed another train at speed really made us jump; Alf had warned us to keep well inside of the cab when a train came from the opposite direction but I don't think we were prepared for the actual event when it came, it was actually quite frightening at first. Keeping a large locomotive satisfied at speed was hard work for Jack as he seemed to be continually shovelling coal into the firebox; the distance from the tender to the firebox was about ten feet so the job of the fireman certainly was hard work. It was very much a question of teamwork and there was no doubt that Alf and Jack worked very well together.

Unfortunately all good things have to come to an end. After stopping at Crowhurst, where passengers for Bexhill left the train to join a 'push and pull' two coach little train which was standing in the adjacent bay platform, we were on our way to Battle and to the stop where we would have to leave the train at West St. Leonards. Alf would have been in big trouble I guess if he'd tried to take us all the way into Hastings, which was actually only about two miles further on. We'd had a journey to remember and were eternally grateful to these two men for letting us accompany them and couldn't thank them enough when the time came to get back into the passenger compartments; it did seem tame sitting in the coach in relative comfort when we considered all the action we had just experienced on the footplate of the locomotive. We never forgot it and I'll always be in debt to Alf and Jack for breaking the rules and letting us ride on 'Sherbourne'. Both Jack and Alf had insisted we purchase return tickets for our journey so in that respect we were not breaking the law.

I was, I think, very lucky to get the footplate rides that I did. When you think that the locomotive crews who agreed to such things were in fact putting their jobs and their careers 'on the line', to coin a phrase, I was extremely fortunate. There was one other trip that stays in my mind and that was riding the footplate of the 'school special', from Tonbridge to Sevenoaks via the notorious Sevenoaks tunnel. I cannot remember how I got the ride; it was just the fact I was in the right place at the right time. I was at Tonbridge one day on my own doing the usual train spotting, how I happened to be there on what must have been a 'school day' I can't really remember, I certainly hadn't played truant. No doubt due to a cancellation of some kind we had unexpectedly got a free afternoon towards the end of my education. Anyway the Tonbridge to Sevenoaks school special was a typical 'Branchline' operation; a three coach 'push and pull' combination hauled by an 0-4-4- "H" Class, Tank locomotive.

The "push and pull" name came from the fact that (in this case in particular) on the outbound journey, the train was pulled by the locomotive and when it returned, usually along the same route, the train was pushed with the engine remaining at the back of the train. In this mode the train was controlled from the front carriage, where there was a 'driving' position, which signalled the locomotive what was required of it. When operated like that the driver was in the front carriage and the locomotive was under the control of the fireman. This type of operation was very popular particularly on branch lines where it saved the requirement to reposition the locomotive at the end of its journey where not all the stations had these facilities.

The locomotive on the train I was lucky enough to ride on was 31544 and when the driver offered the ride, the only proviso was that the train would not return to Tonbridge until six thirty, its scheduled return time; I would have to think of a good excuse to tell my mother why I was late home for tea but the risk was sure to be worth it. The journey would go through Sevenoaks Tunnel in both directions and although the thought was somewhat daunting, Sevenoaks Tunnel being one of the longest on the Southern Railway, it was a chance too good to miss in my opinion.

It was the first time I had ridden out of Tonbridge heading up the line, all my previous journeys had been in a southerly direction and being the first time on the footplate of a tank locomotive, made it all the more memorable as it was a more intimate environment than on the open footplate of locomotives like the 'Schools' class which I'd had rides on before. Our first stop was Leigh where a fair number of our passengers got off and then it was on towards Sevenoaks via the notorious tunnel. As we approached the tunnel the driver hinted at the fact that it may get a little claustrophobic in the cab as we ploughed through the tunnel and that if necessary, I was to sit down on the floor towards the rear of the cab where there was the chance of some better air. I must say that I was suddenly overwhelmed by the feeling of, 'What am I doing here?' but by then it was too late and we were into the tunnel.

I had ridden through the tunnel several times but always as a passenger in the relative luxury of being in a coach.   Nothing could have prepared me for the experience of that day; it is hard to imagine the lack of oxygen and the claustrophobic environment that exists on the footplate of a locomotive as it works hard through a very long tunnel. The only light on the footplate came from a small oil lamp in the cab and from the small gaps in the firebox door. It wasn't long before I realised why the driver had told me to squat down at the rear of the cab as it was hard to see where each of us were and I guess my being where they told me to be meant that they at least knew where I was.   It seemed an eternity before it was just possible to make out the small chink of light that indicated the end of the tunnel. It had never felt so good to emerge into the late afternoon sunshine and fresh air; and lots of it!

I guess the driver and his mate saw the funny side of it but when I asked them for their reaction when they first had travelled through the same tunnel.   I got the idea that they also may have felt much the same as I did but they were not going to admit it to me.   They offered me a seat in the train for the return but I wasn't going to give up the chance of going back the way we had come.   As it so happened the return journey actually seemed shorter; or was it a case of I knew what I was in for and that helped.   On the return with the 'push and pull', with the engine at the rear of the train, the exhaust went rearwards, so I was pleased to find that ventilation on the footplate was greatly improved this for trip.

However I was very grateful for the once in a lifetime experience and, so many years after the event I can still remember it so well today.   When I eventually got home and told my parents and Trev about it, initially they didn't believe I had done the trip, and my mother thought I had only gone to Tonbridge(after school) as was previously planned. When my mother checked my shirt, which bore all the indications of having been in the cab of a steam engine, they didn't question it further and wondered how I had been so lucky to get the ride in the first place. I was lucky really; and I'll never forget it.   When I look back to the opportunities given to Trev and myself I do realise we truly were fortunate at the time.

Our regular visits to the engine shed at Tunbridge Wells West continued. Sunday afternoons were a favourite time to go there as with the Sunday timetables in those days with reduced services, a lot of locomotives would be "on shed" and therefore it was an ideal place for spotters.   There would be types of locos laying over there that were not part of the usual motive power allocation to shed '75A', Tunbridge Wells West and it was not unusual to see the odd Bullied Pacific there at those times.   With a lot of engines there, many were being prepared for services the next morning with low fires burning.   Many of these engines would be parked adjacent to the entrance we used so we were able to get into the cabs, usually with the railwaymen's permission, and we would imagine driving such wonderful machines.

I remember one Sunday afternoon in particular because, as we approached the shed area, we were staggered to see that a locomotive had come through the brick wall of the shed and was suspended between the end of the shed and the ground; about 10 feet below!   The incident had happened some time before we arrived.   No action was being taken at that time to recover the locomotive. The locomotive fortunately wasn't in steam at the time of the incident so must have been pushed through the wall by another from the rear. In talking to one of the railwaymen, he said that recovery would commence once they received the heavy lifting equipment which had to come from Brighton, but that wouldn't be until the Monday.   By the time we got there on the Monday after school, hoping to see it all happening, the engine was back in the shed and builders were reinstating the wall.

The engine concerned was one of the D1 4-4-0T tank locos, and was one of the oldest still in service at that time having been built in 1873.   Unfortunately, after the above incident it was sent for scrap.

The subject of this chapter is really about school days drawing to a close however I seem to have talked of nothing else but railways. They certainly did take up a large portion of my leisure time but in the interests of the reader, I'll look back on other things that were happening at this time of my life.

It was in 1948 that Trev and I had our first holiday away from Tunbridge Wells.   Christ church, in association with other churches in the town, arranged a camping holiday for its young choir members at Cooden, near Bexhill-on-Sea. This was looked forward to with eager anticipation and some apprehension, as having never been away from home before, it was something of an adventure, not that Cooden was likely to be the most exciting place on earth in those days. Obviously some contribution towards the expense of the trip was made by the parents and my Mum and Dad were keen for us to take part.   We weren't to travel in luxury however; the transportation for the journey was to be in one of Gilbert's large Bedford Removal Lorries.

Being a camping holiday, it proved essential that we should take a lot of the basic things with us that we would need. Things like towels, toiletries, blankets etc., so as you can imagine, it was to be a little cramped in the back of the lorry. There were masses of personal belongings as well including basic camping equipment, food and cooking pots, etc., so all in all, rather crowded.

Cooden is only about thirty miles from Tunbridge Wells so it wasn't that long a journey although with the roads of the day it took longer than one would expect today. The journey was fun however. There were about thirty of us youngsters travelling in the vehicle and I must say that we enjoyed the ride. The vehicle was a very large panel lorry, typical of those still used for furniture removals so the only light we had was at the rear of the lorry where the driver had left the top half of the tailgate open, so we at least had some fresh air and daylight.

One of the adults who was in charge of us tried to initiate the singing of hymns but he didn't get any success with that as all we wanted to do was sing the popular numbers like 'Roll me over, in the clover' and 'Ten green bottles'. The 'Roll me over' number was the favourite as it had a certain rude version, which all the lads seemed to know well, I wonder why. Anyway it was aired repeatedly en route much to the disgust of the adults in charge; it wasn't quite what they had expected from 'refined and gentle' little choirboys. It was a good thing that our choirmaster, Mr. Pallant, wasn't there to hear us; he'd certainly have 'blown a gasket'.

Anyway, the songs helped the journey along and all the boys enjoyed themselves, I can't say that the adults did though. In a way it was a bit of a let down when we finally arrived at Cooden. Our camp site appeared totally dedicated to hosting religious get-togethers and was located in a farm field that wasn't that near to the sea and did not exactly come up to what we had expected and hoped for. We had heard that the beaches would by now be clear of barbed wire and thought we would have been closer to the sea. This was the first time any of us had been away from home let alone camping at the seaside. I don't actually remember that much about the week we spent at the site but I do know that Trev and I didn't like it at all. It was heavily religious, not that we were adverse to that but it was too serious and we felt pressurised by it all. The people there I guess thought they were doing a good job and I suppose on the whole they were. What we really couldn't get on with were all the religious lessons that were given to us at all hours of the day and even before you went to bed. As far as I can recall even the games that were held around the campfire in the evenings were the same and it was just too much. I can remember one evening about halfway through the week parents, if they had transport, which the majority did not, were able to visit the site for an hour or so. My mother arrived with good old Bob in his ever faithful Austin 8, EOD 502. It was so good to see them that we would have given anything to have gone back to Tunbridge Wells with them right then, in fact, we did ask if they'd take us but my Mum, who was a very honourable person, wouldn't give in and told us to make the most of it as chances like that were few and far between and she didn't think it fair to the people who were trying to give us a nice time if we just got up and left.

I guess Mum was right really but it didn't make it any easier, we really weren't having a good time and couldn't wait for the end of the week to come. Of course we did get to the sea on some occasions, it was about a mile from where we were staying and I can remember us all making our way there with the adults leading the way. It was the first time either Trev or I had been actually in the sea; you have to remember that the war had been over for nearly three years at that time but it took a long time to remove the sea defences that were put in place all along the South Coast. The weather was not all that warm that week so we did not particularly enjoy our few 'swims' in the sea only to feel frozen when we got out of the water!

As I mentioned earlier in this work, we had been to the sea with Bob in his car a year or so earlier to Rye, but at that time, there was still barbed wire and other obstacles in place so access to the sea was extremely limited. Fortunately, by the time we went to Cooden, most of that stuff had in fact been removed so the sea was there for all to enjoy, weather permitting. I do recall it taking us ages just to get in.

As far as Trev and I were concerned, the best part of

that holiday was the journey there and back, sitting in the back of 'Gilberts' removal lorry!

With my school years slipping away and the fateful age of fifteen approaching when I would either go on to further education or find a job, it was becoming decision time. In many ways, I would have preferred to have gone on to further education and I did my best to get a place at the Tunbridge Wells Technical School, which in those days, was located in Monson Road, next to the Swimming Baths. The school curriculum in our last year at King Charles, included examinations for places at the 'Tec and I did well enough to pass the written part of the examinations only to fail at the oral; just as I had done with my attempt to go to Skinners from Christ Church School, five years earlier.

This was a real disappointment to me as I still had strong ambitions to become an 'engineer' and saw the process through the Technical School as the way ahead for me. The fact that I got so far and fell at the same hurdle as previously was hard to take but my family and friends were great in their support and assured me there were other ways of becoming an engineer and this was eventually, to be the case. At that time with all young men of eighteen having to undergo National Service, unless in 'reserved occupations', chances of getting a good start in a career were limited.

The last months at King Charles were some of the best I had at school; it was probably brought about by the fact that as 'senior' pupils at the school, we would often get involved in things other than direct learning. These roles, fully supported and encouraged by 'Clacker', would see us visiting some of the businesses that flourished in the town and assisting in setting up certain functions that took place in King Charles Hall, which was adjacent to the school. These activities helped us to realise that there was life outside of the insulated environment of school.

A further relief on that front came at the time I was in Class Four when the West Kent Education Committee opened up a site near Culverdown Park called 'Huntley's'. This was to be a coeducational establishment with the prime responsibility of giving hands-on practical training and tuition to schoolchildren. For the boy's schools, it would be subjects such as Wood and Metal work and for the girls, Cooking and Needle work. The place even had some limited sports facilities, which allowed us to get a game of football, or in the summer, cricket. Things really did begin to look up at that time and we really did enjoy the chance of getting stuck in to making things; you have to remember, this was a wonderful opportunity for us after the limitations we had at our main school and the days at Huntley's were always looked forward to.

The funny thing was that although we were sharing the facilities with girls, we were kept well segregated and I didn't get the chance to strike up a friendship with a member of the opposite sex; I can't speak for Trev though.

As I have said, I enjoyed the days there very much. In Woodwork I made a wooden stool with a cord base and was very proud of it. It gave a real feeling of satisfaction and I was very proud the day I took it home. Actually the type of stool I made became the standard model for all those who followed us and I can recall that Robert made one exactly the same several years later; I still have the stool and guess it is with many other unused things in the loft at home. In Metalwork I initially produced a copper ashtray, again, this was a stock standard exercise, and I think it was a choice of making the ashtray or a fire poker as it was used as a means of establishing one's aptitude to metalwork. Afterwards we were allowed to choose what we would like to make and I elected to make a tin plate motor boat which would eventually be powered by an electric motor and a couple of U2 batteries The manufacture of this boat was to take almost all of my remaining sessions at Huntley's. It was a finicky process that involved a considerable amount of soldering, for instance, the sides of the boat had to be soldered to the keel and then the top and soldering in those days didn't benefit from the use of modern flux's that are used today; so it was a very time consuming process.

I did in fact complete the boat before I left school although it never ventured onto the water; it was very successful though and I was pleased with it. The last I saw of it was when I think it finished up with Robert after I left to join the Air Force; I don't know whether he ever sailed it though.

In our final year at King Charles School, 'Clacker' introduced us to boxing! Not for us the use of such a thing as a boxing ring, we had to make do with the floor of the Church Hall and the 'ring' was the circle made by fellow students. I think the idea behind 'Clackers' boxing tuition was to teach some form of self defence to us as we approached the outside world which in many ways was a very good idea.   However, the actual boxing matches were something else.   Having received a very brief session of instruction in the art of boxing from 'Clacker' himself, we were matched up to opponent's who were of similar build and stature and the idea was that, and for the want of a better word, a 'knockout' competition would be held to find the 'champions' at the various weight levels.

In many respects it was a corny formula but at least it gave the opportunity for some 'friendly' competition. I remember the day I was selected to take on one of the other lads who was about my size.   Actually I really didn't fancy the experience and had secretly hoped that I might have been overlooked in the competition, although I think that was a forlorn hope as I was one of the lads who stood out in the class as a possible suitable candidate as by then I was tall and from the look of things, probably the right physical build for such a sport. I cannot remember who the unfortunate was who was selected to be my opponent.   I seem to recall it was a chap by the name of Bryan Barnes who hailed from nearby Langton.   Anyway we were matched and so in we went for the mandatory, if one survived, three rounds in the art of boxing. The rounds were timed at three minutes and I will never forget just how long three minutes is when you have two guys trying for all their worth to emulate Joe Louis and attempting to knock the living daylights out of the opponent.

One three minute round seemed like an eternity and the majority of punches from each of us, missed the other guy but the energy expended in attempting to score the elusive knockout, was something else and at the end of the contest, it was declared a draw which I guess was a fair result.   It was a good thing that neither of us connected with the huge uppercuts we were 'throwing'.   It would have knocked the other guy's head off if they'd been on target. It was a good experience but one that I could certainly live without repeating; as for learning anything about self defence, I don't think we achieved that either although the experience was worth it and Bryan and I were still friends at the end of the bout.

The final year at school seemed to pass quickly and before I knew where I was the last term had arrived and the thought of leaving the school suddenly became a daunting proposition.   From not really liking school very much at any time during the scholastic years, I was at the point of leaving what was really a safe environment in order to enter the

outside world and all that that would bring.   I will always be
grateful to 'Clacker' for the way he prepared us to enter our
working lives; he went out of his way in the final few months
to make us all aware of the pitfalls that laid ahead. He was a
very good and man indeed and I will always remember him
when it was Cricket Week in Tunbridge Wells and Kent were
playing Yorkshire, his home county, at the Neville Cricket
Ground, which was located about half a mile from the school.
He would get one of us lads to run up to the ground every
hour to find out the latest score and we all hoped it would be
that Yorkshire were winning as we'd then have a better day.

Chapter 16: Working For My Living

I had hoped at one stage that I would be able to take up a career in motor engineering, commencing with an apprenticeship working for Bob. Unfortunately that was not to be so in the period leading up to my leaving school I spent some time going round the different garages in the town trying to discover what prospects there might be for a school leaver such as me. With few people owning motor cars for pleasure job opportunities in that line of business were still few and far between.

The Careers officers visited the school in the final few months to give advice to us but their success rate wasn't very high and many of my schoolmates were more successful by going out and trying to find suitable vacancies themselves. So it was with me; in the last few weeks at school I too spent my after hours seeing what was available and finally, after a visit to the G.E. Tunbridge garage, which was located next to Christ Church School, I was successful in being offered a job as a U.T. (under training) mechanic, to start two weeks after I had left school.

I was very lucky to find the job and I think the fact that my Dad knew Mr. Tunbridge may have helped me somewhat. Anyway I was grateful to get the offer and I can remember the wages were to be 28/-d (twenty eight shillings was equal to one pound, forty pence these days) per week before stoppages.   At the interview with the workshop Foreman I was given a list of hand tools that I would need to have when I first reported to work and he stressed the fact that, "come with no tools, and you don't have a job"   I guess that figures. I also had to provide my own overalls as well, so as you can see there was a considerable expenditure involved before I could actually get a pay cheque.   My Mum and Dad did what they could to contribute and I know that Bob also assisted both with money and by giving me a number of tools he no longer required.   The outlay on tools alone was considerable as they were, and still are, expensive items.

Mum bought the overalls for me in a shop in Camden Road which was an early version of something like 'Millets' would be today. Anyway they were good for the job, which was the main thing and at the end of August 1950 I started work for the first time.   Because I didn't earn that much I also kept on my newspaper round with Mr. Tuppen it was a useful supplement for me. I was grateful for it so didn't mind getting up that bit earlier to do the paper round. I think it was at that time that my Mum used to make me smile when she described the fact that her two sons both did newspaper rounds but that one would be leaving the house to start his round as the other was coming in for breakfast. Can you guess which one was which?

To further supplement my income I set up at home to do cycle repairs. It was something I liked doing and it was an easy way of earning a few shillings; I enjoyed it and amongst my regular customers was Mr. Tuppen, with the trade cycle he allocated to the 'long distance' paper rounds. I also worked on the rounds mans cycles from Raisewells, the grocers in Grove Hill Road. Of course it didn't make a lot of money for me but it did give me an outside interest and a little independence. Some of our neighbours also got me to service their bikes from time to time, although not as frequently as the trade machines, but it meant that I had a number of 'regular customers' which was a good thing. It was about this time that Bob, who had been a regular cyclist, coming into the town from Pembury, decided that he had had enough of cycling and gave me his beloved 'Hercules' cycle. Not having a bike of my own when he gave it to me, it was like winning a jackpot and that bike really came to mean the world to me; at last I had independence and could actually go where I wanted 'under my own steam'.

I could not believe my good fortune. I knew how much Bob had cherished his bike. It was unique in many ways and quite distinctive due to the fact that Bob had installed a wooden box on the rear carrier in which to carry his lunch when he went to work. This was a very useful thing in my opinion and was to prove its value when we went further afield on cycling trips when it was used for carrying all sorts of things and not only snacks.

You may ask how Bob got to work without his bike. By then he was in his sixties and I guess he felt that the time had come for him to use the bus from Woodsgate to the 'Wells as it dropped him at the Central Station. When not driving, his cycle ride from home on the outskirts of Pembury, had included more than one very steep hill and was a fair ride by anyone's standards. At that time he and my Dad were both working for George Coker who ran a Sports Shop directly opposite the station. They both worked in the basement of the building making fishing rods for George who appeared to have an endless backlog of orders. I would often go to the workshop to see them and there they would be, straightening a never ending pile of bamboo canes over gas burners; the job would have driven me absolutely crazy. I guess it was a satisfactory occupation for the two of them but I still don't know how they stuck with it for what would be many years.

My Dad still had regular speaking engagements with the Conservative Party and virtually every Thursday he would don his one and only suit and a tie and would catch the train up to London to speak at places like Lincoln's Inn Fields, Woolwich Arsenal and Speakers Corner in Hyde Park. In the summer he also had speaking engagements on Sundays so the additional income was much appreciated as the job at George Cokers did not pay that much and families cost a lot of money then just as they do now ; albeit in a simpler way.

As for 'my bike', I really treasured it and as I earned money, spent a bit on upgrading it. Things like a dynamo lighting set installation and a rather complicated B.S.A. four speed gearing system which I fitted to it in the hopes of my more easily tackling many of the hills for which Tunbridge Wells was notorious. My supplier for bicycle parts was a little cycle shop in Monson Road, next to the Public Swimming Baths and over the time before I joined the Air Force my cycle repair business was going fairly well so I think I was one of the shop's best customers. My Dad used to make me smile when he'd describe my bike as one of the most complicated things he'd ever laid eyes on. My Dad certainly had no 'mechanical' aptitude so the various additions I had made were quite beyond his understanding or interest.

With Trev having access to using Mr. Tuppens tradesman's bike at weekends and out of hours we at least had the opportunity of getting out and about on our bikes together and it was surprising the distances we used to travel on them. One of our favourite visiting places was to the RAF Station at West Malling, near Maidstone. It was a very active Night Fighter station and over the years we went there, we were to see various types of World War II aircraft ranging from Lancaster's, Mosquitoes, Spitfires and the early jet aircraft like the Vampire and Meteor. We managed to find a way into the airfield through a break in the perimeter fence and had a grandstand view, from a discreet distance, of the aircraft taking off and landing and also turnaround work on the ramp. It was a perfect spot and many would be the summer afternoons we'd spend there laying on the grass and enjoying watching the aircraft.

We liked our little luxuries as well. I'd purchased a methylated spirits camping stove through a mail order catalogue of my mothers and it came complete with a little kettle with which we used to brew up a pot of tea and that, supplemented by a few biscuits, made our cycle trips to West Malling something to really look forward to. You can see now that the box on the back of my bike had come in useful for carrying these items. When I look back we really got our enjoyment from the simple things on life. I have such nice memories of our trips out like that; they didn't cost us anything other than the energy to peddle our way there and back, but the memories are as clear to me now as they were then. We really enjoyed ourselves. In many ways we were lucky not to get chased out of the airfield by the RAF Police.

They must have known we were there but considered us to be totally harmless. There was a large sign attached to the perimeter fence which clearly warned trespassers that they would be subject to harsh penalties if found on 'Ministry of Defence Property'. Fortunately we never once had a confrontation with the authorities. I guess we got away with it because when we were there, we never got up to any mischief. All we wanted to do was to see the aircraft.

Those were the days of the 'Weekend Fliers' so there was always a lot of activity around the place. 'Weekend Fliers' was the name given to the Royal Auxiliary Air Force who turned up on Saturdays and Sundays to keep their hand in with flying the aircraft after the war finished.   There were many 'Auxiliary Air Force Squadrons at that time made up of front line aircraft. You have to remember that, at that time, the British were getting over the confrontation with the Germans and with the 'Cold War that existed between the West and the Soviet Block, it was deemed sensible to have a strong Air Force at immediate readiness.

Hence the activity at places like West Malling was typical of numerous RAF stations throughout the country. At least the need for these aircraft to fly was much appreciated by the aircraft enthusiasts; particularly us. Unfortunately, such high activity did incur losses, particularly amongst the auxiliaries. On one occasion the RAF held a type of air race which had received some coverage in the local press and a number of people turned up to see it. The crowds certainly weren't in the extremes they are today as I guess the level of enthusiasm was at a considerably lower level than now and viewing of the event had to take place

outside the perimeter fence.   However we all went along to
see it and to the best of my recollections, apart from Trev
and myself, there was Wack Warrener and a girl by the name
of Mary (more about Mary later).

From what I can recall the 'air race' was really an inter
squadron competition that tested the preparedness of the
crews to react to an emergency call-out and consequential
'scramble'. This must have been about the time that the first
jet aircraft were being allocated to the auxiliaries, probably
around 1951 as the aircraft used in the event were De
Havilland Vampires, a single seat, twin boom fighter bomber.
Although I preferred the beautiful sound of the Rolls-Royce
Merlin piston engines used in the Lancaster and Mosquito,
the jet aircraft were certainly more exciting to watch.   On
the day in question we had watched several aircraft
'scrambled' and after take off they made a wide circuit of the
airfield probably within about fifteen miles of the field and
the object was that having followed the course, the first
aircraft back on blocks after the flight, were the winners.

It was all good stuff to watch and quite exciting until
we noticed that soon after one of the Vampires took off
pieces started falling off the aircraft and we watched
dumbfounded as it continued in flight and turned on course
out over Paddock Wood and towards Horsemonden when it
then suddenly plummeted straight into the ground with a
resulting flash and plume of smoke. The early jet aircraft did
not have ejector seats installed so it was obvious that the
pilot did not get out of the aircraft and this would be
confirmed   in   the   following   mornings   newspapers.
Immediately after the accident, the rest of the competition
was cancelled and we made our way back home in a
somewhat deflated spirit.   To add to the general air of
depression the weather broke and we got rather wet making
the return journey home on our bikes.

There   were   in   fact   several   accidents   to   aircraft
operating out of West Malling over the years; one of the
worst was a Lancaster that came down shortly after take off
and narrowly missing Mereworth Church, it crashed in a
nearby wood killing all ten persons on board.   Fortunately
we weren't at the airfield that day as that would have left a
lasting impression on us.   That particular church was less
than a quarter of a mile from where we used to sit and watch
the aircraft operations.   At the time the accident to the
Vampire played on our young minds as one didn't expect
such things to happen, unfortunately real life does have a

habit of waking you up to facts and when I was in the RAF a few years later, accidents, like the one we witnessed became all too frequent an occurrence.

My first days spent working for my living at Tunbridge's didn't inspire me all that much. I think this was due to my being the 'junior' and consequently, I got all the 'dogs-body' jobs. I recall arriving all keen and keyed up on my first day there and was ready to take part in all the aspects of automobile engineering. My first morning should have warned me that the path to actually carrying out mechanical tasks myself, would start with my only being allowed to carry out all the dross jobs. When I arrived the Foreman told me that I'd have to start at the beginning and it would be some time before I would be able to actually work on the vehicles. At the time I think I was more annoyed by having had to scrimp and scrape along with help from my parents and Bob to get together the tools I was expected to have with me on day one. As it turned out, it would be some time before I'd actually get to use them on the job.

My job at Tunbridge's concentrated on washing the customer's cars and when required, filling up passing motorists cars with petrol; these were the days before 'self service'. When not engaged in car washing I would be responsible for making the tea for the morning and afternoon breaks and for popping out to shops like the Neville Bakery, to get the men buns and cakes, and when I had the time, to keep the place tidy. As you can see, these jobs really didn't tax the brain and it was a pretty soul destroying occupation. I know that it was the 'juniors' job to do these things and I'm sure it happened to countless youngsters setting out on a career path but of course at that time, you really didn't see it as constructively as that. There were good sides to the job, the workforce, which numbered about ten, including the Foreman weren't a bad bunch and all in all we got on well together.

Tunbridge's, apart from being the main Austin dealer, also took in work on all sorts of cars and was also the main agent for BSA and Velocette motor cycles so the opportunities for a good future appeared assured and it was good to have the full spectrum. Of course there was bound to be the 'induction' of beginners and I wasn't to be spared that experience. One day I was asked by one of the men working on one of the new Velocette 'LE' motorcycles to assist him with a job he was doing on the engine. I should have smelt a rat as this was during the afternoon tea break.

Anyway I agreed and he asked me to hold a part of the engine distributor whilst he turned over the engine with kick starter.   Well for those not knowing much about internal combustion engines, as I didn't at that time, the distributor is the unit which feeds the high tension electrical supply to the engine spark plug at the correct time during the engine compression cycle.   The power comes from the magneto which generates the current when the engine is 'kicked' over. I duly complied with the guy's request and like a lemon held the spring loaded terminal in my hand as he turned the engine over with the kick start.   Within a split second I felt the effect of 15,000 volts which really woke me up! It was a shock to put it mildly, fortunately, without any amperage which could have been a different story. I wouldn't get caught so dumb again believe me; the rest of the men thought it a great joke but I really didn't see the funny side of it.

In my opinion the car wash job was the most tedious of occupations as it seemed as though you no sooner finished one car and there was another waiting to be done; at least I guess I learned the right way to wash cars which has stayed with me ever since (just ask my family. It is a joke with all who know me that I still just love cleaning the family cars). The owner of the Garage, Mr. Tunbridge, was a big built guy who drove cars as though he was on a racetrack.   Rumour had it that he had at sometime in the past, actually raced cars at Brooklands. I guess he was in his early forties at that time but his reputation, as a bit of a maniac, and something of a Casanova to boot, preceded him.

As the agent for all the latest Austin cars he would always drive the most modern cars and at the time I was working there, his favourite car was the Austin Atlantic which was a sports saloon and considered a fast car in those days. One of his favourite tricks was to drive this car reasonably fast into the garage on arrival and onto a turntable which was located just at the beginning of the vehicle maintenance area; he timed it perfectly, the inertia of the car stopping on the turntable, gave enough impetus for the turntable to revolve the desired 180 degrees at which point he accelerated off the turntable, back the way he had come in. He really had it off to a fine art believe me because if he had misjudged his exit he would have accelerated straight into the line of cars in the reception area of the garage awaiting work.

Apart from the fact there were men working in the

vicinity of the turntable we all thought it extremely dangerous as a slight slip would have written off a fair number of customer motor cars; I guess we secretly hoped that he would one day miss–time the procedure and do exactly that but it didn't happen during my time there.   The location of the garage was right next door to my old Primary school, Christ Church, and it certainly brought out memories of my time there when I heard the children out playing in the yard.   Sometimes, when I had a few minutes of free time I would pop in to see the teachers who in the main were the same ones who'd taught both Trev and I some years earlier. They always made me welcome and it wasn't unusual to be paraded in front of the top class as one of the 'ex pupils'.

When I'd been at the school I had always got on well with the teachers and as my mother also had got to know some of them, this made a total family connection so they always made me welcome; I never stayed that long as the Foreman would get a little upset if he couldn't find me.

Getting back to Mr. Tunbridge, he drove cars like a bit of a madman and I suppose it was only to be a matter of time before he tried to do the impossible somewhere and this turned out to be the case one night on the Pembury to Hastings road when the Austin Atlantic left the road at high speed and finished up in a field upside down.   I didn't know anything about it until I went in for work the next morning and on entering the garage the car wreck was parked just inside the main door, having been recovered the night before. It was the first time I had seen a wrecked car and it was a bit of a shock and from what I saw, I assumed Mr. Tunbridge didn't make it but was assured by one of the men who went out to recover the vehicle that he had gotten away with just a few scratches and shock.   To me it seemed unbelievable as the driver's side of the car had taken the full impact of contact with an immovable object, later established to have been a large oak tree.   Mr. Tunbridge had a remarkable talent for survival or I guess, just plain good luck as this, by all accounts, wasn't the first car he had written of. He came into the garage later that same morning as though nothing had actually happened.

Between car washes I did enjoy it when I got the opportunity to actually work on the cars and now and again, the motorcycles.   One of the lads there, who's name I cannot now remember, had bought himself an Ariel 350cc motorcycle which he used for getting backwards and forwards to work as he lived in Langton.   These days, it would be real collector's item but at that time it was a useful and economic means of transportation and I must admit, I did envy him the machine. Obtaining a Driving Licence in those days was a little easier probably than now and it was before learner drivers were limited to machines of limited engine size whilst learning; he was very much at home on this particular bike and I secretly yearned that one day I would have a motorcycle of my own but that would come some time later.

One of the jobs I did enjoy was going out on the 'recovery' vehicle to collect broken down motorcycles. The recovery vehicle itself was a BSA 650cc single cylinder motorcycle with a sidecar converted into an open box unit large enough to take a motorcycle or two. I would sit on the pillion of the bike and the sound of the big four stroke engine, and of the wind rushing through my hair, was my idea of heaven. This was in the days before it was made compulsory for riders to wear crash helmets. The regular driver of the combination was a young chap who really had a great flair for driving this type of machine which certainly wasn't one of the easiest vehicles to drive. (I would learn this some years later when Leila and I had one as our first mode of 'family' transportation.) The more involvement I had with the bikes the more I liked them and my prime objective became that one day I would actually own one for myself.

Another friend of mine, who lived in the St. John's part of the town, was also into motorcycles and owned a BSA 250cc machine. My induction into semi long distance motorcycling came with his offer to ride pillion with him to see the 'Old Crocks' run from London to Brighton, one Sunday in November 1951. At the age I was, the idea superseded all others and the question as to just how safe it was never came into the equation. The fact that I didn't have the right type of clothing for such activities never came into the reckoning either. The necessity for proper clothing would become very obvious to me very soon however. The 'Old Crocks' run, or Veteran Motor Car Rally, to give it its correct title, takes place in November, so as you can imagine the weather was likely to be less than summery and quite likely to be wet and cold for this my first decent run on a bike. On the day of the trip I wore the outer garment that was typical for that era, namely my faithful raincoat. This would not now be considered an ideal garment by any means although when we started off for Epsom, where we'd planned to watch the rally, the weather was dry but unfortunately not for long!

It was great fun though and although a two fifty in those days wasn't the most dynamic piece of machinery, we chugged along at a good rate and both of us really enjoyed the ride. Motorways were unheard of at that time and there were far less motor vehicles on the road so the old 'A' class roads really weren't a problem to motor cyclists. We made Epsom in good time to watch the early 'old crocks' making their way towards Brighton and enjoyed sitting on the side of the road eating the sandwiches that our mothers had made up for us. Mothers tended to really care of their families in those days of there only being one breadwinner for most families.

My friend then suggested we follow the 'old crocks' and go on to Brighton to see them arrive at Maderia Drive; it sounded good to me but we had forgotten all about the considerable distance (for ill equipped motorcyclists!) and the weather. I cannot remember just how far we had gone when the rain started; we were in the area of Preston Park, which is in the suburbs of Brighton and as we were almost there, decided that it was more sense to press on than consider aborting the journey. What did we have to lose? We were going to get wet either way we played it.

On our arrival on Brighton sea front the weather had driven all but the stout hearted away from the rally and into the town in search of a warm and dry refuge. We were both well and truly soaked, cold and already feeling hungry having devoured the sandwiches sometime earlier. With limited funds between us and remembering we had to get fuel for the bike on the way home, we elected to go to the cinema in an attempt to warm up and dry out. It was a good decision as the cinema seats only cost us one shilling and three-pence each (about six pence in today's money) and we still had sufficient money left for a little snack as well! We actually did dry out pretty well whilst in the cinema but on coming out were met with a cold, wet and very dark evening. The thought of now riding over thirty miles on a motorcycle, which would take at least an hour, was not the most inspiring thought and I think it was a feeling of desperation that finally got us on the bike and on our way back home to Tunbridge Wells.

I think that journey was the longest thirty miles of my life. My friend was a good rider so it really wasn't dangerous, (or so we thought) but more of an endurance test and it really had to be a case of mind over matter. At times I thought we were the only vehicle on the road as we didn't see many other road users en route. Finally we arrived back home. What a wonderful relief and my parents, who had been a little concerned as to where we had been all day, were very pleased to see me turn up in one piece. My Dad had his usual lively fire going in the Kitchener and the warmth of the place was like paradise to me after the nightmare of that motorcycle journey. Mum had kept my Sunday dinner, which she warmed up on top of a saucepan, on the on the stove and I virtually swallowed the meal, plate and all! Never had the simple things like a good meal and warmth felt so good before.

That journey was enough to kill anyone's enthusiasm for motorcycling but I'm glad it didn't.

My friend Wack (Jack Warrener) was also in the motor trade working for a firm by the name of Oliver and Rush. They had workshops in Little Mount Zion and also at the far end of the High Street behind the White Bear public house. Wack had actually left school six months before me and was therefore a bit of a veteran in the trade compared to me and by what he said, his opportunities for working on the cars were certainly better than what I was experiencing with the never ending car washing as my prime task at Tunbridge's. I guess I was about sixteen at that time and already I was feeling as though I needed more of a challenge in the job I was doing.

The problem with the job at Tunbridge's was that I could see no future with the company. I realised that the only way to get on in any occupation was to get settled into an apprenticeship; every time I raised that point with the Foreman I was told that "next year we'll see what we can do". In other words, it was very much a case of promises, promises. It was obvious to me that they had no intention of employing another 'junior' to allow me to concentrate on an apprenticeship, so about that time I started to look about me for another job.

My folks were very supportive of my concerns but didn't have any ready solutions; it was up to me. I think it was Wack who told me that Oliver & Rush were looking for someone and the chance existed in that company to become an apprentice. It was just what I was looking for and it would be great to work with Wack and the opportunity of really learning a trade looked within my grasp. I managed to be selected for interview at their main works located in Little

Mount Zion.   The Foreman's name was Oscar Huntley and he carried out the interview.   My first impression of him was that he would be frank and fair to work for.   He explained to me that the vacancy actually existed at their facility located at the end of the High Street which was where most of their routine servicing was carried out.   This was fine with me because he did confirm that I would be taken on as an apprentice and would be released to attend the Tunbridge Wells Technical School, every Thursday, in Monson Road. The moment I met Mr Huntley I liked him, and I was to see quite a lot of him over the next year to eighteen months when I not only worked under him but was to go out with his daughter.   But more about that later.   He was a big man, completely bald, but always very jovial and saw the funny side of things.   He was to introduce me to such things as Motor Racing, Motorcycle Trials and Scrambles and how to take real care of a motorcar.

I was over the moon with the thought of actually getting to grips with the trade and it was with little regret that I handed in my notice, of one week, to Tunbridges.   In a way, from what he said, I think Mr. Tunbridge was sorry to see me go but of course he accepted my resignation.   His company could not offer the professional training that I wanted.   You have to realise that these were the years straight after the war and British industry was finding it very hard to recover from the effects of the years of conflict.   A lot of people were out of work and service industries were not the thriving examples they are today.   Most folk believed one should always hang onto a good job if you had one but I could see that this would not be in my best long term interest.

However, before I was to start work at Oliver & Rush, my mother arranged with her older brother Arthur and his wife Renee, who lived in Eastbourne, that I would spend a week or so with them as a holiday.   From a job point of view this worked out fine for me as the couple of weeks between would be an ideal time to take a break.   Holidays, in those days, were far from being frequent events for most people and certainly were rare for us.

When Mum first mentioned the idea, to me, of a break in Eastbourne, I have to say that I was less than enthusiastic having never been away on my own before but at the age I was, it was not a bad idea and the thought of being near to the sea really appealed to me, so I decided to take up the offer.   On arrival at Eastbourne station I was met by Uncle

Arthur. A short bus journey took us to where the family lived at 25 Rotunda Road, which was at the eastern extremity of Eastbourne and adjacent to the 'Crumbles'.

At the time of my visit the 'Crumbles' was a vast expanse of pebbly beach. They made me very welcome and I was soon introduced to their own family who were Ruth and Jim.   Unfortunately they were six to ten years older than me and had jobs, so it was obvious to me that I would be spending quite a bit of time on my own.   I wasn't too concerned about that as there were a lot of places to go to see within a short distance of where they lived.   The unspoilt and rugged beauty of the Crumbles itself was a real attraction for me.   This area, which spanned most of the land mass between Eastbourne and Pevensey Bay, began within a very short walking distance from Uncle Arthur's house.   There was something magical about the place. There was no commercial aspect to it at all and apart from a few broken down war defences and the Napoleonic Martello towers that had survived decades of wear and tear, it was left completely to nature and its elements.

The Crumbles became my second home as I explored all it had to offer. Fishermen operated there and on a couple of occasions they gave me a few Herring or other fish made a tasty addition to our tea.   Auntie Renee was always appreciative of them. I used to walk miles as the Crumbles alone covered a huge area.   Or I would walk in the opposite direction into Eastbourne itself; usually along the seafront to the pier as there was always much more going on there than where I was staying. Mark you, compared to holidays these days, it was still extremely unspoilt and laid back. I usually returned to Rotunda Road by bus having walked enough. Eastbourne Busses operated regular bus services to the 'Archery' area of Eastbourne, along 'Seaside', which was still about a mile from where I was staying so it still left me a long walk to do.   Some services did in fact operate to a stop near to Rotunda Road which was in those days the extremity of their operation.

I remember than Jim had a 'James' 98cc two stroke motorcycle which he used for getting to work and one day he offered me a ride on the back of it into Eastbourne as I was wanting to go to town that day.   Having only once before ridden on the pillion of a motorcycle, this was something for me to look forward to!   However what I didn't have was any experience of how to ride pillion properly.   As we approached the town along Seaside we came to a right hand bend in the road. As Jim leaned into the bend I put my right foot down.   That is something you just don't do when riding on the back of a motorcycle.   How Jim managed to keep the bike upright I will never know but he pretty annoyed.   Afterwards, apart from really giving me an earful he said that would be the last time he'd take me out on the bike. I cannot recall why I did what I did, it was just impulse, I suppose, but it could have had serious consequences and we were lucky. Poor old Jim.

It was whilst I was staying at Uncle Arthur's house that, one wet afternoon, I went to the cinema.   In those days, there was a cinema at the 'Archery' so it wasn't too far away. I decided to go to see the latest horror film which was called 'The Thing from Another World'.

Although it had an 'eighteen' certificate, being tall for my age, I was able to get in without any problem.   Well maybe I should have thought more before I saw it as it really gave me a dose of the frighteners.   The film was set in the Antarctic where some scientists located the remains of a flying saucer and extracted the frozen body of the creature from the wreckage.   I still recall the point in the film where 'the Thing', having been frozen in ice for years, was then placed in a storeroom with one of the group to keep watch over it. Well after a time and whilst the 'watchman' dozed, the ice melted and this horrible creature got loose.   To me, it was and still is, one of the classic cinematic 'frights' and it was all very well done considering that film techniques were not very advanced when this film was made.   However it wasn't such a good thing for me later on, when I tried to get to sleep that night.   When I told my aunt and uncle they had a good laugh but I blamed myself for being over enthusiastic about going to see the film in the first place.

My uncle, who was an active member of the Eastbourne Police Force, was also a keen gardener and Bee keeper. His small but highly productive garden kept the house well supplied with vegetables and I was fortunate in staying with them when he harvested the honey from the bee hives. Having never seen this done before I was fascinated by the use of a hand operated centrifuge which extracted the honey from the honeycomb. The job of cranking the centrifuge was given to me with guidance from Uncle Arthur and I was delighted. Naturally Uncle Bob did not have any protective clothing! As a reward, when I returned back home, he gave me a jar of honey to take with me. This my folks really enjoyed because, for us, with most things still being on ration, honey was a real luxury. Coupons from ration books would only permit one to buy the basics.   My uncle also enjoyed singing in the church choir and attended whenever his police duty roster would allow.   I went to church with them one Sunday evening and it was a change, for me, to sit in the congregation and hear a good choir in operation. (Unfortunately, a very few years later on, my uncle unexpectedly passed away in the middle of his singing Stainer's 'Crucifixion' at the same church.   It must have been a terrible shock for my poor aunt Renee)

Having so enjoyed a really nice holiday with Uncle Arthur and Auntie Renee in Eastbourne, I returned home to a minor shock.   My mother, judging that young men of my age were past the soft toys period, had, in my absence, disposed of my two Pandas and a beloved toy Camel.   It may sound silly but I was really upset by this as these three comforters had survived the trauma of the war years with me and although they didn't mean as much to me at the age I now was, I was still sentimental about them and really had not wanted them to be got rid of.   Surely, such toys were just typical of what so many youngsters had been given. One of the Pandas in particular, and probably the original one I'd had, had needed to have a knitted coat sewn around it just to hold the thing together.   Nobody else would have wanted it.   For obvious reasons when I was young, children had not received the huge quantities of toys that succeeding generations were to receive.   I didn't fall out with my mother about many things but did so on this occasion.   In hindsight I do believe that she did come to regret her actions but by then it was too late.

The Oliver & Rush Garage in the High Street was a small organisation which acted as a satellite of the bigger works in Mount Zion.   Staff strength was really minimal with a total work force of about eight men.   Apart from Wack (who, as it happened, had been transferred there from Mount Zion) and I, there was a funny little bloke, whose name to the best of my recollections, was George. He thought, or acted as if, he owned the place.   There was also a lead mechanic by the name of Norman Bennett (no relation to Gordon!) and three or so other guys who were general mechanics.   The owners of the company were a Mr Oliver, who was a poor mans imitation of Errol Flynn and drove to work in a vintage SS Jaguar saloon, and a Mr. Rush who spent all his time at the Mount Zion garage.   It seemed to me that this arrangement was intentional as I never saw Mr. Rush at our site and Mr. Oliver rarely went to Mount Zion.

Mr. Oliver really fancied himself and it was so obvious when a lady customer brought her car in for work. He would almost run out of his office to meet them and give them the full works of gentlemanly assistance. It was so over the top that we would often watch his performance from behind a parked car just to have a really good chuckle! The location of his office was close to the main entrance which meant that he saw all comings and goings at the garage so could, if he wished, always be the first on the scene when a customer arrived. I guess he was an attractive man to women as apart from his very confident attitude his looks resembled the famous film star of the day, Errol Flynn. I think he overdid it a bit to the point whereby he could sometimes be very arrogant indeed. This was probably left over from his wartime service as an officer in the British Army.

I must say I did enjoy the job there, yes I still had the occasional car to wash but on the whole I was allowed to get hands on experience with car repair and servicing. Norman, another motorcyclist, was a inspiration to me and went out of his way to explain things; he was a good engineer and when things were on the quiet side we would tinker with his motorcycle, a Norton 500cc machine. Unfortunately one day when he was working on the bike adjusting the timing chain, with the engine idling, his hand slipped and the next thing we saw was a finger lying on the ground underneath the engine! On this occasion Mr. Oliver really turned up trumps as before we knew where we were, he'd gotten Norman into his Jaguar, we'd picked up the finger and wrapped it in a clean cloth and off they roared to the local Kent & Sussex hospital.

I think the quick action on Mr. Oliver's part probably went a long way to Norman having his finger reattached and eventually he was able to use the hand again; almost to its fullest extent. As young mechanics this accident proved to be a good example of what can happen when you try to do things the quick way without taking proper precautions. It really made an impact on us and would have a lasting impression on the way we would do things in our careers.

I am glad to say it wasn't long before Norman was back to work. He assured us that he wouldn't be making such a silly mistake again. Norman lived in Wadhurst and relied on his trusty Norton to get backwards and forwards to work which in the winter, was no joke with icy roads. Not long after the finger incident, he hit black ice on the way to work one morning and took a heavy tumble from the bike finishing up once again in the Kent & Sussex Hospital, fortunately, without serious injury.   He was a glutton for punishment though, and as soon as he could after this latest accident he was back on the bike again!

Oliver & Rush's breakdown recovery vehicle was a classic machine.   It was a 1926 Austin 16 converted into a recovery vehicle complete with crane and towing equipment. It was a magnificent old thing and these days, would have been a real collectors item.   It had large cast iron spoke wheels which fooled everyone when snow was on the ground as these big wheels meant that when we had snowfall, it was virtually the only vehicle that could keep going in the conditions.   One of my jobs was to start the thing up every morning to ensure it was in a go condition when required. It didn't have a starter and relied solely on cranking the engine with the starting handle which was permanently attached to the front of the vehicle.   To allow one person to start it, it had a hand throttle and ignition advance and retard control located in the centre of the steering wheel. Once you got to know the vehicle you knew exactly where to set these controls and she would start quickly; after a couple of cranks on the starting handle.   I got quite expert at it and took a pride in the old Austin always ensuring she was in a good clean condition ready for service.   Not being old enough I never had the opportunity to actually drive her on the road; with a crash gearbox that required double declutching through all gears, I don't think a learner would have coped with her.

We did have another vehicle which was used more as a runabout collecting various spare parts etc.   This was a Vauxhall car that had been converted into a pickup truck and it would in fact be the first vehicle I would actually drive on the road.   Having obtained my Provisional Driving License I was allowed out in the Vauxhall under supervision whenever they needed spare parts and I wasn't doing anything else.   I enjoyed it very much and used to make the Vauxhall 'sing' when I was at the wheel much to the alarm and consternation of other staff members who happened to be with me at the time.

One of our customers was a Mr. Bridger who owned a Plumbing Supply business almost opposite the garage, usually sent his car to us for servicing and attention.   This was some motorcar.   It was a 1938 Talbot London Sports

Saloon finished in an immaculate metallic grey condition. It was magnificent; a real class motorcar with wire spoke wheels, leather upholstery and classic lines.   I once went with Norman when he took it for a road test and it was to be the fastest car ride I had ever travelled when we achieved 92 mph down the Eridge Road! It would be a long time before I exceeded that speed and the thrill of riding in such a lovely car at high speed was a memory to stay with me for a very long time.

As I was officially an apprentice in the company, I spent every Thursday at the Tunbridge Wells Technical School, initially when it was located in Monson Road but later on, when the facility moved, I went to the top end of Upper Grosvenor Road for instruction. I enjoyed 'going back to school' as the subjects were all related to engineering and, as a form of homework, we were set some very interesting projects to do in our spare time.

We were all tasked to carry out an engineering feasibility study based on an original idea of our own. This was to be presented for evaluation at the end of the tutorial year.   My idea was to attempt to design telescopic front forks for a pedal cycle. Being a bit of a cycling enthusiast at that time the idea of some improvement in the suspension of pedal cycles, really did seem to have been overlooked I guess mainly because cycles were supposed to be a very economical form of transportation and luxuries, such as I envisaged, would have pushed up the price. I put a lot of thought into the idea I had and the further I got into it, the more involved it seemed to become.   Starting off with just the front forks eventually led me to look at the whole frame and also, to compare it with the frame used on motorcycles where 'sprung frames', of a sort, were becoming standard. On reflection it would have been easier to design a full 'sprung frame' for a motorcycle as weight and dimensions gave that much more tolerance.   The problem with pedal cycles, certainly at the time I was doing my project was the fact that they were basically a lightweight construction and installation of telescopic forks could have been impaired due to the lightweight structure you were working with.

I put a lot of thought into the project and honestly believe I would have got it to work eventually; given the time. Unfortunately this was not to be as my apprenticeship aspirations were to be cut short well before fruition, but more of that a little later on. (What was frustrating is that I really believed that I was onto a good idea regarding my cycle project as it has only been within the last few years that cycle manufacturers have marketed a cycle with frame suspension and, from what I've seen of them, they are not far removed from what I was in the process of designing!)

In 1951 the British Government set up and hosted the 'Festival of Britain'. It was a very elaborate affair with all sorts of activities throughout the British Isles to celebrate the occasion. It was years in the planning and in London, on the South Bank of the River Thames, a whole site was established with futuristic buildings and a large exhibition area. Apparently it was to be the biggest exhibition held in the United Kingdom since the Crystal Palace Exhibition of 1938. I cannot remember exactly what the Festival of Britain was supposed to celebrate but it was seen as a tonic for the people after the years of war and the post war recession, which followed. There were celebrations throughout the country and Tunbridge Wells played its part in them but the main thrust of the festival was at the South Bank exhibition in London. They had built a very modern (by 1951 standards!) theatre, which is still there and known as the Festival Hall; in the exhibition area which was adjacent to the Festival Hall, there were things like the Space Needle and other futuristic exhibits and people came from all over the world to see it all. It was a wonderful display of things 'British' and, at that time, was a real tonic for the masses.

I took a day off from work to go to the London exhibition. Unfortunately it meant going on my own as Trev was at school and Wack couldn't make it. I did at least have the company of my Dad on the journey to London as he was going off to one of his speaking assignments but after leaving him at Charing Cross Station, I spent the rest of the day on my own. Don't get me wrong, I enjoyed it very much but I believe you enjoy such outings much more with company and with my being a bit of a stranger to London it was a little daunting and awe inspiring being on my own. It was the first time I had visited London apart from with occasional school outings several years previously.

The exhibition was fascinating although many of the exhibits were based on futuristic things it is amazing for me to now realise, that since 1951, just how many of the ideas on show have actually happened during my lifetime. There were things like supersonic air travel, space exploration and moon landings, electrically powered cars, computers, Jumbo Jet airliners etc. It all seemed so far away and just futuristic gobbledegook back then. With my enthusiasm for railways never diminishing, one of the exhibits there was one of the new 'Britannia' Class Pacific locomotives, number 71004, 'William Shakespeare'.   In many ways, the journey to the Festival was worth it to me just to see this magnificent locomotive and it is still one of the things I remember most about at the 'Festival of Britain'.   Unfortunately along with virtually all of her sister locomotives, 'William Shakespeare' had a rather short life as steam was to end on British Railways in the mid 1960's after a life span, for her of only fifteen years.

1951 was a good year. We had a pretty good summer and all the 'Festival' activities meant that there always seemed to be something happening in the town, and especially in the 'Calverley Grounds' where special events like Band Concerts, outdoor shows and the like took place. On the whole, life was pretty good to us at that time.

I have already mentioned my cycle repair activities, which I continued working at.   I acquired some of the neighbours as customers, several had cycles and so I was kept fully occupied. I still did my newspaper round before I went to work. Then I'd be arriving home from my round just as Trev was setting out on his; things hadn't changed although I now had to be at work by eight o'clock.   One day he was a little later than usual in setting out on his round and I remember pulling his leg that he'd be late for school if he didn't look out.   As I've said, he had taken over my old long distance round that took in the top of Grove Hill Road and Camden Park where, because it always tended to be gloomy and dark, and especially so in winter due to all of the trees in that area, Trev used to fly round as though Old Nick himself was following him.

I must say I had always been glad to get the Camden Park section of the round over with when I was doing it. It could be quite creepy of a damp and misty morning in the shadow of the trees when you hardly ever saw a fellow human being out and about so early in the day. I truly believe there were less dog walkers around in the years following the war so the streets were virtually empty until much later on and cars, of course, were still few and far between and very few parked along roadsides. Thinking about it, it must have been difficult to have kept pets fed during the shortages England had been through. Our own little cat 'Tibs,' had apparently managed well enough with the scraps we had all left him to eat.

Well this morning in particular Trev was going hell for leather on the big old tradesman's bike down the hill that leads from the top of Grove Hill to 'Charnwood' and 'Hollyshaw'; it was quite a steep hill so Trev must have got up a fair speed. Unfortunately, there was a man riding his cycle in the opposite direction coming from Hawkenbury and their paths met at the foot of the hill when Trev cannoned into this guy and they both went flying! The first we knew of it was when someone phoned Mr. Tuppen at the shop and told him of the accident; this person had also called an ambulance which subsequently took Trev and the other guy off to the Kent & Sussex Hospital.

As it turned out neither were badly injured thankfully and I think the bikes came off worse; Trev had mild concussion and bruises but I think the other man had a broken nose. Of course he blamed Trev for the incident and accused him of riding too fast! Really! Fortunately no action was taken by the police in the matter so apart from sore pride, it was all soon forgotten. To the best of my recollections, I think Trev gave up that particular paper round once he was back on his feet, I don't know whether it was due to the crash or because of the spooky households he had to deliver to!

It became obvious to me that Oliver & Rush, certainly at their High Street branch, weren't doing that well in the motor repair business and it wasn't long before they transferred Wack to their Mount Zion garage. As I had to go there from time to time, we still saw plenty of each other as we continued to walk to work together in the morning and often got together in the evenings to either go to the cinema or meet up with the rest of the 'gang'. There really wasn't a lot to do in the evenings particularly in the winter; so we took advantage of events at Christ Church Hall which I got to know about as I still belonged to the choir. There were various events held at the hall ranging from Slide Shows and Missionary talks to activity evenings for youths of the parish. At all events in the hall there was the never ending cup of tea and sometimes a biscuit, which always went down well. I had begun Confirmation classes about this time in readiness of being confirmed by the Bishop of Rochester at a later date; the classes were normally held at the Vicarage in Claremont Road.

We all thought that the vicar was my mother's 'heart throb'. The Rev. John Smith had discussed confirmation with Mum and so she became particularly keen for me to attend the classes.   The idea had not come from me.   I didn't really object to the thought of Confirmation as still being a regular church attendee through my choir appearances, it seemed the logical thing to pursue the vows made on my behalf by others when I was Christened.   I can't say I found the classes very entertaining but I understood why it was necessary to sit and talk about the need and the importance of Confirmation.   But it wasn't until 1952 when I was actually confirmed by the Bishop at a big service which was held in Christ Church.   Of course my Dad had no time for it at all and when discussed with him he ridiculed the pomp of the church and the people in it; and especially the higher clergy. To give my Dad credit though, he knew it was something my mother wanted and never once tried to dissuade me from going through with it.   Funnily enough I don't remember Trev having to do it.   (Possibly he was confirmed later on, during the time when I was away in the Royal Air Force)

Apart from doing my paper round, after I started full time employment, I also continued to work with Herb on the railway delivery vehicle most Saturday mornings.   I think I kept it up for the social aspects as it wasn't that I earned much working with Herb, all payments he made came out of his own pocket! It was just that I liked doing it and Herb was a very nice guy and more often than not, over the weekend, I'd go to their house in St. James Road for tea.   As I've said they were a really nice family and I always enjoyed the time I spent with them.   These were the days before Television was available to the masses so you had to find other things to do during the evening. We would play games such as 'Monopoly' or 'Totopoly' (a horse racing game) or else we played simple card games.   Whist Drives were popular with the older folks.

All my activities meant that time rarely stood still and that on the whole life was very enjoyable.   Of course Christmas was always a family affair although we didn't see that much of my Grandparents who lived further down Grove Hill, socially but my Dad would stop by to see them, and we did occasionally too.   When it came to Christmas I think my Grandmother always accepted the invitation of her daughter, who lived in the St. John's part of town.   I think this used to be disappointing to Dad but he never complained about it in front of us.

As you know we really didn't have that amount of room at number 32 for five of us, let alone for any visitors so all our socialising had to take place in the kitchen which itself wasn't that large.   Mr. & Mrs. Freeman lived in the top flat and they used to pop down early on Christmas Day for a seasonal chat before spending the day on their own or out with friends.   Miss Pope, in the flat above us, used to go to her family at Hurst Green for Christmas.

My folks knew the people who lived in number 30, just below us, and I remember they used to ask us round sometimes on a Christmas morning and they would give us some sweets and fruit which we appreciated.   They were an older family than us and I believe their two sons ran a prestige car agency in Crescent Road.   Tragically at some time over the Christmas period, I believe it was in 1951, they had gone along the Pembury Road in an Allard sports car which they owned lost control and hit a lamp post.   In those days the Allard was one of the fastest cars produced and I believe it was an unforgiving car at times; it certainly was on this occasion.   I cannot remember if both of them were killed, certainly one was, but at the time the news hit us all very hard and their family were shattered.

Christmas memories are usually good and certainly were in my case.   We didn't have a lot of money so the extravagances we take for granted today were unheard of in my youth.   The funny thing was that you didn't expect so much and what you did receive certainly meant a lot and you treasured it; a far cry from what happens today and although that is no criticism of anyone, I think it reflects how times have changed.   These days I often look at TV adverts at Christmas time and sympathise with families who don't have much money.   I see advertisements aimed at children and when you read the small print it can well state that "prices start at eighty pounds"!   So I am glad that Trev and I had a far simpler boyhood.   We did enjoy life.   The fact that I was earning and still had various small sources of income as well, including Christmas boxes, all meant that we could help out with things for my parents, although, there really wasn't a lot you could buy in the way of food and sweet treats as we were still rationed at that time.   I was able to get a few under the counter things from Mr. Tuppen at the paper shop, such as some chocolates and candies.   This all helped to make Christmas special for us.

So far I haven't mentioned 'Loppy' my rabbit.   I cannot remember exactly where I got him from but I guess I must have had him for at least a couple of years.   He lived in a converted tea chest in the derelict greenhouse at the back of our ground floor flat.   It was a case of spoiling the animal like mad when I first got him but when other interests took over, he went to the bottom of the list and it fell to my parents to ensure the poor thing received the basic necessities, such as food and water.

When I became a parent, exactly the same thing happened with the rabbits our children had!   Leila will verify that fact as she had hands on experience in looking after them!   All four hutches of them – and breeding regularly thanks to the occasional greetings sessions the children encouraged amongst the rabbits who were normally split up with boy rabbits being in one hutch and girl rabbits in another!   The local pet shop got to know Leila and our family quite well and finally had to refuse to take any more baby rabbits off our hands.   But I digress forwards so I will return to the days of my growing up and to poor old 'Loppy'!

My not taking much interest in 'Loppy' resulted in my Dad telling me, one evening, that a man he knew would buy the rabbit from me for ten shillings (fifty new pence) and I agreed.   Unfortunately, when I thought about it later, I think he finished up as rabbit stew which would not have been uncommon in days of food rationing!

My mother also had a love of cats and as far as I can remember there was never a time when the family moggy wasn't around.   In the early fifties, it was a tabby named Tibbs, and he had been around for a long time.   So the evening one of my friends knocked on the front door to tell us that he had found Tibbs laying in the path that led to the back of the houses in Mountfield Road, we all ran to find out what was wrong with him. When we got there poor old Tibbs was already dead; my Dad took one look at him and reckoned he'd eaten poison but we never really confirmed this.   We buried him in the back garden of number thirty two and all shed a few tears that night.

It wouldn't be long before we had a cat to replace Tibbs and my Dad came home with a pure white cat which we named Snowy.   He was a lovely cat and like Tibbs, would fortunately be around for quite a number of years until well after Leila and I were married.   Cats had a good home with my Mum and we nicknamed her the 'Cats Café'; that name would remain associated with my Mum just about all her life as even in later years when she didn't actually have a cat of her own, she would feed all the neighbours cats and they would come around home expecting it! She made them all very welcome.

At about the time in question I didn't help the pet situation much when one day, whilst I was out for a ride on my bike in the Mayfield area, I stopped at a house with a sign up advertising 'Kittens – Free to Good Homes'. I selected a lovely Tabby kitten and it fitted perfectly into the wooden box that was attached to the rear carrier of my bike; an ideal means of carriage for it. The lady of the house gave me a left over sausage from their lunch to keep the kitten interested during the ride to Tunbridge Wells; and with a piece of cardboard placed over the top of the box, the kitten was secure.

When I got home and pushed my bike into the back garden, I took off the cardboard cover to find the poor cat absolutely petrified after what must have been a bumpy experience for him. He hadn't really enjoyed the ride as he'd urinated in the box and had had to sit in this mess for the long journey home, together with the sausage. My Dad came out to meet me and when he saw what I had in the cycle box he was less than enthusiastic, in fact he was totally unenthusiastic. I think his first words on seeing the cat were "and you can take that back to where you got it from". This was to be the case as he meant what he said and lo and behold, I had to pedal back to the house which being near Heathfield made for a fairly lengthy and hilly cycle ride. Thus it was on the following day that I, with one cat but minus sausage, made the return trip. Fortunately the lady who had given me the cat didn't seem to mind taking it back again. I think she had a chuckle at the thought of the poor bedraggled animal bouncing about in the cycle box. Though I felt sorry for the cat I had not much enjoyed the whole event myself at all.

Chapter 17: Girls!

As far as I can recall, the first girl I had anything to do with was when I was at Christ Church School. Her name was Cynthia Appleton. We really only got to know each other because we were in the same class, it was as simple as that! It most certainly was not a 'lovey-dovey' type of relationship at all.   I guess I was in Class 4 at the time so that would have made us both about nine to ten years of age at the time. These were the war years and it was the rule that you went home directly after school had finished so it wasn't a case of walking her home or anything like that, not that that really came into the question. We were too young to think of things like that. As far as I can remember I believe she was the daughter of a friend of my mother. They lived in Dudley Road which was located at the top of the town opposite the Opera House, the name of a cinema and sometimes was also used as a theatre for pantomimes and occasional amateur dramatics. It was one of four cinemas in the town in those days,

I think the only time I ever saw her outside of school was when she attended my birthday party.   In my school years, with so many outside activities, I didn't pay much heed to girls. The "friendship" between Cynthia and I faded away after I started at King Charles School and as I have already said girls really didn't figure in my life at that time.   Our "gang" did associate with a girl who lived, I believe at number 52 Grove Hill Road which was a little further up the hill. Her name was Nadine Tollet. The Calverley Grounds, being near to all our homes, was a neutral territory which was freely available to us all to gather in especially during summer evenings and at weekends. Nadine, and latterly, a brunette who lived elsewhere in the town, joined us regularly for various innocent activities in the grounds and they even joined in with our games of football and the cricket matches we continued to play there knowing full well it all annoyed grounds men.

Nadine was quite a nice girl really and I don't remember anything much going on with her and the rest of the gang; don't forget, these were the days of innocence.   Her friend, however, was a completely different kettle of fish and in fact, in my opinion, she was a little odd.   She was the sort who would tease the lads and then lash out at them.

We nicknamed her the 'Wildcat' as in many ways her dark looks matched her temperament. Please don't get the wrong idea, when I said that she'd tease the lads, it didn't mean any more than verbal spats. She did have a very odd way of behaving. It wasn't just when she was with us either; I recall we used to go to the Youth Club, that was held at the Grosvenor Hall, at the bottom of Camden Road. There her attitude was no different than when she met up with the "gang" in the Calverley Grounds.

I guess in some ways I did try to befriend her as she gave the impression of being a very lonely type of person. At the Youth Club, which was held every Tuesday evening, I tried to get her interested in playing Table Tennis with me and just when you thought that we were coming around to a normal type of relationship, off she would go in one of her moods. That relationship surely wasn't one that was going to work out and in the end I never pursued it.

In many ways, although he was younger than I, Trev really had a way with girls and was a bit of a boy when it came to the opposite sex. I remember his relationship with the daughter of the publican who ran a Public House at the end of the High Street, opposite to where I eventually worked. Her name was Ann Robus and she and Trev were friends for a long time. My mother had a soft spot for a girl by the name of Mary, who lived on the Ramslye Estate down the Eridge Road and she was a regular visitor to our house when I was in my teens. I think Mum befriended her when Mary's family lived through the Grove in Mount Zion and Mary proved to be a great help to my Mum in helping with Robert and taking him out in the pram to the park. My mother was suffering from the effects of having a baby late in life, her mid forties and, as I was to learn later, had ulcerative legs. These were to plague her for the rest of her life. Having a willing helper around from time to time, like Mary, was just what she needed.

Mary used to virtually live at our house; apart from the help she gave to Mum, I believe all wasn't that well for her at home and she was happier away from it. Her presence at home came to be taken for granted and coming in from school one would expect to find her there helping Mum. She really seemed like part of the family. Mary was older than me by about two to three years but around the time I was about to leave school, I noticed her more as a girl than as a home help to my mother. During summer evenings she would join up with the rest of us as we spent most of our time out in the Calverley Grounds just doing the scatty kind of things one normally associates with youngsters. By that time, I guess, I was one of the older members of the group and Mary felt more at ease with me so we were able to talk together about things of mutual interest. As I have said earlier in this work, she accompanied us on many of our cycle rides to places like West Malling airfield, and was always good company.

Sadly, in common with many youngsters at that time, she didn't enjoy the best of health and there were many times when she'd not come to our place for several days at a time; unfortunately, that was to be the story of her life. I believe she was tubercular and her chest was weak. Up to that period of time milk was known to carry the infection but gradually most milk was tested for T.B. which was a great step forward.

She was a good cyclist and when the family moved to the 'Ramslye Estate' she relied on her trusty cycle to make the journey to our place. That was fine in decent weather but during wet weather the bus was a better means of transportation for her. As I gradually got to know her more, I would always walk her home. She was an interesting person and the times spent with us walking alone but together really gave me my first experience of discussing things feminine; this was a real change for me after non stop railway and masculine subjects. I have to admit to the fact that Mary was the first girl I ever kissed! The first time it happened it all occurred quite naturally and almost took us both by surprise, as I hadn't anticipated it. It took me back a little as she was the one who led me, not unwillingly, into it!! After that first time, thereafter it happened every time I took her home and I must say that I began to look forward very much to our lengthy walks very much indeed. There was life outside of the Southern Railway after all!

She was attractive in a certain way; not the sort of girl you would actually call glamorous but with a personality that made up for not being particularly beautiful. As I have said she was a few years older than I so the relationship was never to be anything other than "just good friends". I think my mother paid her for her time helping with Robert; it was a good arrangement. I gathered that her mother was a single parent with the odd boy friend and her brother was a handful with various encounters with the police which didn't help towards a settled home life for them.

I never really dated her, the most time we ever had on our own were the walks back to her home but she was someone I really liked. Later on, with my time in the RAF, and then with my going to work away from home, I lost track of her. Unfortunately I believe her worsening state of health became more of a problem to her as she got older. I will always remember her gratefully as being the first girl who really made me realise that it was good to have a girl friend.

Wack and I got into the habit of walking up the town of an evening. There we always called in at the Italian coffee shop at the top of the town which was very much the in place for the young people to meet up in. These were the years leading up to the "Mods and Rockers" era and whereas public houses are the 'in thing' with youngsters today, in our time the Espresso Coffee establishments were the usual meeting places. It seemed the thing to do, to walk the town, see some of your mates and all finish up at the cafe.

To be open about it, we were always on the lookout for girls and I can still remember Wack dressed up like a dandy with his quiff hairstyle which was all the rage in those days. He was a real smoothie and I guess we were as attractive to the opposite sex as any other couple of guys doing the same thing.

We often chatted up suitable girls but when I look back on it, it was a bit of a mugs game as I think the girls were only interested in getting a free cup of coffee or a seat in the cinema, after which you'd never see them again. I can still remember times that having met a girl the night before and then arranging to meet her the next evening, I'd go waiting at some agreed rendezvous point and to stand there for literally ages only to find that she had no intention of turning up.

I sometimes thought that they did it as a dare and would probably go to the meeting point but kept well away so as not to be seen, and have a good laugh at the twit standing there waiting for someone who wasn't going to arrive. Believe me; it happened to me a number of times like that so in the end, I would be the one who'd fail to arrive. Being the innocent youth I was at the time, and honestly believing that they would eventually turn up, it was normal for me to wait for in excess of one and a half hours for some mysterious girl who had no intention of turning up!

Summertime gave added opportunity to meet girls at

the Andrews Fun Fair which took up residence for long periods on the Lower Cricket Ground, opposite the Pantiles. It was there that I met what appeared to be love at first sight, a nice quiet, red headed country girl named Barbara. (In many respects she was virtually the image of Sarah Ferguson, who became the Duchess of York)   She lived with her parents in a farm tied cottage between Frant and Wadhurst and had a wonderful 'Sussex' country accent.   From the moment we got chatting at the fair, I got the feeling that she was not going to be one of those mysterious types who, after having a good time, at my expense, wouldn't bother to see you again.   Ironically, Barbara and I got on extremely well from the beginning and having met on a Saturday evening, I was a little shocked when she invited me for tea at her home on Sunday afternoon.   We agreed a suitable bus time from the town and I duly arrived at the stop to which she had directed me; she was waiting for me when the bus drew in and I must admit, looked very nice in a light summer dress which complemented her red hair.

I was the real gentleman and had bought her a small bunch of flowers for which she was very pleased.   Her house was about half a mile from the bus stop so we were able to take a pleasant country walk to where she lived and being a very nice day, it was the ideal thing to do. As I was not really a confident socialite, in some respects I was dreading meeting her family having had rather limited experience with meeting strangers up until that time. The walk to where she lived was most pleasant; it was a beautiful summer's day and it was a lovely part of the country. We chatted about all sorts of things and what surprised me was the fact that we really got on well together which made conversation very easy.

What we actually talked about I cannot remember but the fact that we were able to get on well really broke the ice and gave me the required confidence for my meeting up with her family later on that afternoon.   What I did like about her was that she was not pretentious in any way and didn't try to make something of herself that she wasn't.   She had an aura of honesty about her which I liked. I guess that is what made our first real meeting together go so well.

She was a real advert for a 'country girl' with her fresh outdoor looks and a mass of red hair, and her family were typical country folk as well.   If you can draw a comparison, they remind me now of the Larkins family in 'The Darling Buds of May'.   When we arrived at their house I was welcomed by her mother and father and two brothers (fortunately, younger than I) as though I was some sort of long lost family member they hadn't seen in ages.   The welcome came as a great relief to me as it was apparent that there were no inhibitions with them, they were very much down to earth country folk and took people at face value; if their daughter wanted to bring a boy home for tea, then that seemed fine with them.

When I look back what impressed me was the fact that they had gone to a lot of trouble to make me welcome and apart from laying on a typical Sunday family tea with lots of home-made cake. there was a genuine feeling of true hospitality which I hadn't experienced before; you have to remember that this was my first real date and I had not been called on to 'meet the family' before.   I guess I was a little naive in many respects and should have wondered why I was feted to such a welcome on my first visit, remembering the fact that we had only met for the first time the night before!! But I didn't query it and just accepted the pleasant situation. With Barbara being such an attractive girl; what more could I ask for?

I made my departure for the bus stop later that evening and as offered by her family, promised to go to tea again in the near future.   Barbara walked with me to the bus stop and for the first time in my life, I had a girl who was asking me when we could meet again!   I gathered that she wasn't working full time and relied on doing a part time job in one of the village shops during the mornings so she was free afternoons and evenings. So it was really up to me to make the next date! I didn't want to push things too quickly, as this was only our first meeting, so we agreed to meet on the following Wednesday evening after I had finished work; she would meet me outside of Oliver and Rush's at five thirty. Then I offered her some tea at our house so that we could go to the cinema afterwards.

After saying our farewells and politely exchanging kisses, I set off home. When I got home, my Mum and Dad were eager to know how my first real date had gone and my mother was only too pleased to offer tea the following Wednesday. She was delighted to have the opportunity to meet 'the girl friend'. This was all quite a relief to me.

Whereas my Mum didn't try to pry much out of me about Barbara, my Dad was quite the opposite and was very keen to hear all about her. He didn't get very far as I was reserved about the whole thing but must admit I did look forward to meeting her again.

The following Wednesday she arrived at the garage quite a bit earlier than I had asked her. I didn't know she had actually arrived until one of the other guys mentioned a girl waiting outside the garage and asked me if I knew who she was. On investigation I found it to be Barbara so had to ask her to go for a walk around the Pantiles or somewhere to kill the time until I got off work. This she did and she was back to meet me at five thirty. Although I had a quick wash at work before I left, I didn't feel good walking her up the High Street to my home still smelling of motor oil and petrol but fortunately she didn't mind. We got to number 32 where my Mum was ready with a nice table laid and immediately made Barbara feel at home. To me this was quite an event as she was the first real girl friend I had ever taken home! She got on well with my mother immediately. I guess they were both countrified people so that helped a lot with breaking the ice.

Trev, who was still at school in those days, was occupied with homework and my Dad came in from work soon after we arrived. I must give my Mum credit, she knew I wouldn't be able to have a good wash when I got home, as the kitchen also doubled up as our bathroom when it wasn't being used either as a kitchen or living room. (We had lost the use of the front room when Robert arrived)   To overcome this problem Mum had arranged with Miss Pope that I could use her toilet for a quick wash and brush up which I appreciated very much indeed. Although I used one of Miss Popes spare bedrooms on a permanent basis, this luxury didn't extend to the toilet facilities so Mum's thinking in this matter was right on the ball.   Anyway, I guess my absence upstairs for a little while gave my mother an opportunity of forming an opinion of Barbara.

I guess it was over tea that I got the impression that Barbara had serious intentions in attempting to form a strong relationship as within no time at all, as far as I was concerned, she was offering to come into the town afternoon's to help Mum with Robert or with doing any shopping she required. Initially, I thought it to be a very generous offer and I think Mum saw it that way as well as at that time Mary was unwell and hadn't been around to help my mother for quite some time.   So Barbara's offer came as a blessing in many respects.

I really didn't think too much about it; I was glad in

many ways to have what appeared to be the beginning of a steady relationship with a girl, my parents seemed to like her so all in all things looked very good. We enjoyed our tea and Mum suggested we could get off out as we'd planned to go to the Great Hall cinema to see an Errol Flynn film which we subsequently did and enjoyed it. I saw Barbara onto the last bus which fortunately left from just outside the cinema and agreed arrangements with her to meet again on Saturday afternoon.

I was keen to get home to find out what my Mum and Dad thought of my girl friend and was pleased to hear that she had won them over during her first visit. Trev was somewhat non committal on the subject though and summed her up as not his type.

Barbara and I met on regular occasions after that and at times she'd turn up in the town unannounced and I wouldn't know she was around until I got home from work where she would invariably be waiting for me. Something like "surprise, surprise". At first I thought she was genuinely coming into the town to help my mother by taking Robert out in the afternoons for her. With Mary still poorly and not having been around for a while at that time, Mum was glad of the now regular assistance. Barbara was now becoming like part of the furniture in some respects. Sometimes, she'd surprise me by turning up at the garage with Robert in the pushchair which the other guys didn't mind but to which I was not the best pleased. A couple of times Mr. Oliver was there when she came into the garage and I could see from his expressions that he preferred she didn't do it. He never actually said anything but I could see her being there wasn't really the right thing.

From my mothers point of view though I guess Barbara's various ways of helping out suited her. But I was beginning to get slightly apprehensive about the relationship in more ways than one. Firstly I got the feeling that Barbara was trying to strengthen our relationship by getting around Mum; and that she was always 'there' and no arrangements needed to be made for us to see each other. I felt that I was being manoeuvred into some sort of permanency with the girl and the more she worked her way into my family, the more I was looking for a way out.

The other thing with Barbara was that she was what I can only describe as a 'man eater'. Bearing in mind the fact that she was the first real girlfriend I'd had, and I must admit, I certainly wasn't an expert in the art of handling girls, there were times when her eagerness to be alone together became a cause for concern in my opinion. Like all young couples a healthy walk in the country or over the 'common was something to look forward to; unfortunately, to her, it was a case of once we were alone together then she made it quite clear that there were other things in a relationship, of a more intimate nature, than merely holding hands and kissing!

Things were going too fast for my liking and the feeling I had was that this particular relationship was not what I had expected and not what I really wanted. Today, the attitude of Barbara would be the normal thing, I guess, and you could say that her forwardness was actually ahead of its time but back then, I really couldn't accept it. I did not accept from her the closeness that she was looking for and together with her apparent objective of getting totally serious, I was back-peddling as fast as I could. I think my mother noted what was happening with Barbara with her virtually living at our home almost every day.

It got to the point where I would come home from work with my fingers crossed hoping that she'd not be there. When I raised the matter with my mother, she also confirmed her concerns about what Barbara was actually looking for in the relationship. She knew that I was trying to cool the affair but Barbara was a very determined character and one of those people who wasn't easily deterred from their objective.

Let me just say once again, Barbara was an extremely attractive girl and as far as my work mates were concerned, she was a "nice piece of homework", but I was only sixteen and a half and far too young to get into the sort of relationship she was obviously looking for. I guess she just wanted to find someone who she could settle down with; but no, I didn't think I wanted to be that one at my age.

Things finally had to come to a head; it was obvious that my mother was getting concerned from what she saw of the relationship and knowing I was less than keen, wasn't surprised when I told her I was going to tell Barbara that we really couldn't go on as we both wanted different things and I certainly wasn't looking for a serious relationship so soon. I took the opportunity of telling her we were through during one of our walks over the common near the Higher Cricket Ground. Her reaction was one of total and utter amazement as she thought what she'd been doing was what we both wanted; how she got that interpretation I will never know. She took it badly and there was quite a scene but I stuck to my guns that it was over between us; she surprised me when she said she'd still like to come during the afternoons to take Robert out but I feigned a white lie by saying that Mary was now well and back on the scene to do that.

I must say I didn't like doing that to her as basically she was a very nice girl and I guess she thought that by helping my mother with Robert and being nice to me that she was doing all the right things but in fact, the opposite was the case. It took a time for her to actually give up on the subject though as once or twice, she did come into the town and stopped by home to see my Mum; she even came to the garage a couple of times but I was eventually able to convince her that there was nothing between us and soon afterwards her visits to the town ceased. I wonder what happened to her in the end; I do hope she found some country lad who wanted to settle down, have a family and is probably a contented Grandmother now; at least I hope that is what eventually happened for her as that was obviously all she really wanted in life.

After Barbara, I didn't chase the girls for a while and was very content to meet up with Wack in the evenings for our walks around the town and the invariable cup. It had been a case of "once bitten, twice shy"!

We were frequent cinema goers and one of our favourite places was the Kosmos Cinema in Calverley Road, opposite Marks & Spencer although it has long since gone. The 'Kossie' as we called it was also known as the 'flea pit' but we liked it as it showed the kind of films we liked, good thrillers, horror stories and the occasional 'X' Certificate attraction. We were regulars there and I must admit it, it was the only cinema that I have ever been thrown out of. (without them giving us our money back as well!) I cannot remember what the main attraction was on the night of the incident but the supporting programme included a short film on road safety and this was the source of our upsetting the manager.

In the road safety film it gave a graphic example of cycling without due care and attention and illustrated this by showing some guy, suitably dressed in the proverbial raincoat and wearing the customary Trilby hat, cycling flat out, head down, straight into the back of a parked van. We split our sides laughing about the scene as it was just so funny in our opinions and we couldn't stop laughing about it;

the image of this guy going along with his Trilby hat forming part of the required 'slip streaming' in those days with head down and 'WHAM', he hits an immovable object. I can remember it as clearly now as I did then and can still conjure up smile when I think of it; I know the film was trying to make a point and it was an effective bit of reconstruction, but it just seemed so funny to us.

Unfortunately, the manager didn't share our sense of humour and his dark shape at the end of the row of seats with the message "Oi you two, out". As we left the row he grabbed us by the collars, much to the applause of the audience, and in no time at all, we were out in the cold of Calverley Road wondering what the main film would have been like!

Wack and I were avid cinema goers and often went twice a week as Tunbridge Wells had in those days, no less than four cinemas in the town. The Ritz, Opera House, Great Hall and the Kosmos. The ultimate to us was working our way in to see 'H' (Horror) category films which today, having once been certificated as 'X', are now category 'R'.

The criteria, as now, was that you had to be eighteen years old to get in but Wack and I didn't have a problem as I guess we looked old enough to be allowed in. Actually there were times when I wished we hadn't got in to certain horror films as they left quite startling impressions on your minds especially those with Boris Karlof, who used to play the legendary 'Frankenstein' and other nice characters which usually gave us both the creeps.

Funnily enough Wack didn't appear to have a lot of success with the girls at that time. Although he was older than me by about six months, he gave girls a low priority whereas I was keen to get the company of the opposite sex but after the experience with Barbara, I must admit I was a little put off and didn't go out of my way to seek them out.

That did not last long though as I soon noticed a rather attractive girl who lived at the back of the Oliver & Rush garage and eventually I made tentative overtures to her hoping to set up a friendship. Coincidentally her name was also Barbara but fortunately that is where the similarity ceased!

What was a change compared to her previous namesake was that I had to do most of the running and I didn't mind that. She was still at school and was a pupil of Rusthall Girls School. They had previously lived in Rusthall, I was to learn, and to save too much disruption to her education her parents elected to leave her there to complete her education. She was an extremely attractive girl and had looks like Rita Hayworth, the film star but without the long red hair; hers was dark brown. There was one problem though. When I met her I was sixteen but I found out that she was only just fourteen which proved to be a problem with her parents. She certainly looked older than she was. The age gap was a significant one in those days when people frowned at girls of that age going out courting with someone over two years older. It wasn't until the second or third meeting with her that I was to find out exactly what her age actually was; the subject had never come up before. As she was a tall girl I honestly thought she was around my own age as I realised that many youngsters were still at school beyond the mandatory age of fifteen.

We got on well together and I began to think I could look forward to a long friendship with her. Things went well for the first few meetings until one day when I popped into 'Jacks Café'. This was located at the back of our garage and along a passage way that also led to the house in which she lived. Here she waylaid me to tell me that her parents wouldn't let her see me again. They were concerned about the age gap and she really didn't have any choice in the matter. It wasn't what she wanted but she couldn't disregard her parent's wishes. These protective wishes I can now better comprehend. We both wanted to keep the friendship going but with the pressure from her parents was impossible. The only way we would be permitted to meet up would be by our always being accompanied by a friend; this was the only compromise her folks would allow to us meeting and I can still remember very pleasant walks to such places as the High Rocks and Happy Valley. These were suitable places for a "romantic" walk but with the proverbial 'friend' of hers accompanying us somewhat less so! It was not the best way to get to know each other and as much as I hated to admit it, with such restrictions, the friendship was doomed to failure. The constrictions upon our innocent friendship prevented real communication and eventually, sadly, we packed it all in which, as far as I was concerned, was a great pity.

Soon after this I began to get friendly with Oscar Huntley, a big burly sort of guy who was in fact a real gentle giant. Oscar was the Shop Foreman at the Oliver & Rush

Garage in Mount Zion where Wack worked and actually lived in a house in Hawkenbury facing that of my Grandparents.

Oscar had one of the most perfect motor cars I had ever seen. It wasn't that it was something out of the ordinary, far from it, it was only a Morris Minor 8 with a soft top but it was the most immaculately maintained car imaginable. Even the 'prop shaft', that drives the rear axle from the gearbox underneath the car, was polished. He really did think the world of that car and spent a lot of pleasure in entering it for various car rallies where it would usually walk away with the top honours in the Concours De E'legance; quite an achievement for something that was really only a family motor car.

I got to know Oscar when I was despatched to his workshop, from the High Street branch where I normally worked, and the workload dictated additional resources for his shop. The catalyst of his living so near to my mother's old home had something to do with our building up the friendship. Of course I was extremely interested in all things mechanical and especially in his car so, in the manner of the times, it was not long before I was invited to his home for tea one Sunday. He had two daughters, the oldest was a girl named Margaret who was in her last year at the Tunbridge Wells Girls Grammar School, and I took a particular liking to her. She was the image of her father, but better looking, and enjoyed good conversation and also enjoyed doing things involving motor vehicles; she was his prime support in keeping the car looking as nice as it did. As a family they were all interested in motor sport, particularly motor cycle motor cross and trials events. I think the first subject of our conversation when I first went there for tea was about the various names participating in the above sports. At that time they were totally unheard of strangers to me. Motor sport in any shape or form, was something totally new to me then. This was not long after the war and such sports were still very much in the doldrums due to lack of funding and limited dedicated circuits being available for the sport. What venues there had been in the pre-war years had been taken over by the military and the return to normality was extremely slow. Motor cycle 'trials' were actually very attractive to keen participants as apart from furnishing the actual motor cycle and suitable clothing (such events usually took place in quiet and unspoilt parts of the countryside, well off the beaten track), it was a fairly economical form of motor sport for the rider.

The first evening I went to Oscar's home was like a form of brainwashing or initiation of the ignorant. I knew absolutely nothing about motor sport but Oscar's eldest daughter certainly did and I felt a bit of a lemon really. The only way such an ignoramus as I could be "initiated" into the sport was to go along to one of the 'trials' with them and that was arranged for the following Sunday when a big event was taking place near Ticehurst. All I had to do was to show up at their house at a certain time on the day, and off we would all go.

Mrs. Huntley would arrange the picnic lunch and we'd all go to the event in the Morris Minor, which, when you think of it, would do extremely well to carry five adults. I guess this was in the early part of 1952. "Trials", it seemed, took place in winter months so good winter clothing was essential for spectators and in particular, good strong footwear. They really made me feel one of the family and during that winter when I went out with Margaret we went to many motor sport events. When the following summer arrived the trial events handed over to track racing; particularly at Brands Hatch where the grass track was eventually replaced by a tarmac surface and my fascination with speed began. Over the years I was an avid Brands Hatch supporter and this was thanks to my indoctrination by the Huntley family. Anyway, I do not mean to deviate from my relationship with Margaret so I must get back to that!

The aspects of all things 'motor' seemed to dictate my relationship with Margaret Huntley. I do admit that I was becoming a real enthusiast, at that time, but there were times when all I really wanted was Margaret's company and not the automotive subject. Don't get me wrong, we did get on well together but whereas I imagined young couples would get out and about together, we were destined to either be accompanying her folks on days out or were talking motor cars or helping Oscar to keep his car in pristine condition. Of course we were both very young and serious relationships were really not suitable but by our not being able to spend time on our own, as time went by, the strain of constant company began to affect our friendship. As a boy, girl relationship we were really going nowhere and eventually the time came for us to part which we did as very good friends. Looking back, Margaret's parents were also gently being protective of their young daughter as was the way of parents of girls when we were young. I was always grateful to Oscar and his family as they were really nice folk and their introducing me to the thrills of motor and motor cycle sports was one of the best things that happened to me. My working with Oscar meant that we did keep in touch with sporting matters and he was a good boss to work for when I was allocated to the workshop in Little Mount Zion. I still popped into to see him and his family when I went up to Hawkenbury to see my Grandmother so we kept in touch after I parted from Margaret.

After I packed up with Margaret there was a lull in my associations with the opposite sex and I concentrated on my job at Oliver & Rush hoping for serious consideration of me as an apprentice. Even at that young age the need for security was paramount in my mind and the fact that the job I was doing gave limited instruction contributed to my feeling of insecurity. I got to the point where I asked to see Mr. Oliver in order to discuss my concerns. I felt it better to get the subject out into the open. If you remember earlier I said that they had promised me an Apprenticeship when I went for the interview! In business matters he was a negative sort of person and from what I learned later in life, a poor man manager. However he did reluctantly agree to release me once a week to attend the local Technical School to pursue some suitable instruction. I guess I did achieve something; but not an actual apprenticeship scheme. I would now say that I had been 'fobbed off'!

Trev and I still went around a lot together. You may well ask why I have not mentioned him for a while? It was possible that 'girls' had been taking up some of our leisure time separately from time to time. Summer holidays would usually see the pair of us purchasing a Railway 'Runabout' ticket which was valid for a week. This ticket allowed one to unlimited travel in certain regions of the "Southern". Our usual trip was the area covering as far East as Hastings and as far West as Worthing so the places in between like Eastbourne, Newhaven, Seaford and Brighton, were all included which gave us a good field of choice. We certainly made the most of the tickets and did get our moneys worth and covered a lot of miles. Unfortunately on one particular trip we made, Trev and I fell out! It was a Sunday and we had travelled by train to Seaford and then planned to walk the 'Seven Sisters', a beautiful part of the South Downs between Seaford and Eastbourne. All went well between us for the first two thirds of the hilly and undulating walk until we stopped for our lunch which Mum had kindly provided. For some reason or other we got into an argument over something I cannot even remember and Trev 'stormed off' on his own. I decided to stay where I was assuming that he would return after a while and we would then make up our differences and press on with the walk. Well he didn't come back and at that point I realised that he had gone off, accidentally, with the railway tickets.

Panic set in and as time was getting on and I still had a long way to walk to Eastbourne railway station I hastily set off expecting I would at least see him in the distance but that was not to be so!   The last train for Tunbridge Wells left Eastbourne at seven thirty and I eventually got to the station to see it steaming out of the platform. The walk we had started together was a very lengthy one by anyone's standards. We may well have underestimated how long it would take to do. I had no way of knowing if Trev was on the train or not; I certainly didn't see him.

I went to the Station Master's office and reported my predicament. He already knew all about the about the problem and waved my ticket at me as I spoke to him. Earlier on when Trev had arrived at the station, he had sensibly handed my ticket to the Station Master rightly assuming I could not have already gone home on an earlier train. That was all very well but now the last train to Tunbridge Wells had departed. The railway people were very good and arranged for me to travel to Lewes where I could catch the late train from Brighton to Tunbridge Wells. To make sure I didn't get lost again they first of all phoned the Police in Tunbridge Wells to get them to stop by my home and let my parents know that I was OK and would eventually get to the West Station about eleven p.m. Few ordinary people had telephones in their homes and mobile phones were decades away in the future. To insure that I did get there they arranged that I would travel in the 'care of the Guard' on both sectors; I guess I really couldn't blame them, better to be safe than sorry.

When the train eventually arrived at the West Station; there waiting for me on the platform was my long suffering Dad!   Actually he wasn't too upset about it really as he was probably relieved to know that we had both got home all right but I must admit it was an experience. The down side of this particular story is that somewhere between Seaford and Eastbourne I lost a lovely brass and leather telescope. This telescope had been given to me by a lady on my newspaper round and I thought a great deal of it. It had been contained in a little brown, thick cardboard attaché case (an article that was typical of the period) which we had used for taking our lunch with us on the day out. Back packs were unheard of then as were 'Cool boxes'! At some point after Trev and I had parted company, and I had eventually set off to catch up with him, the hinge on the attaché case had broken, without me knowing it, and the case halves had opened ensuring what items were in the case progressively fall out.

I didn't realise this until I got to the outskirts of Eastbourne by which time it was too late to backtrack over the route to find the contents. Somebody would have probably found them by then anyway so it would have been a wasted exercise even if I had had the time to retrace my steps; which I hadn't. I was really upset when I realised what had happened, losing the remains of our picnic had been bad enough but losing the telescope was a real disaster for me.

I guess it was destined to be one of those days! Maybe I might have been better off with a girl for company – if only her parents would have agreed to us tracking off on our own.

Chapter 18: Decisions

As I was saying in the last chapter, the feeling of insecurity in my job at Oliver & Rush was an increasing source of real anxiety to me as I looked at the future. National Service was still in place in those days. It was intended for all able bodied, healthy, youths at the age of eighteen, who did not have a 'reserved occupation'. It was not a case of not wanting to go into the armed services when my time came but I was very determined to try to get a career. I had heard too many stories of lads going into the services for the two years and having to find a totally different sort of job when they came out. More worrying too was the fact that employers were under no obligation to offer you your original job back when you were 'demobbed'. With the 'family' motor car still very much in its infancy the trade I had chosen as a career path was not secure at all and the numbers of motor mechanics required was quite limited. My training had not taken off as I had expected either. Bob's experience should have warned me that times were hard and one had to be very careful of what job decisions one made and then to stick with them if you could; hoping things would eventually improve.

Working at Oliver & Rush, in the High Street, as I did, I felt there was no long term future for a young lad but not having a great deal of choice at the time I planned to stick it out and see how things developed.   We were not very well paid and I only earned about one pound and ten shillings a week (one pound fifty by today's standards) and I still really needed any extra income I could make from my usual sources of extra income. My Dad was very friendly with George Coker who ran a sports shop opposite the Central Station. Coker's was a really thriving shop as at this time people and were looking more to outdoor sporting activities.   The shop appeared to be doing quite well. Eventually Coker's expanded into manufacturing its own fishing rods and Dad went to work for George Coker on a full time basis when they set up the workshop. Soon after this he was joined by Bob. It was a family concern too.

George Coker had a brother by the name of Jim, and as far as I can remember, he was the travelling salesman for the company and he drove around in an old blue Hillman van which was always in need of some repair or other, mainly to the bodywork. To save maintenance costs, my Dad had the brain wave that I could do the odd jobs on the van during the evenings or at weekends and the Coker brothers jumped at the offer.

I didn't object in the least as every penny it earned me was appreciated. It became a regular thing for Jim to drive the van up to Meadow Hill Road, which was adjacent to the passage way that led to our back gate at No. 32, in the evening after he had finished his rounds and, within my limited capability, I would endeavour to do whatever needed to be done on it. (Less equipment was required in those days which made home repair work possible in many cases). With good planning, if I was told early enough about what required doing on the van, I could borrow any special tools from the garage and that together with my own tool kit, usually meant that I could handle quite a variety of jobs and I really enjoyed it.   The biggest job was trying to keep the thing in one piece as it was suffering badly with corrosion which took the majority of my time to keep under control. These were the days before M.O.T. Tests were introduced so there wasn't the legal requirement that vehicles had to be to a certain standard to continue using the roads.   The arrangement worked very well for everyone. The old van kept me well occupied, along with my continuing upkeep of the bikes of various neighbours. Jim Coker was an eccentric and quite the opposite of his brother who was the real business man in the family. I don't think I ever saw Jim without his pipe in his mouth and invariably wearing a long overcoat, which he appeared to wear year round with the proverbial cap. He was a very likeable sort of bloke though and you always had a laugh when he was about. Often, if I had done some work on the van and there was still some evening left, when I had finished and particularly in the summer Jim would come to collect the vehicle and would invariably offer to take the van for a 'test drive'.   But remembering that there were only two seats in the van, he would still invite my mother and father to come along with us too.   His favourite test run was to the Huntsman pub at Eridge Station where we'd all have a 'quick one', which he usually generously paid for.

I can remember one funny occasion when, after having our half pint, we all got back in the van, which I can assure you was a bit of a squeeze as apart from the two seats in the front which Jim and my Mum usually had, meant that the rest of us had to travel in the back of the thing. When we began our journey back to the 'Wells, we had to negotiate the hill that led towards the town; the pub at Eridge Station is located right at the bottom of the long hill and on this particular evening it was dark when we began our journey back home. (That hill was the 'Old Road'. There has been a by-pass road built which is now roughly a hundred yards away from the pub and the station).

As we began to ascend the hill Jim became very concerned about a 'vehicle' coming in the opposite direction which appeared and would not dip its headlights. We actually couldn't see the other vehicle but some lights were apparent as we approached the brow of the hill. From our seat in the back of the van we could hear him getting more and more annoyed about "that other bloke who won't dip his flaming headlights." He kept on about this and I could hear him cursing this 'other vehicle' to the point where he drew into the side of the road and said he couldn't see where he was going because of the glare of the oncoming lights.

He said he would stop to allow the vehicle to pass before we went on. (Those were the days) We had at that time, not even seen the vehicle to which he referred, only seeing the glow as we approached the top of the hill. Having stopped the van we waited for this mysterious vehicle to pass us but nothing came at which point Jim said that it must have pulled into the side for something or other and had left its lights on full beam. As we were now stopped I offered to go and see what the other 'vehicle' was doing as Jim was adamant that he would not go on until it had passed us.

I ran to the top of the hill but well before I reached it I could see what the other light source was, it was a solitary street light and there was no sign of another vehicle! When I got back to the van and told them what it was, everyone split their sides with laughter much to the embarrassment of Jim Coker. I don't think we stopped laughing until we got back home! It was only when we'd got safely back home that Jim told us he had 'never driven in the dark' before. (I wondered whether he was joking!) My Dad, who was never the best passenger in any sort of road vehicle, went white and I thought for a minute he was going to hit Jim. Dad certainly never went out in the van with him again afterwards. The rest of us saw the funny side of it and we would still have a laugh about it many years later.

When one compares the crowded modern roads it makes one think! Fortunately the incident on Eridge Hill really only came about because there were so few cars on the road and even fewer street lights.

The old blue Hillman and Jim himself are memories I treasure. His sense of humour matched his appearance. One wouldn't see his type around these days. I still have a smile about Jim and even these days, Trev and I still have a good chuckle about him when the subject comes up. Jim was definitely one of nature's gentlemen.

At this time, I was enjoying my one day a week at the Technical School and around this time, the facility was moved from Monson Road, adjacent to the swimming baths (in those days), to the top of Upper Grosvenor Road where there was considerably more space after having been quite congested at the old site. I kept up with my project to design sprung front forks for a bicycle and I think that even the instructor was a little impressed with the idea.

Unfortunately job security at Oliver & Rush didn't improve and it was apparent that the throughput of vehicles for jobs wasn't making ends meet for the company. I still had the odd mechanical job at the branch in Mount Zion when they had a peak workload and I would get to working under Oscar Huntley again which was always a pleasure but on the whole, the operation in the High Street was turning into a bit of a dead loss.

The Foreman at the High Street branch was a wizen little bloke named George. It was obvious that his knowledge of motor vehicles was extremely limited and funnily enough he spent most of his time serving petrol on the pumps. Surely this was hardly a job for a Foreman. I think George was the first person I met who fell into the category of a 'two faced, report all happenings to the boss', type of individual. In other words the rest of the men working there would not trust him any further than they could throw him and it was very obvious that as soon as Mr. Oliver drove into the garage, George would be in his office and my work colleagues would be saying 'I wonder who he is running down today'.

Of course these goings on did nothing for the overall morale of the men working there and when they got the opportunity some of them managed to find jobs elsewhere. What followed next was to put the tin hat on it as far as I was concerned. One morning we were all summoned to Mr. Oliver's office to be told that, as if we didn't know, business was not going that well and the company had decided to concentrate vehicle maintenance at the Mount Zion works and had successfully tendered for, and won, a contract to manufacture parts of shell case sections for the Royal Navy. This work would be allocated to the High Street branch which would cease carrying out motor vehicle work almost as soon as the lathes and other specialist equipment had been installed in the place.

At that time, I think, there were only about five of us left working in the place. With George the foreman, a man called Norman, Wack and myself we were rather few to produce many shell cases at speed. I had to smile to myself when Mr. Oliver said that they would not be employing additional staff as he considered the work could be handled by the staff who were currently there; all I could say is that I was glad to know there wasn't a war going on at that time as I didn't see us lot as England's front line force in the manufacture of munitions! This must have been in the summer of 1952 and it was then I decided that there was no way I was going to become a production line worker doing a totally thankless, boring and in my opinion, soul destroying job of standing over a lathe all day cutting out shell case parts. We were assured by Mr. Oliver that this was the only way we would remain employed in the company.

Wack and I both took the same attitude about the situation we found ourselves in but we knew we had to stay put for the time being as with our lack of qualifications, the chance of finding another job was remote. As it so happened, Wack actually wasn't too worried about the short term prospects as he was facing the prospect of National Service early the following year when he would be eighteen. He hadn't pursued a planned career path in the automobile industry, as I had hoped to achieve, so was resigned to stay put for a few months until he joined up. With him being about five months older than me, he would be the first of our group to go into the services. So, for him anyway, it was a fait accompli.

I remember going home to my Mum and Dad at that time and telling them the news that I was going to be forced to become a production line worker. Unfortunately as my Dad tried to point out to me I would just have to hang on in there to at least earn a wage. I knew times were hard for my parents as they were for many other people at that time; my Dad was, in my opinion, doing a job well below his capabilities although, to be fair to him, he never complained. That was the thing about my Dad and I respect him for it more than I can say.   He was his own man. It was a case of him doing what he had to do; in order to earned sufficient to allow his family to live as well as could be expected.   He couldn't have cared less what other people thought.   Bob was of similar nature in many respects. I now consider that for many years he had been a personal chauffeur to the Morton family, had run his own business until financial pressure brought about by bad payers, certainly none of his own fault, had put an end to that. He was one of the best engineers I have ever met.   He and Dad were now both prepared to stand over a gas flame, every day, straightening out bamboo canes for fishing rods. I could accept what they had resigned themselves to do but at my age, and with no dependants, I just did not want to go up a dead end path as well.

Bearing in mind what I have just said I reluctantly agreed to give the lathe operator job a try but I can assure you, it was only a stop gap as far as I was concerned.   The lathes duly arrived on site and were installed in the workshop area.   We were given a simple overview of what we were expected to do and within a month from the time we were first told by Mr. Oliver, the Oliver & Rush Munitions Factory started production. The job was a really simple one. All we were expected to do on the lathe was to run down the rough outer casing of the metal ingots, to established dimensions, and then send them on to another factory (where this was I do not know as its location was kept secret!) for turning out the interior of the ingot for the ultimate insertion of the explosive charge.

Within a very short time it was obvious that the work we were doing was required no skill whatsoever; just plain boring production line activity that a monkey could have done. We worked to templates which meant that one really didn't have to be a genius to produce the end product. We did still get the odd minor jobs on customer cars when they happened to drop in without notice but on the whole, it was just the very repetitive lathe operation; day in and day out. As I worked I gave serious thought to my future career path which, it was now obvious, would not be in the motor trade. My resolve was strengthened when Mr. Oliver called me into his office one day to say that the company would not be able to continue releasing me for my day a week at the Technical School. That was the final straw. The pity of it all was that I really had wanted to finish my idea on the bicycle 'sprung frame'; you never know it may have been a great success. One never knows and now never will. I thought it was workable though.

I still kept up my interest in railways and together with Trev, spent time at all our favourite haunts whilst still chasing those elusive engine numbers. At about this time there were some quite innovative ideas coming along on the railway scene; particularly where locomotives were concerned. O.V. Bullied, the designer of such classic Southern Railway locomotives as the 'West Country', 'Battle of Britain' and 'Merchant Navy' Pacific class engines, came up with the idea of the 'Leader' class of steam locomotive which was put on trial in the region between Tunbridge Wells West, Brighton, Eastbourne.

The 'Leader' did not have the conventional classic steam engine lines at all, in fact it looked very much like one of the early Diesel's with a box like body, large driving wheels and a cab at either end. The idea behind this layout being that the engine did not require turning as it could be operated from either end. It was not the prettiest of locomotives and with the boiler and firebox located in the centre of the unit, its resemblance to a dirty, long box on wheels was obvious.

At the time the 'Leader' was introduced it was seen as the steam locomotive of the future. It was a fascinating engine to watch in action and we were lucky that it seemed to spend a lot of time at the 'West. In fact two engines were built but from the outset they gave a lot of trouble, particularly with overheating due to the location of the hot sections of the engine being located in the centre of the unit. They were poor steamers as well probably again due to the layout of the boiler and their operational lives were to be short indeed. Without a doubt their design was to be the last 'revolutionary' steam engine design embarked on by British Railways before steam was eventually replaced by diesel traction in the mid 1960's. We were lucky to have seen these engines during their short lives; unfortunately their failure in operation was to lead to the rather rapid fall from grace of their designer Mr. Bullied, which was a great shame. Apart from the 'Leader' fiasco, his streamlined Pacific's which were known as 'Spamcans', were proving to be temperamental and it wasn't to be long before British Railways modified a lot of them into conventional outline locomotives which proved to be exceptionally good. It is however reassuring to know that today, there are more Bullied Pacific's in preservation than any other type of steam locomotive. I guess that says a lot for the man who had such futuristic ideas. Unfortunately, neither of the 'Leaders' made it to preservation.

In those days Tunbridge Wells used to hold a large annual Fete and Sports Meeting at the Neville Cricket Ground which was always very popular. This usually took place in mid summer and was always well attended. Apart from the usual stalls and various money making fete type activities there were a considerable number of competitive events which would be thrown open to 'all comers'. These usually produced partisan support from the crowd when local favourites competed against town and county 'stars' and particularly so in the track events. Unfortunately on the day in question Trev and I, for some reason or other, didn't go to the event. I think we were off on some railway jaunt or other.

However my Dad, who had got into the habit of going out on his own whilst Mum chose to stay at home with young Robert, actually went to the gathering at the Neville Cricket Ground, totally unbeknown to either my mother or to us. In fact we didn't know anything about it until the evening when we met up with some members of 'our gang' in the Calverley Grounds and were completely taken aback when I think it was Nadine Tollet said to us, 'what do you think about your Dad going in for the five mile race at the Neville today'? We thought she was joking but soon realised that she was serious!

Apparently in our absence Dad had entered for the race wearing his old baggy trousers and vest; he didn't have running shoes so ran in his bare feet; fortunately it was on a grass circular track! My Dad, who was well in to his fifties by then, and to the best of my knowledge had never been much of an athlete had, for some reason or other decided to go in for the big race. Nadine had been there so gave us a full report on what had happened. It appears that Dad who was known to many in the crowd was cheered on. He did it for a joke more than with any serious intent. The amazing thing was that he completed the course, albeit, some time after the other competitors had finished, to the rapturous support of the crowd who gave him a fantastic ovation as he finally crossed the finishing line.

In many ways this was very typical of my Dad; he was one of the original nonconformists who clearly did not feel a need to follow the 'party line'. Although he would go off every Thursday to speak at Lincoln's Inn Fields in London (paid to do so by the Conservative Party), and every so often, to a speaking engagement at Speakers Corner in Hyde Park, he was the sort who would often shock us with his individuality.   Really and truly, we were not that surprised when we heard of what he had done at the Neville and it was not very long before all the neighbours were talking about it. There was also an article referring telling of Dad's exploits in the race, in the edition of the 'Kent & Sussex Courier' which came out the following week.

Another thing about Dad was that he could take a joke. Bu the time he reached middle age he had lost of lot of his teeth but would never go to the dentist to get a set of false ones made up. 'Crowns' work was unheard of then and would have been very expensive in any case.   I can remember my mother going on at him that he should go to the dentist.   The funniest thing would be to watch him attempting to chew meat with what were probably about only two or three good teeth! We actually nicknamed him 'Fangy' which was hardly complimentary but described him to a tee. Mum did eventually get him to grudgingly get a set of false teeth but these he never wore for eating but on occasions he would put them in for appearances but would take them out to eat a meal! If he did wear them for a meal he would often intentionally drop one of the plates out of his mouth when my mother wasn't at the table and imitate Winston Churchill with his famous gummy manner of speaking.

(Churchill was famous for portentously speechifying with an enormous cigar stuck in his mouth which distorted his speech).   'My friends', he would pronounce, gummily. 'Never in the field of human conflict ....', and so on!   This would result in Trev and me splitting our sides with laughter as we watched Dad acting the Churchill role with one half of his dentures protruding from his mouth! My mother got to know when he was doing this when she heard us laughing and would then tell him off.   But she could not fail to see the funny side of it and it became one of Dad's famous party pieces thereafter.   When I look back at my parents, I must say that I consider myself blessed to have had such really wonderful people as my Mum and Dad.   They were not perfect but then who is?   They were wonderfully natural human beings with hearts of gold and, as I saw it, all the right priorities.

Yes, we had hard times throughout my childhood, money was always in short supply and at times Bob was a true benefactor to us all. But we never missed what we never had. What was a fact was the pride in all both my mother and father had towards us as their children and I can assure you Trev and I were hardly angels. In later years Dad's patriotism of us was sometimes an embarrassment, especially so when I joined the R.A.F., when some of his stories about my activities in the service, as told to friends and neighbours would stray somewhat from the facts but it was all because he was so very proud of us.

I know that many a time I would find myself in a difficult position when meeting an acquaintance who had been told things about me by my father. I would have to try to get around what he had been saying with neither admitting I had not done what he thought and without admitting that Dad had been a bit elastic with the truth either. With Dad knowing a lot of people these instances occurred quite often but I never got around to complaining to him about it. I took it as another example of his love for us and provided I could go along with what he was saying to a certain extent, I was not going to put him on the spot. He meant well but I can recall some quite famous exaggerations I do assure you!

I know my mother used to get on to my Dad about his exaggerations and I can remember her saying to him 'Dodd's, (that was another of my mothers nick name for my Dad), you will have to answer for all these stories you tell one day', to which Dad would usually come back with the statement that when he reached the final reckoning, God would see the funny side of it!   That was typical of him! Really and truly he was anti the establishment such as the Church of England. I am sure he held many genuinely Christian beliefs in his heart as he would never do anyone down. If we are to be judged one day, I think it will be on the way we lived our life whilst on earth. My Dad was a person who ridiculed the pomp of religion as he saw it as a way for a lot of hypocrites to make a living off of the gullible and to keep the poor in their place. He used to give examples of those who fell into this category, one of his main targets was the Archbishop of Canterbury of that period who particularly annoyed him with his policies. Whereas people like the vicar at Christ Church, the Reverend John Smith, were the type of people Dad considered to be genuinely religious and had the interests of his parishioners at heart. I recall that previously when I went forward to be Confirmed and attended Confirmation Classes at the Vicarage, I remember Rev. Smith raised the subject of my Dad's attitude towards the church on more than one occasion and I got the impression that he really had some level of understanding of my father's way of seeing religion in action in the higher echelons.

From the earliest time I can remember my Dad was a regular contributor to the 'Readers Letters' page of the local newspapers, especially the 'Kent & Sussex Courier'.   He would write almost weekly about a large variety of subjects and it came to the point when if he did not have a letter printed, it was unusual; it was almost like him having his own column in the paper!   What used to amaze me was the wide variety of subject matter he would write about; I know he was well read, taking full advantage of the free lending library in Tunbridge Wells, and that definitely came across in his letters.   He used to get replies from other readers which was very interesting and he really thrived upon this unpaid sideline.   After he died (in 1974), there were several letters from readers saying how they would miss my Dad's letters and that was an enormous tribute to him.

My mother, on the other hand, was a great believer in regular church attendance and along with Miss Pope, her long time flatmate and neighbour, would go to church as often as she could.   That is not to say Mum was anything other than a genuinely generous and warm hearted person who believed in practising what she preached.   I recall her saying 'We were put upon this earth to help each other'.   She was musical and having played church organ a bit in her youth, she enjoyed the hymns and organ music of church services.

Yes I was still a fairly active member of the Christ Church choir as my voice hadn't broken to the point where I was at least valued to make up numbers.   Actually Trev and I were the two longest serving members of the junior choir and wore the blue ribbons around our necks to show 'service'. (I think that in those days you had to be in the choir for a minimum of three years to get a Cathedral choir ribbon).   We would be at the front of the choir procession as it entered the church, walking side by side, right behind Reg Manktelow carrying the cross, and with the rest of the choir following us.   Often would be the time that, just prior to entering the church, we would share a joke and still have the grins on our faces as we led the procession!   We were hardly images of reverence. The choir master, Mr. Pallant, must have had nerves of iron to put up with us and it still wasn't beyond him to throw a hymn book or something at us if he saw us playing the fool.   Fortunately this normally only happened during choir practice but there was one day when he threw something at us whilst the vicar was giving his sermon, which was all rather embarrassing. This was because all of the choir, including the eight adult men, virtually split their sides with laughter much to the disgust of the assembled congregation.

Mr Pallant who was, if you remember, also the hairdresser in Grove Hill Road, usually got his own back on us when we visited his shop for a haircut! Having asked us how we'd like our hair cut he would proceed to cut it as short as he could get away with and I often sensed a smile on his face when I looked at him in the mirror as he worked away. I'm glad I didn't have to go to him for a shave.

Towards the end of the summer of 1952, with Wack just a couple of months away from beginning his National Service, I wrote to the R.A.F. Careers Department for information on opportunities for Aircraft Engineering in the Royal Air Force. The reply I received made it abundantly clear that the service was looking for career airmen and as I was only just turned seventeen at the time I could if I wished, join up as a Volunteer at seventeen and a half if I passed the required interviews and medical tests. Having made it clear that I was very interested in joining up and wanted to get involved with aircraft, I was asked to attend an interview in Chatham which was the regional recruiting centre for the Air Force. As it happened Wack and I found we were to attend interview in Chatham on the same day so were able to go together which was something of a bonus. Travel passes were provided and we set off on the number seven Maidstone & District bus to see what was in store for us. We had to each take one day's leave from Oliver & Rush so as not to give Mr. Oliver any idea what his staff were up to although that Weasel George would have given his right arm to know what it was.

We both duly arrived at the recruiting centre along with a lot of other young men like ourselves; all destined for the same nerve wracking experience. As I was a 'volunteer' and Wack was National Service, we were split up when we got there and would not see each other until later in the day when the tests had been completed. I got the feeling that the Air Force was very keen to attract youngsters like myself who they probably saw as the 'career airman' types as opposed to the National Service guys who could be expected to just carry out the basic requirements of their two years service and get it over with. I must have been why they had two different interview methods. Of course, I was to later discover the reality of air force life was to prove to be completely different to the impression deliberately given to us at the interview.   We were called 'Mister' by the servicemen and officers who did the interviews and all in all, the impression I got was that life in the R.A.F. would be far better than the uncertainty I had of trying to pursue a career in civilian life; especially at Oliver & Rush.

Wack and I went our different paths when we got to the interviews although we did bump into each other at one point where the medicals were taking place but we didn't get much of a chance to compare notes at that point.   From all that I could recall of the events of that day, I did get a favourable impression that the R.A.F. would offer a much better opportunity of obtaining a decent career even if one was not intent on taking out a very long term engagement, which from what I discussed with the careers officers, was something they tried hard to get chaps like myself to agree to.   Maybe they were on a bonus system with extra perks if they got some willing person to sign away twenty five years of his life.   To be fair to them though, at that specific time, they did not exert much pressure to make you do that.

The next hurdle was the medical which took place after a lunch break and I proved to be perfectly fit and healthy.   I was offered a career in the Air Force and would start as an 'Aircraftsman 2' (A/C 2) grade which would qualify me as an Aircraft Engine Fitter after training!   The proviso to being able to join the career path of my choice was that I had to agree to a minimum of four years which, at my stage in life and with the knowledge that it would actually give me a profession, I agreed to. Actually, at the time of my interview, I was a couple of months short of the mandatory seventeen and a half age minima to be able to join up right there and then and of course, I had to get my fathers permission to join anyway.   The plan was that I could 'join up' on January the first, 1953.   I was pleased with myself as I left the interview room with the necessary forms for my parents to sign and met up with Wack, as we had planned, for the return journey on the bus back to Tunbridge Wells.   The good news when we met was that he had passed all the required tests to allow him to start his National Service on the same day as I did so; New Years Day in 1953 was to be a big day for us both.

Actually, Wack had also opted for a tradesman's occupation in aircraft maintenance but because he was only due to be in the service for the mandatory two years of his National Service, his training path was expected to be different to the one I was scheduled to do but at least we would go off to the Air Force Reception camp on the same day together. We would be able to help calm each other's nerves down a bit prior to our going our separate ways. It would be quite a big step for us to leave our families to go into the world and to travel on our own.

When I got home my enthusiasm was not completely shared by my mother and father. I guess my mother, rightly, saw it as her son leaving home and that nothing would ever really be the same again; actually, that was to be the case as after joining the R.A.F. in 1953, I was never to live at home on a regular basis again. My father saw it in a more practical way, as he had spent many years as a young man in the Merchant Navy with very lengthy periods of time spent away from home. So he more easily accepted the facts that the same thing could happen to his son(s). Both of my parents were realists which helped and they knew that, in those days, there was little future in a career path in Tunbridge Wells so it was inevitable that I would have to go away, at some time, to get a decent career. And even if I didn't join the services as a 'volunteer', I would eventually have had to go for my National Service anyway; so they accepted my decision.

The key thing was that both Wack and I didn't want to lose our jobs at Oliver & Rush until it suited us; we knew that if Mr. Oliver or his pet Ferret George, got to know our intentions, they would fire us out of spite. Although we were going to leave anyway after a couple of months, we wanted it to be in our own time as it would be impossible to get a job for a month or two before we joined up and we needed the money to get the things we would need to go away with. We managed to keep it a secret from our work colleagues and management for some time but it was inevitable that at some point, the boss would get to hear about our plans and take appropriate action.

Actually from a legal point of view, certainly in the case of Wack who was going to leave to do his National Service, they would have been out of order in firing us but we were a 'non union' firm and what the boss wanted to do he could do, unchallenged to a certain degree. All he had to say was that we were being made redundant due to a downturn in work and nobody could do anything about it; and that is exactly what they did. In early December 1952 we were called into Mr. Oliver's office and told that as there had been a reduction in work they could not retain our services.

It came as a bit of a shock to us both even though we had been fearful of some kind of repercussions. It still hit us a bit 'below the belt' when the crunch came! We didn't even have to finish the week, we were paid off there and then and it was a rather odd feeling as we walked home together that dark winter evening, knowing that our life was about to change drastically in the weeks ahead of us.

My Dad was absolutely furious when he came in from work, and I told him what had happened to us both. It had been a shock to my mother when I told her but she said she thought that something like that might happen when our employers found out even though, as I have said, they were quite out of order in doing so. My Dad said he would go and see Mr. Oliver the very next morning and give him a piece of his mind which he subsequently did but of course it had no impact at all on the outcome.   I wouldn't have wanted to go back there anyway. As it happened Wack and I were both fortunate really as the Post Office was looking for their usual Christmas Rush temporary staff and the morning after we had left our old jobs, we were first in line at the Post Office hoping to be selected as Temporary Postmen.

We were lucky and both of us were selected and very pleased about it, at least we would have some money for Christmas and to buy the things we would need when we went to 'join up' on New Year's Day. I was given a postman's round that included the area beyond Mount Ephraim; places like Moleneoux Park and the area around the Spa Hotel.   It was a round spread over quite a large distance and took an average of about four hours to complete. On days when there was a considerable load, I would have to split it up into two, with a post van meeting up with me half way round, to hand me the second section. I guess having been a paper boy all those years made me an ideal candidate for a postman's job and I recall that I really enjoyed it. My round included some very nice houses and I guess the area I had to work in was one of the more affluent areas of the town with some important people living there; if the size of the Christmas mail they had was anything to go by, they certainly knew a lot of people!

To allow me to do the post office job, I had to reluctantly give up my paper round and it was with some regret that I did so although it was inevitable with my R.A.F. service coming up, but bearing in mind that I had been a paper boy for over eight years it was a bit of a wrench to finally stop doing it, especially at the period of Christmas and Christmas boxes!

Trev took over my paper round as he had, by now, improved at getting up in the morning, so it was possible for him to combine it with what he was already doing, which certainly pleased Mr. Tuppen as he didn't want to be let down just before Christmas. Trev made a very nice gesture to me when he took over the round by sharing the Christmas boxes with me; a true mate as well as brother! As I said, I really enjoyed the Post Office job; getting there early in the morning was not a problem either to Wack and I and usually, before we set out on the round, we would grab a quick cuppa in the Post Office canteen so that we could at least have a chat together before going our separate ways.

Wack's round was more in the town than mine which suited him; I was more of the country type so my round suited me perfectly and especially because they had given me a bicycle to help me carry out the work. As the Christmas period approached we were expected to do a second delivery as there was a considerable load to be distributed. These were the days when the Post Office had the monopoly of letter and parcel postage, not like today, so there was a lot to do. One of the houses that I had to deliver to was 'Chancellor House", a block of expensive apartments located behind the Spa Hotel on Mount Ephraim. A long time business friend of Bob was Mrs. Horne, (I mentioned her earlier on when I talked about Bob and his garage) who lived in one of these apartments.

I think Bob must have told her that I would be doing her postal route because she always welcomed me with some small refreshment when I got to her flat and this was very welcome indeed. One needed the energy on that job so what she so kindly offered did not go amiss. She had been a long time friend of the Bob Hulme and his wife, I think it originated from the days when Bob was chauffeur to the Morton family who were somehow connected with her. With her being a wealthy lady, I seem to remember she always looked after Bob at Christmas time. I remember he certainly did all the work on her car when he was in the motor business and they remained good friends until she died some years before he too passed away when well into his nineties.

Being the festive time of the year, when the time approached Christmas, I did very well for Christmas boxes on the round I did, which I guess was a little unfair on the regular postman but I wasn't complaining. I wasn't to know it at the time but the Christmas that was fast approaching then was to be the last Christmas I would spend at home for three years. The fact that I was going into the services gave me the incentive to make sure we all had a nice Christmas and the post round had paid very well so I was able to splash out a bit and help Mum and Dad with some of the expenses that Christmas invariably brings.

It was a little like the feasts in Dickens, 'A Christmas Carol', after Scrooge learned the error of his ways and tried to make it up to the Cratchet family; not that we were characters from Dickens but with the uncertainty of the future, we decided to have an extra special Christmas and, although I wasn't to know what the future was to bring, it did seem to be the right thing to do.

Although we had all been special friends with Bob for many years, we somehow never saw anything of his wife. It would not be until 1955, when Trev and I were asked to their place at Woodsgate, Pembury, for tea, during Christmas, that we would meet her for the first time; and we both thought her to be a very nice lady indeed. What I am trying to say I guess is that Bob obviously did not join us over the Christmas but I can remember that after a glass of Ginger Wine on the Christmas Eve, Bob made us all laugh when out of the blue, he came out with his story of the old postman at the Central Station who used to collect the mail bags from the train when it arrived. Bob said he would load his barrow with the mail bags and begin pushing towards the lift to take it up to the mail van at road level. As there were always a lot of people about, he would shout out "Bye leave for His Majesty's Mail, Bye leave for His Majesty's Mail----well get out the bloody way then"! I can remember it now as clear as when he said it. It was completely out of the blue and we all fell about laughing at the way Bob had told the tale. I guess the Ginger Wine helped but I'll never forget it. Those little gems stay with you over the years and I guess it was more the fact that it was unexpected that made the impact of his little story that much more effective.

It was a good Christmas and was to be marked in other respects as being the last Christmas that rationing was in force as in early in 1953 rationing, introduced just before the start of the war, came to an end. I remember we heard it on the radio news; just after I had joined the R.A.F. I suppose with that news people finally knew then that the war was over as although nothing exceptional happened with regard to freedom to buy what you wanted, it was, I think, the realisation that life was, at long last, finally 'back to normal'.

Anyway, back to Christmas 1952.   Mr. Tuppen had allowed Trev and I to buy a lot of things 'off the ration' over the years and Christmas 1952 was no exception!   All in all we had a lovely time.   My Granddad came to dinner for the first time that I could recall, as previously my Dad's parents had appeared to spend every Christmas with their daughter Vera, and her husband and son Peter at their house in Grosvenor Road.   I guess that with things being a little cramped at number 32, with the five of us living in three rooms, it had been understandable in many ways for my grandparents to go to Vera.   With Grand dad now widowed things were changing somewhat.

My Grandparents had always been very welcoming to us but there was no closeness between Dad and his sister Vera.   My aunt had been able to send their son Peter, to Skinners School whereas we would have found that to be a struggle financially.   As it happened my cousin grew into a bit of a loner.   Trev and I had met up with him from time to time, during our school days, usually at the Central Station where we shared the same interest in railways; at least we had that interest in common.   Unfortunately I lost touch with him when I went into the services but after Vera and her husband died, he didn't stay on at 'Sunny Ridge' and I don't know what became of him.

The time between Christmas and the New Year went by rapidly and it was not long before the fateful day for Wack and I to leave home in order to join up came along.   In those days New Years Day was not a Public Holiday as it is today so following a totally uneventful New Year's Eve, as was typical in those days, I got an early call from Mum, at about five thirty on a cold, wet and totally dark January the first.   I left home at six twenty to catch the number seven bus to Chatham.   My Dad even got up.   Now that was something of a miracle as he loved his bed.   So it was that, suitably supplied with sandwiches and snacks from Mum, I left home for a new life.   As I walked down Grove Hill Road towards whatever the future had in store for me, it was an extremely emotional time.   I had a lump in my throat the size of an egg but I didn't want to let my parents see that the decision I had made was as upsetting to me as I'm sure it was for them.

In a way, I was glad to turn the corner at the bottom of Grove Hill towards the bus stops located at the bottom of

Mount Pleasant.   I wasn't glad to leave Mum and Dad, Trev and Robert behind, in fact it was the opposite, but as I walked away from the part of Tunbridge Wells that had been my life, and which had so many memories for me, it was as though a new life was beckoning me from the moment I stepped on the bus and it began its arduous journey to Chatham.   He didn't have to say anything but I knew that Wack felt the same way.   For once we were lost for words!

Leaving my family, and the town of Tunbridge Wells which I loved, was a hard experience.   It wasn't that I wouldn't be going back there again in the years to come; I think it was more a case of realising that I had come of age and the future, whatever it had in store for me, meant that things would never be the same again.

But that is another story!

'EPILOGUE'

When I look in the Dictionary, I see that the word 'Epilogue' means 'conclusion' or 'postscript'.

It seems a long time ago when I started to think about the idea of compiling a 'book', similar to what (if you have actually read the thing) I have tried to do here. Would you believe that according to the reference page in my Computer 'MultiMate' Programme, the old programme I used to compile the majority of this record on, the first 'key applications' (computer keyboard) are recorded as having taken place on February 21st., 1991, whilst I was working in Dubai! At the time of adding these few pages, it is late 2004! How the time has flown! I now use a much more modern computer and programme as well!

I know I am not a fast typist but to be absolutely fair, I have not been 'at the book' constantly during the years it has taken me to compile it. I have found that I have often gone for long periods without doing any work on it at all; this has been brought about by my work which at times required me to be away from 'home' a lot, and at other times, not having the inspiration or mental resource to press on with it. Please do not get me wrong, it has been a labour of love in many respects as I have really wanted to try to get all my thoughts and experiences from when I was young into something like this.

The problem with taking so long on it and having considerable breaks in between is that you can fall into the trap of repeating yourself and I do hope I have not done that too much. When I edited the book, I did find that there were areas where I had in fact said the same thing twice; where it was possible to edit out those instances without having to practically rewrite the whole chapter, I have done so but I doubt if I have been completely successful so please bear with me if you do (did) find examples of repetition in it.

I felt it necessary to add a 'postscript' mainly because when I went through the book, I did find questions that I felt needed answering and some of these are as follows.

You will find that reference to my Grandparents is somewhat limited. Whereas I have mentioned quite a few things about them, I realise that I have also missed out certain aspects as well. That was not intentional but was more a case of not really having all the facts to give you. In the case of my father's parents, we did associate with them as children and it was as children that they treated us. That was to be expected and I am sure that if one asked my own grandchildren about me, they would probably have similar types of memories of me not unlike those I had of my grandparents. What one has to remember is that children see things differently to adults and really only recall things that actually directly affect them or in which they have been closely associated.

In some respects these are the 'missing' links in the book. For instance, if I look back at my Grandmother Gardner, she was always the same in her attitude to Trevor and I and that is how I remember her. What I find missing however is detail as to when she actually died. To the best of my recollections she did in fact die of cancer whilst I was still at school but for some reason or other, my parents never really involved us with the loss. We certainly never went to the funeral.

Although I did not mention it in the book, I was actually at my grandparent's house the night Granddad Stringer died. Again I cannot recall the year of this but it took place in the evening and all the family were there but I was the only one from the Gardner household. I believe that came about because I had cycled up to Hawkenbury on the off chance to see them not realising that Granddad was very ill. Again, I have to ask myself why my parents did not mention this or why I was unaware of the situation as I am sure my Mum was not there when the old chap passed away. I remember cycling home to tell my family the bad news and as I cycled home, the night was crystal clear and looking up into the heavens at the stars, I imagined that Granddad was looking down on me from his place in heaven. Childhood impressions!

What I have tried to do in this work is really to try to describe what things were like for me as firstly as a child and then as an adolescent. As I said in the introduction, the things I have written about happened to me and in many respects, to Trevor. Chronologically the dates referred to herein are as near to the actual events as far as I can recall. Apart from the loss of Grandmother Gardner and my Grandfather Stringer whilst I was a boy, the only other bereavements are as I have described herein.

My father died in 1974 and my mother in 1990. Bob died in the mid 1980's. I have been blessed with a wonderful wife and family and will always be grateful that I was able to actually spend the time to tell my story. I do hope you have enjoyed my return journey to the Tunbridge Wells of my boyhood. The ride has been a good one for me.

<u>ACKNOWLEDGEMENTS</u>

No literary work can be complete without the help of others and this work is no exception. I would therefore like to thank the following people who have given great help to me in the compilation, editing, formatting and general constructive comments to allow me to produce the finished article.

Richard Guzovich, for all his help in achieving the required computer format for publishing. Bearing in mind that when I started the book many years ago, the computer programme then in use was 'MultiMate'. Transferring this to the required 'Word' format was no mean feat!

Dr. Margaret Norris, for all her time consuming patience in proof reading the book for me.

Patrick Coulcher, for giving the benefit of his experience in publishing a work like mine.

Leila Gardner, my wife, for all her help and support especially when at times I wondered whether it was really worth pursuing the book to its conclusion.

Thank you all.